SOCIAL IDENTITY, INTERGROUP CONFLICT, *and* CONFLICT REDUCTION

RUTGERS SERIES ON SELF AND SOCIAL IDENTITY

RUTGERS SERIES ON SELF AND SOCIAL IDENTITY   *Volume 3*

SOCIAL IDENTITY, INTERGROUP CONFLICT, *and* CONFLICT REDUCTION

Edited by

Richard D. Ashmore

Lee Jussim

David Wilder

OXFORD
UNIVERSITY PRESS
2001

OXFORD

UNIVERSITY PRESS

Oxford   New York

Athens   Auckland   Bangkok   Bogotá   Buenos Aires   Cape Town
Chennai   Dar es Salaam   Delhi   Florence   Hong Kong   Istanbul   Karachi
Kolkata   Kuala Lumpur   Madrid   Melbourne   Mexico City   Mumbai   Nairobi
Paris   São Paulo   Shanghai   Singapore   Taipei   Tokyo   Toronto   Warsaw

and associated companies in
Berlin   Ibadan

Library of Congress Cataloging-in-Publication Data
Social identity, intergroup conflict, and conflict reduction / [edited by] Richard D. Ashmore,
Lee Jussim, and David Wilder.
    p. cm.—(Rutgers series on self and social identity ; 3)
Includes bibliographical references and index.
ISBN 978-0-19-513743-9
1. Group identity. 2. Conflict management. 3. Ethnic relations. I. Ashmore, Richard D. II.
Jussim, Lee J. III. Wilder, David, 1949–   IV. Series
HM753.S6197   2001
302.4—dc21   00-053761

Printed in the United States of America
on acid-free paper

Preface to Volume 3

This volume is important to me both professionally and personally: it is a significant part of my evolving life story. At the same, my co-editors and I believe that this book provides a start toward an important new perspective on intergroup violence, a problem that brings extensive material destruction and widespread human suffering around the globe.

In the spring of 1964, while still an undeclared and uncertain history major, I read Gordon Allport's *The Nature of Prejudice* for a course entitled, "Medieval Anti-Semitism." It was an epiphany—I would become a social psychologist, and I would seek to understand the causes and cures of intergroup conflict. That summer I enrolled in my first psychology classes, finished the psychology major during my senior year, and went on to get my Ph.D. in social psychology with a specialization in intergroup relations.

When I read Allport and chose my occupation and specialty area, I did not know Erikson's seminal work on identity development. As I look back, though, his ideas about adolescent identity search fit my experience very well. Becoming a social psychologist and seeking to understand prejudice and discrimination allowed me to bring together my *childhood* identifications (with two parents who were simply good people, with a succession of outstanding teachers [from Mrs. Cirino in the fourth grade to Professor Lewis Spitz at Stanford who, to this day, provides the model for how I teach a large undergraduate class]), my then *current* concerns and values (I believed in 1964 that conflict among groups was the greatest problem facing humans; I felt that we should and could do something about this), and my *future* work (becoming a scientist and uncovering why people engage in group-based harm-doing).

Now it is 2000. With many twists and turns, I today still see myself as an intergroup relations researcher. And I continue to believe that intergroup conflict is the major problem facing the world. What is different, one of those twists and turns, is that I now consider myself also an identity researcher. This volume allows me to bring together, then, my personal life story, especially my commitment to understanding intergroup conflict, with my evolving professional self-definition as a social scientist who studies self and identity.

Although the world today is, in many ways, quite different from that of almost 40 years ago, group-based violence, aggression, and suppression are no less in evidence. Although the global cold war has ended, we now experience a seemingly never-ending succession of small and local "wars." These are global in a new way—group-based strife occurs on all continents and every corner of the world and yet, because of powerful new communications technologies, the whole world often is involved if only as CNN viewers.

Since I entered the field in the mid-1960s, the social and behavioral sciences have made great strides in seeking to understand and ameliorate intergroup conflict. At the same time, there are still many gaps in our knowledge.

My co-editors and I believe that social identity may provide a powerful perspective for filling in some of these gaps. Social identity has certainly been implicated in past work on group strife, but these efforts have been piecemeal and isolated from one another across disciplinary boundaries. Our goal in this volume was to bring together scientists from diverse social and behavioral sciences to address the multiple ways that social identity and intergroup conflict are interrelated. We believe that our contributors have done an excellent job, on the one hand, of highlighting major current theories, concepts, and methods and, on the other, of identifying the crucial issues that need to be addressed if we are to develop a more complete and coordinated social identity perspective on intergroup conflict. We hope that this volume contributes to the development of such a paradigm and that it, along with other approaches, facilitates social technologies that significantly reduce the incidence and intensity of people harming others because of group membership.

Piscataway, New Jersey   Richard D. Ashmore
May 2000

Acknowledgments

Many individuals and organizations helped us as we planned and carried out the Third Rutgers Symposium on Self and Social Identity and produced this volume. We thank you all. We received so much help from so many sources that we are sure to have forgotten to mention some here, and for that we apologize.

We first thank the symposium speakers/chapter authors. They were chosen because they each have distinguished scientific careers, and that past behavior predicted their performance in this endeavor. They produced high-quality symposium presentations and excellent chapters appearing in this book. In addition, they had to deal with fairly picky editors. We thank each of you for sticking with us and producing the present polished contributions.

Next, we wish to thank our publisher, Oxford University Press, and our editors there, Joan Bossert, Philip Laughlin, and Catharine A. Carlin. Joan has been an invaluable source of guidance and support since she first received the proposal for the *Rutgers Series,* and Philip and Catharine ably assisted us as we moved the present volume from an idea, to a conference, to a book.

There are many people to thank for sharing their ideas about the topic of social identity and intergroup conflict, for suggesting speakers/authors, and for providing comments on chapter drafts. We especially wish to thank the members of our editorial board, who provided valuable feedback on initial and revised proposals. In addition, the following people provided input concerning one or more facets of the conference/book: Myron Aronoff, Mahzarin R. Banaji, James Jones, Louis Kreisberg, B. Ann Bettencourt,

Yael Zerubavel, David Sears, Daniel M. Ogilvie, Jessica Heppen, and Rick Lau.

This volume, as with its two predecessors, deserves to be part of the Rutgers Series on Self and Social Identity. We have been helped at every step of the way by the faculty, staff, students, and administrators of Rutgers–The State University of New Jersey. The following members of the Rutgers University community were particularly helpful: Steven Lione, Thelma Collins, Deana Guden-Pagnozzi, and the staff of the University Inn and Conference Center; Stacey Hersh-Ehling of the Rutgers News Service; Joanne Aguglia of the Douglass College Center; Rosemary Manero and her colleagues in the Rutgers Dining Service; Marc Beebe, Justine Cardone, Kathy Maloney, Rae Frank, Maria Brewer, Anne Sokolowski, and Alison Smith, all of the Department of Psychology, who exhibited patience and good humor in their extremely efficient handling of day-to-day tasks and deadline pressures.

Other members of the Rutgers community deserve special thanks. First, Charles Flaherty, chair of the Department of Psychology, has supported the Rutgers Series since its inception, and he made departmental staff and other resources available for our use in putting together the third symposium and present associated book. Second, we express our gratitude to the faculty and graduate students of the doctoral program in social psychology. Members of the Social Psychology Area served as hosts for speakers, helped with symposium registration, transported speakers to and from airports and train stations, directed traffic between symposium sessions, and helped conduct myriad other essential tasks. Third, we thank the following members of the Rutgers community for their generous financial assistance: Joseph J. Seneca (Vice President for Academic Affairs), and Richard F. Foley (Dean, Faculty of Arts and Sciences).

We are also grateful for grants from the National Institutes of Health (R13MH60129-01; Carolyn Morf, Chief, Personality and Social Cognition Program) and from the National Science Foundation (SBR-9811485; Steven J. Breckler, Program Director, Social Psychology) that supported both the Third Rutgers Symposium and the production of this volume.

Contents

Contributors

Richard D. Ashmore, Department of Psychology, Tillett Hall, Rutgers, The State University of New Jersey, 53 Avenue E, Piscataway, NJ 08854-8040. E-mail: ashmore@rci.rutgers.edu.

Marilynn B. Brewer, Department of Psychology, Ohio State University, 1885 Neil Avenue, Columbus, OH 43210. E-mail: brewer.64@osu.edu.

Jack Citrin, Department of Political Science, 210 Barrows Hall #1950, University of California, Berkeley, Berkeley, CA 94720-1950. E-mail: gojack@uclink. berkeley.edu.

Brian Duff, Department of Political Science, 210 Barrows Hall #1950, University of California, Berkeley, Berkeley, CA 94720-1950. E-mail: duff@socrates. berkeley.edu.

Thomas Hylland Eriksen, Department of Social Anthropology, University of Oslo, Moltke Moesvei 31, Eilert Sundts hus, 6th floor, P. O. B. 1091 Blindern, N-0317 OSLO, Norway. E-mail: t.h.eriksen@ima.uio.no.

Jessica Heppen, Department of Psychology, Tillett Hall, Rutgers, The State University of New Jersey, 53 Avenue E, Piscataway, NJ 08854-8040. E-mail: jheppen@rci.rutgers.edu.

Lee Jussim, Department of Psychology, Tillett Hall, Rutgers, The State University of New Jersey, 53 Avenue E, Piscataway, NJ 08854-8040. E-mail: jussim@rci. rutgers.edu.

Herbert C. Kelman, Psychology Department, Harvard University, Cambridge, MA 02138. E-mail: hck@wjh.harvard.edu.

John R. Petrocik, 210 McAlester Hall, Department of Psychology, University of Missouri-Columbia, Columbia, MO 65211. E-mail: PetrocikJ@missouri.edu.

Jim Sidanius, Department of Psychology, 1285 Franz Hall, P. O. Box 951563, 405 Hilgard Avenue, Los Angeles, CA 90095-1563. E-mail: Sidanius@psych. ucla.edu.

Ervin Staub, Department of Psychology, University of Massachusetts, Amherst, MA 01003. E-mail: estaub@psych.umass.edu.

Robert W. White, Department of Sociology, Indiana University at Indianapolis, Cavanaugh Hall 303, 425 University Boulevard, Indianapolis, IN 46202. E-mail: rwwhite@iupui.edu.

David Wilder, Department of Psychology, Tillett Hall, Rutgers, The State University of New Jersey, 53 Avenue E, Piscataway, NJ 08854-8040. E-mail: wilder@psych-b.rutgers.edu.

Cara Wong, Department of Political Science, 210 Barrows Hall #1950, University of California, Berkeley, Berkeley, CA 94720-1950. E-mail: cwong@bravo. berkeley.edu.

SOCIAL IDENTITY, INTERGROUP CONFLICT, *and* CONFLICT REDUCTION

Lee Jussim
Richard D. Ashmore
David Wilder

1

Introduction

Social Identity and Intergroup Conflict

Intense conflict between nations, ethnic groups, and political groups has created some of the most enduring and lethal social problems humans have ever faced. Slavery, conquest, exploitation, war, mass murder, and genocide are among the most extreme manifestations of intergroup conflict. Such conflicts remain as much a part of the human condition today as ever.

Over the last two decades, social and behavioral scientists have increasingly emphasized the role of self and identity in the causes and consequences of intergroup hostility and harm-doing. This is, in part, because issues of self and identity occur at multiple levels of analysis: individual within a social context, groups within a society, and nations of the world. At the level of individual within a social context, ethnic identity may contribute to both in-group bonds and hostility toward other groups (Jones, 1997). At the level of groups within a society, social identity theory and self-categorization theory emphasize the potential for group-based identities to foster support for the status quo among higher power and status groups, and to foster intergroup competition and movements for political change among lower power and status groups (Tajfel, 1981; Thoits & Virshup, 1997; Turner, 1987). Finally, at the level of modern nations, identity is implicated in a variety of conflicts—state violence against internal minorities (e.g., Goldhagen 1996; Staub, 1989), armed uprisings by ethnic groups against central governments (e.g., Gurr, 1993), and international conflicts (e.g., Greenfeld & Chirot, 1994; Keegan, 1993). Furthermore, addressing issues of identity may be necessary to reduce certain conflicts between groups (e.g., Kelman, 1997; Kriesberg, Northrup, & Thorson, 1989).

Although self and identity play a critical role in some (perhaps most) intergroup conflicts, social scientific analyses of that role have thus far been largely isolated from each other. This is unfortunate because, just as the scientific analysis of conflict has blossomed in recent years, so too has there been a resurgence in work on self and identity (Ashmore & Jussim, 1997). Multiple and diverse lines of contemporary social science research and theory demonstrate that self and identity are central to the understanding of human thought, feeling, and action. They are also crucial in accounting for interrelationships between the individual and larger sociocultural institutions and systems (Holland, 1997; Tajfel, 1981; Thoits & Virshup, 1997). Thus, there is much in the areas of self and social identity that might inform our understanding of intergroup conflict.

The main purposes of this book are to elucidate ways in which:

- Social identities create and exacerbate intergroup conflicts.
- Intergroup conflict influences social identity.
- Addressing social identity issues might help reduce some intergroup conflicts.

To achieve these goals, we invited a group of talented social and behavioral scientists to address relationships between intergroup conflict and identity. First, we asked them to address the *locus* of social identity. Are social identities primarily phenomena of individual psychology or are social identities primarily phenomena that reside in the larger social structure? That is, do social, group-based identities occur primarily in the minds of individual people? Or are they embedded in the culture, language, norms, and social practices of a group of people? Or do social identities emerge from some combination of individual psychology and socio-cultural discourses, beliefs, and practices?

Second, we sought contributors whose work addresses different types of intergroup conflict. Although developing a taxonomy of the dimensions on which intergroup conflicts may vary is beyond the scope of this book, it is clear that social identities may be involved in a great variety of intergroup conflicts. For example, whether it is "identity politics" in American elections, ethnic cleansing in Yugoslavia, or riots targeting Muslims in India, group-based identities often play a critical role in maintaining, and sometimes exacerbating, intergroup conflicts. Although addressing all types of intergroup conflicts is beyond the scope of any single book, we sought contributions that would address a wide range of conflicts: conflicts played out within normal legal structures; conflicts involving illegal acts of aggression; conflicts over symbolic and ideological issues; and conflicts over concrete resources and power.

Although each contributor did not address the role of identity in this full range of conflicts, the contributions addressed many different types of conflicts (rather than focus on a single type of conflict—e.g., genocide). Therefore, the first pair of contributions (by Brewer and Eriksen) focuses on identifying broad principles or common themes underlying a range of intergroup conflicts. The second pair (by Citrin, Wong, and Duff, and Sidanius and Petrocik) focuses on the extent to which ethnic identity in the United States remains strong and predicts strength of attachment to U.S. political institutions and culture. The third pair of contributions (by White and Staub) addresses the role of social identity in lethal violence by and against the state. The seventh chapter (by Kelman) addresses the role of social identity in reducing intergroup conflict.

In setting the stage for the chapters to follow, we address the following questions: What do we mean by social identity? What do we mean by conflict? What is the organizational scheme for this volume? What specific topics do the chapters address?

What Do We Mean by Social Identity?

Self and identity are not simple concepts with widely agreed upon meanings. As we pointed out in the first volume in this series (Ashmore & Jussim, 1997), the terms have been used in a bewildering diversity of ways. Sometimes, the same word or phrase is used by different writers to refer to different concepts; sometimes different words or terms are used to refer to what appears to be the same construct. To make matters worse, self and identity are both *evolving* concepts, which have meant different things in different historical epochs (Baumeister, 1997; Danziger, 1997). Self and identity are also *doubly contested* concepts today. First, the nature and meaning of group-based identities, such as national, ethnic, or gender-based identities, are often contested in the context of sociocultural discourses (for example, consider the potentially strong reactions, both pro and con, that the statement "My country right or wrong" sometimes evokes). Second, the meaning and nature of self and identity as social scientific constructs are contested among researchers from different traditions (Danziger, 1997; Holland, 1997). Social constructivists, for example, often argue against the possibility of even studying self and identity objectively (Holland, 1997), whereas many psychologists and sociologists implicitly assume that self and identity can be studied objectively (Jussim & Ashmore, 1997).

This volume, however, does not attempt to address the multiplicity of controversies surrounding self and identity (though see Ashmore & Jussim, 1997, which does just this). This volume focuses on *social identity* (and its role in intergroup conflict). Social identity is a narrower and more specific subset of the phenomena included under the general rubric of "self and identity." As such, it may be at least somewhat easier to introduce the term in a way that will meet with some agreement across disciplines and perspectives.

Within psychology and sociology, one of the clearest and most common definitions of social identity was provided by Tajfel (1981, p. 255): "that part of an individual's self-concept which derives from his knowledge of his membership in a social group (or groups) together with the value and emotional significance attached to that membership." Thus, according to Tajfel, social identity has two components: belief that one belongs to a group (e.g., "I am an American") and the importance of that group membership to one's self (e.g., "and I am damn proud to be a citizen of the greatest country on earth").

We have not insisted that the contributors use this definition; they were free to define social identity in the manner they saw as most appropriate to their work. Nonetheless, five of the seven contributors cite and use Tajfel's definition. Limitations to this definition, however, were implicitly highlighted by the two authors (Eriksen, Kelman) who did not use it. Tajfel's definition is almost purely *individualistic*, focusing exclusively on how the individual thinks and feels about group memberships. Both Eriksen and Kelman suggest that ethnic and national identities are not purely individualistic—that such identities emerge within specific sociocultural contexts. Sociocultural discourses, national myths, and intergroup relations are all essential to the creation of any particular ethnic or national identity, so that, according to Eriksen and Kelman, social identity resides at least partly within one's national or cultural community, rather than exclusively within the individual.

What Do We Mean by Intergroup Conflict?

Conflict, of course, can occur between almost any type of groups (e.g., sports teams, corporations, university departments, nations, political parties, ethnic groups). The chapters in this book, however, primarily (but not exclusively) emphasize conflict between ethnic, racial, religious, and national groups. This emphasis reflects some of the dominant concerns within the social sciences. Those concerns, we suspect, have largely been motivated by a longstanding desire to understand some of humanity's deepest and most tragic social ills—war, genocide, mass murder, and institutionalized oppression.

Within social psychology, conflict is often defined as some sort of incompatibility of goals, beliefs, attitudes, and/or behavior (e.g., Myers, 1999). The nature of the conflicts addressed in this volume are many and varied. Some address economic and political discrimination within a nation; others address how such discrimination can flare up into murderous intergroup violence. Five chapters focus on specific, real-world conflicts. Eriksen addresses conflicts between Serbs and Bosnians; Fijians and ethnic Indians in Fiji; Hindus and Muslims in India. Citrin et al. and Sidanius and Petrocik address conflicts between white Americans and ethnic minorities in

America. White discusses the multi-sided conflict in Northern Ireland, and Kelman describes his own workshops focusing on reducing the conflict between Israelis and Palestinians.

Three chapters (Brewer, Eriksen, Staub) seek to provide broad, general insights into the intersection of social identity and intergroup conflict. Brewer develops a theoretical perspective on the steps leading to progressively greater intergroup hostility. Eriksen derives general insights into intergroup hostility on the basis of his analysis of three real-world conflicts. Staub focuses specifically on the origins of genocide and mass murder.

The starting point for understanding intergroup conflict often varies across the different social science disciplines. Within social psychology, conflict of some type or another is often addressed, implicitly or explicitly, in theories and approaches to intergroup relations (e.g., Allport, 1954; Oakes, Haslam, & Turner, 1994; Sherif, 1958; Tajfel, 1981). The goal of such research is typically to provide broadly applicable general explanations of phenomena such as bias, prejudice, and discrimination. Social psychological theories customarily provide *individual-level* explanations for conflict and the method of choice is, in general, laboratory experimentation. The starting point for many such perspectives, therefore, is the accumulated experimental evidence addressing issues such as stereotypes and prejudice.

This is in stark contrast to many of the other social sciences, such as anthropology, political science, and sociology. Work in these disciplines often focuses on understanding the history, sources, and nature of particular intergroup conflicts. When general principles are sought, however, the starting point is usually real-world conflicts between nations, ethnic groups, or religious groups. There is often more emphasis on organizational, institutional, and sociocultural levels of explanation. The methods of choice tend to be surveys, interviews, ethnographies, archives, and other sources for historical analysis. Consequently, the literatures addressing intergroup conflict in the different social sciences have developed largely independently, and often may appear to be talking past one another. One purpose of this book, therefore, was to begin to redress this tendency by drawing contributors from several social sciences (anthropology, political science, psychology, and sociology).

Themes Underlying This Book

Several themes provide the framework for the specific topics addressed by the volume: (1) identity issues are important to diverse intergroup conflicts; (2) conflict influences social identity; (3) social identity can contribute to intergroup conflict; (4) addressing issues of social identity may be useful or even necessary for reducing some conflicts; and (5) to understand how identity figures in intergroup strife, it is necessary to consider multiple levels of analysis.

Identity Issues Are Important to Diverse Intergroup Conflicts

Regardless of whether intergroup conflicts are played out peacefully in cultural and political arenas, or become violent and murderous, social identity is usually involved. On the peaceful side, consider the various conflicts within the United States over issues such as affirmative action, immigration, and official use of the English language. These conflicts often seem to involve social identities—with policy preferences and attitudes often varying among different ethnic groups in such a manner as to enhance the power, status, or privileges of one's own group.

Or consider the more brutal side: the various incidents of mass murder and genocide that have occurred throughout human history. In many cases, extreme nationalist movements link a deep commitment to a national or ethnic identity to hatred of a minority group—a pattern that can be found in the Turkish genocide of the Armenians, the German genocide of the Jews, and in Serbian mass murder of Bosnians.

Conflict May Influence Social Identity

People are usually affected, sometimes deeply, by intergroup conflicts. Cultural stereotypes and prejudices can lead members of stigmatized groups to disidentify with and disengage from tasks in which they are most heavily stigmatized (Steele, 1997). Some African-American youths, for example, disengage from academic achievement because negative intellectual stereotypes about African Americans are too threatening and because high achievement may be seen as "acting white" (Fordham & Ogbu, 1986; Steele, 1997).

Furthermore, groups that have once been victimized by conquest, enslavement, or genocide may, in turn, undergo identity changes that render them more vulnerable to *committing* atrocities against other groups in the future. At least sometimes, a "we better get them before they get us" attitude becomes a critical component of a national or ethnic identity. When such an attitude takes hold on a large scale, the society may become less likely to consider making peace with enemies, more likely to seek violent solutions to conflicts, and more likely to commit genocide (du Preez, 1994; Goldhagen, 1996; Staub, 1989).

Social Identity May Contribute to Intergroup Conflict

Intergroup violence can be fostered by social identities as well as stem from group-based self-interest (the notion of realistic group conflict [Ashmore & Del Boca, 1976]). For example, the recent Serbian-Kosovar conflict was started over a material issue: who, Serbs or Kosovars, would have political authority over Kosovo? But one of the reasons this was important to the Serbian government was the historical linkage of Kosovo with Serbian identity (it was the location of a 600-year-old stand by Serbs against invading Turks).

Addressing Issues of Social Identity May Be Useful for Reducing Some Conflicts

At the same time, social identity can assist in alleviating intergroup conflict. For example, Sherif's (1958) classic work on "superordinate goals" demonstrated that members of two groups in conflict can work toward a shared goal. Doing so can involve a new sense of "us," which likely contributes to the lessened hostility that "superordinate goals" produce (cf. Gaertner, Dovidio, Anastasio, Bachman, & Rust, 1993).

To Understand How Identity Figures in Intergroup Strife, It Is Necessary to Consider Multiple Levels of Analysis

The incorporation of the final organizing variable—level of analysis—underscores that the links of identity to intergroup conflict cannot be reduced either to the characteristics of individuals or to the qualities of groups. Fortunately, however, different social and behavioral sciences tend to emphasize different levels of analysis. Thus, it was necessary that contributors to this volume come from diverse academic disciplines that cover the full continuum—from those that focus primarily on the individual (as most psychologists do), to others that emphasize understanding the relationship of individuals to institutions and social structure within a society (as do many sociologists and political scientists), to still others that investigate multiple societies (as do many anthropologists).

The Chapters in This Volume

Three sections, each including two chapters, address different aspects of relations between identity and conflict: (1) general analyses of how social identities contribute to conflicts between groups and how conflict can influence social identity; (2) analyses of the extent to which ethnic identities influence degree of patriotism and attachment to mainstream American political culture and institutions; and (3) perspectives on how social identity contributes to lethal intergroup violence. The fourth topic is conflict resolution, which is addressed in a chapter that describes a specific conflict reduction intervention and the role of social identity in this intervention.

How Social Identities Contribute to Intergroup Conflict

The first section analyzes the role of identity, as both a group- and individual-level variable, in contributing to intergroup conflict. Ethnic and national rivalries have a long history of leading to intergroup conflicts with horrendous consequences. In the extreme, ethnic identity has led to mass murder (e.g., in the former Yugoslavia). National identities, especially in the form of aggressive nationalism, have contributed to genocides and global war (e.g., the Nazi Holocaust and World War II). Ethnic identities have also contributed to slavery, discrimination, and exploitation.

In chapter 2, Brewer reviews the psychological research on social identity and intergroup strife. Social psychologists have long studied how individuals' social identities and group memberships influence their reactions to, and perceptions of, others. Much work has addressed the role of individual-level stereotypes, prejudice, and discrimination in intergroup conflict. In addition, two related theories—social identity theory and self-categorization theory (Tajfel, 1981; Turner, 1987) have explicitly identified ways in which individuals' group memberships and social identities may lead to intergroup strife. Brewer integrates existing theoretical perspectives on social identity with social cognition research on stereotypes and prejudice and with her own work on optimal distinctiveness into a new perspective. Her analysis suggests that intergroup harm-doing is the end result of a series of progressively more hostile steps that include the psychological categorization of people into groups, ingroup trust and preference, perceived moral superiority of the ingroup over outgroups, and antagonism toward outgroups. She argues that although progression from each step to the next is not inevitable, the occurrence of each step increases the likelihood that the next will occur.

In chapter 3, Eriksen addresses this topic by focusing on three case studies of the role of identity in intergroup conflict: the Serbian-Bosnian conflict; the *Hindutva* movement in India; and relations between ethnic Indians and Fijians on Fiji. In all three cases, Eriksen describes how conceptions of "us" and "them" (social identities and intergroup relations) are influenced by societal/cultural phenomena such as the existing power structure, nationalistic leaders, national myths, and modernization. He then discusses how these socially and historically constructed views of "us" and "them" in turn contribute to intergroup conflict.

To What Extent Do Ethnic Identities Influence Attachment to the Mainstream Political Culture of the United States?

The second section of the book focuses specifically on relations between ethnicity and attachment to mainstream American political culture. To what extent have different ethnic groups adopted mainstream American values and become strongly attached to American political institutions? To what extent does a strong ethnic identity undermine attachment to American political culture? Two chapters address these issues.

In chapter 4, Citrin, Wong, and Duff assess ethnic similarities and differences regarding key, symbolic aspects of American identity. Levels of chauvinism, patriotism, and pride in America are strikingly similar among blacks, whites, Asians, and Hispanics. Personal commitment to an American identity serves to bind Americans to the United States and to bring diverse groups together in providing a common identity, and, to some extent, a common set of interests.

However, alongside this common sense of attachment to America, many people, especially members of minority groups, express a strong sense of attachment to their ethnic groups. Among whites, furthermore, a strong attachment to a white racial identity seems to foster intergroup conflict. Specifically, such whites tend to be most resistant to policies aimed at improving the social and political conditions facing Blacks. In contrast, strong ethnic attachment among minority groups did not seem to foster intergroup hostility.

In chapter 5, Sidanius and Petrocik compare three general perspectives—melting pot, pluralist, and social dominance—regarding relations between ethnic identity and national identity among African-American, white, Latino, Asian, and Jewish United States citizens, and among resident aliens living in the United States They find that: (1) ethnic identities remain strong for many people; (2) ethnocentrism exists among all groups they studied; (3) differences in patriotism between whites and the non-black ethnic groups is small or nonexistent; but (4) differences in patriotism between African Americans and whites are larger. Sidanius and Petrocik interpret these results as most consistent with the social dominance model, which predicts that the strongest support for a society's culture and institutions will be found among those groups that benefit most from that culture and those institutions.

Social Identity and Lethal Intergroup Conflict

The third section of the book is devoted to the role of national and ethnic identity in the instigation of deadly violence. Intergroup hostility, even when intense, does not always erupt into violence. And even when violent, conflicts do not always erupt into mass killing, ethnic cleansing, or genocide. Nonetheless, systematic and widespread state-sponsored violence is clearly one of the ultimate manifestations of conflict between groups. From biblical stories of conquest, to the Romans' treatment of foes and rebellious peoples (e.g., Carthage, Israel), the Crusades, the Turkish slaughter of Armenians, the German Holocaust, the Cambodian genocide, and widespread killings in Rwanda and Bosnia, mass murder and genocide have emerged as gruesome recurrent themes of intergroup relations. Thus, two chapters address the role of social identity in lethal intergroup conflicts.

In chapter 6, White presents an analysis of the ongoing hostilities in Northern Ireland. In tracing the historical roots of the existing conflict, he identifies three primary perpetrators of violence: the Irish Republican paramilitaries, Protestant paramilitaries, and the state's security forces. He analyzes the role of religious, political, and national identities in perpetuating the conflict and the violence. He concludes that: (1) social identities play a crucial role in maintaining the conflict; and (2) very different types of identities underlie each group's involvement. IRA members often view themselves as working for freedom and to overcome the oppression of the Irish by the British; Protestant paramilitary members view themselves as fighting for the defense of their religious/ethnic group; and British political leaders view themselves, at least according to their public statements, as unbiased peacekeepers (a view that White argues is not completely consistent with their actions there).

In chapter 7, Staub presents a social psychological analysis of factors leading to, and preventing, genocide. He describes the social and historical conditions that often predispose a society toward genocidal violence. In so doing, he highlights the various ways in which self and social identity are involved in the processes of mass killing. For example, he concludes that "injured" social identities—the belief that one's group has been unfairly victimized in the past and, therefore, is at greater risk of being victimized in the future—is one major precursor of genocide ("we have to get them before they get us"). Staub also discusses the types of interventions that seem to avert genocide.

Social Identity Approaches to Reducing Intergroup Conflict

In chapter 8, Kelman describes his extensive experience running conflict-resolution workshops for Palestinians and Israelis. Through these workshops, it has become clear that each side tends to have components of a national identity that seem to reduce the conflict to a zero-sum game. Indeed, even acknowledging the identity and existence of the other group has often been viewed as a threat to one's own identity and existence as a nation. However, Kelman also points out that, although the core identity of both peoples may be non-negotiable, there are many peripheral aspects of those identities that have emerged from these workshops as negotiable. Kelman's chapter, therefore, describes the role of identity in both contributing to the Israeli-Palestinian conflict and in seeking solutions to that conflict.

Conclusion

Research on identity and on conflict have long histories within the social and behavioral sciences. Until relatively recently, however, research on relations between identity and conflict has been less common. In the last 20 years, researchers in anthropology, political science, psychology, and sociology have begun to study how group identifications contribute to conflict, how intergroup conflict can influence identity, and, most recently, how identities might be harnessed to reduce intergroup hostility. This volume does not summarize all such existing work. The following chapters do present a sophisticated and detailed analysis of some of the most fundamental issues involved in understanding identity and conflict. Chapters address conflict between ethnic, racial, religious, and national groups; they address ethnic differences in national attachment; political conflicts over territory; and genocidal conflicts. As the chapters take stock of existing work on identity and conflict within several social scientific disciplines, we suspect that both their diversity and some similarities in underlying themes will stand out.

References

Allport, G. (1954). *The nature of prejudice.* Cambridge, MA: Addison-Wesley.

Ashmore, R. D., & Del Boca, F. K. (1976). Psychological approaches to understanding intergroup conflict. In P. Katz (Ed.), *Towards the elimination of racism* (pp. 73–123). Elmsford, NY: Pergamon Press.

Ashmore, R. D., & Jussim, L. (Eds.) (1997). *Self and identity: Fundamental issues* (Rutgers Series on Self and Social Identity, Volume 1). New York: Oxford University Press.

Baumeister, R. F. (1997). The self and society: Changes, problems, and opportunities. In R. D. Ashmore, & L. Jussim, (Eds.), *Self and identity: Fundamental issues* (Rutgers Series on Self and Social Identity, Volume 1; pp. 191–217). New York: Oxford University Press.

Danziger, K. (1997). The historical formation of selves. In R. D. Ashmore, & L. Jussim, (Eds.), *Self and identity: Fundamental issues* (Rutgers Series on Self and Social Identity, Volume 1; pp. 137–159). New York: Oxford University Press.

du Preez, P. (1994). *Genocide: The psychology of mass murder.* Southampton, UK: Bowerdean Publishing Co.

Fordham, S., & Ogbu, J. U. (1986). Black students' school success: Coping with the "burden of acting White." *Urban Review, 18,* 176–206.

Gaertner, S. L., Dovidio, J. F., Anastasio, P. A., Bachman, B. A., & Rust, M. C. (1993). The common ingroup identity model: Recategorization and the reduction of intergroup bias. In W. Stroebe & M. Hewstone (Eds.), *European review of social psychology, 4,* pp. 1–26, London: Wiley.

Goldhagen, D. (1996). *Hitler's willing executioners: Ordinary Germans and the holocaust.* New York: Alfred A. Knopf.

Greenfeld, L., & Chirot, D. (1994). Nationalism and aggression. *Theory and Society, 23,* 79–130.

Gurr, T. R. (1993). Why minorities rebel: A global analysis of communal mobilization and conflict since 1945. *International Political Science Review, 14,* 161–201.

Holland, D. (1997). Selves as cultured: As told by an anthropologist who lacks a soul. In R. D. Ashmore, & L. Jussim, (Eds.), *Self and identity: Fundamental Issues* (Rutgers Series on Self and Social Identity, Volume 1, pp. 160–190). New York: Oxford University Press.

Jones, J. (1997). *Prejudice and Racism* (second edition). New York: McGraw-Hill.

Jussim, L., & Ashmore, R. D. (1997). Fundamental issues in the study of self and identity—contrasts, contexts, and conflicts. In R. D. Ashmore, & L. Jussim, (Eds.), *Self and identity: Fundamental issues* (Rutgers Series on Self and Social Identity, Volume 1, pp. 218–230). New York: Oxford University Press.

Keegan, J. (1993). *A history of warfare*. New York: Alfred A. Knopf.

Kelman, H. C. (1997). Some determinants of the Oslo breakthrough. *Negotiaion Journal, 13*, 327–340.

Kreisburg, L., Northrup, T. A. & Thorson, S. J. (1989). Intractable conflicts and their transformation. *Dynamics of Identity, 4*, 55–82.

Myers, D. G. (1999). *Social psychology* (fifth edition). New York: McGraw-Hill.

Oakes, P. J., Haslam, S. A., & Turner, J. C. (1994). *Stereotyping and social reality*. Cambridge, MA: Blackwell.

Reich, W. A. (1997). An expanded role for identity in the analysis of intergroup conflict. Unpublished manuscript.

Sherif, M. (1958). Superordinate goals in the reduction of intergroup conflict. *American Journal of Sociology, 63*, 349–363.

Staub, E. (1989). *The roots of evil: The origins of genocide and other group violence*. Cambridge: Cambridge University Press.

Steele, C. (1997). A threat in the air: How stereotypes shape intellectual identity and performance. *American Psychologist, 52*, 613–629.

Tajfel, H. (1981). *Social identity and intergroup relations*. London: Cambridge University Press.

Thoits, P. A., & Virshup, L. K. (1997). Me's and we's: Forms and functions of social identities. In R. D. Ashmore, & L. Jussim, (Eds.), *Self and identity: Fundamental issues* (Rutgers Series on Self and Social Identity, Volume 1; pp 106–133). New York: Oxford University Press.

Turner, J. C. (1987). *Rediscovering the social group: A self-categorization theory*. New York: Basil Blackwell.

PART I

THE CONTRIBUTION OF INDIVIDUALS' IDENTITIES AND THE COLLECTIVE IDENTITIES OF SOCIAL GROUPS TO INTERGROUP CONFLICT

Ingroup Identification and Intergroup Conflict

When Does Ingroup Love Become Outgroup Hate?

Social psychologists' interest in social identity and ingroup bias arose in the context of research on intergroup relations (Tajfel & Turner, 1986; Brewer & Brown, 1998). As a consequence, there has been a coupling of the study of ingroup favoritism and outgroup prejudice, the implicit assumption being that the more we know about why individuals become attached to their ingroups, the more we will understand why they come to dislike or derogate outgroups. The present chapter seeks to challenge that assumption by examining more carefully the nature of the relationship between ingroup love and outgroup hate. The basic thesis is that the formation of ingroups and ingroup identification arises independently of attitudes toward outgroups. Attachment to ingroups is presumed here to be the primary process, fundamental to individual survival and well-being. Ingroup identification thus precedes outgroup hostility and intergroup conflict but is not by itself a sufficient explanation for such conflict. Instead, as this chapter will argue, we need to trace the steps that lead from ingroup formation to outgroup hostility, specifying the conditions under which the two become entangled.

Sumner's Theory of Ethnocentrism

An early theory of the interrelationship between ingroup attachment and identification and outgroup antagonism was implicit in the definition of "ethnocentrism" when the term was introduced by Sumner (1906). Ethnocentrism was described by Sumner as a universal characteristic of human social groups whereby a differentiation arises between ourselves, the we-group, or in-group, and everybody else, or the others-group, out-groups. The insiders in a we-group are in a relation of peace, order, law, government, and industry, to each other. Their relation to all outsiders, or others-groups, is one of war and plunder. . . . Ethnocentrism is the technical name for this view of things in which one's own group is the center of everything, and all others are scaled and rated with reference to it. . . . Each group nourishes its own pride and vanity, boasts itself superior, exalts its own divinities, and looks with contempt on outsiders. . . . (pp. 12–13)

The features characteristic of Sumner's ethnocentrism syndrome include negative attitudes toward outgroups as well as positive feelings and evaluations of the ingroup. Further, an explicit negative correlation between ingroup and outgroup attitudes is postulated: the greater the attachment and solidarity within the ingroup, the greater the hostility and contempt directed toward outgroups. This hypothesized relationship between ingroup love and outgroup hate derived from Sumner's functional theory of the origins of social groups and intergroup conflict:

> The relation of comradeship and peace in the we-group and that of hostility and war towards others-groups are correlative to each other. The exigencies of war with outsiders are what make peace inside, lest internal discord should weaken the we-group for war. . . . Thus war and peace have reacted on each other and developed each other, one within the group, the other in the intergroup situation. . . . Sentiments are produced to correspond. Loyalty to the ingroup, sacrifice for it, hatred and contempt for outsiders, brotherhood within, warlikeness without—all group together, *common products of the same situation*. (1906, pp. 12–13, emphasis added)

The last 20 years of social psychological research on ingroup bias and intergroup relations have cast doubt on the validity of the functional relationship between ingroup and outgroup attitudes and behavior presumed by Sumner. Results of the laboratory experiments using the "minimal group paradigm" designed by Tajfel and his colleagues (Tajfel, Billig, Bundy, & Flament, 1971) explicitly challenged the assumption that differential treatment of ingroup and outgroup members derives from cooperative interdependence within groups and competitive relations between groups. In the minimal group experiments, mere categorization of persons into differentiated social groupings has proved to be sufficient to give rise to preferential discrimination in favor of ingroup over outgroup members, in the absence of any differential interdependence (Tajfel et al., 1971; Turner, 1978; Brewer, 1979; Diehl, 1990). Field studies assessing the relationship between identification and attachment to ingroups and discrimination against outgroups have also failed to find any straightforward negative correlation between ingroup positivity and intergroup attitudes (Hinkle & Brown, 1990). For example, in a study of the reciprocal attitudes among 30 ethnic groups in East Africa, Brewer and Campbell (1976) found that almost all of the groups exhibited systematic differential positive evaluation of the ingroup over all outgroups on dimensions such as trustworthiness, obedience, friendliness, and honesty, but the correlation between this measure of ingroup positivity and distancing from outgroups was essentially .00 across the 30 groups (p. 85). Thus, the question of when and how ingroup identification is related to outgroup hostility and intergroup conflict requires further investigation.

Decomposing Ethnocentrism: Ingroup, Intergroup, and Outgroup Orientations

Sumner's definition of ethnocentrism cited at the beginning of this chapter contains four separate propositions. The four distinguishable elements can be characterized as follows:

1. Human social groups are organized into discrete ingroup-outgroup categories (the *social categorization principle*).
2. Individuals value their ingroups positively and maintain positive, cooperative relationships with members of the ingroup (the *ingroup positivity principle*).
3. Ingroup positivity is enhanced by social comparison with outgroups in which ingroup attributes and outcomes are evaluated as *better than* or superior to those of outgroups (the *intergroup comparison principle*).
4. Relationships between ingroup and outgroups are characterized by antagonism, conflict, and mutual contempt (the *outgroup hostility principle*).

In contrast to Sumner's (1906) expectation that these four elements necessarily cohere into a pattern that is universally characteristic of intergroup relations, a review of relevant social psychological research suggests that the components can be distinguished both empirically and conceptually. However, the components are not entirely independent features of ethnocentric attitudes, either. Instead, I propose that the elements represent a systematic progression along a continuum of possible relationships between ingroup formation and intergroup behavior in which each element in the progression provides a necessary but not sufficient condition for occurrence of the subsequent elements. Within this system, the first two elements are probably universal characteristics of human social groups (as Sumner postulated), but the third and fourth elements require additional social-structural and motivational conditions that are not inherent in the processes of group formation itself.

Social Categorization: The Basic Substrate

Virtually all current theories of social identity and intergroup relations recognize social categorization as the basic cognitive process underlying all intergroup phenomena (e.g, Allport, 1954; Tajfel, 1969). Categorization (a) partitions the multidimensional variability among human beings into discrete subsets, accompanied by (b) accentuation of perceived intracategory similarities and intercategory differences (Doise, Deschamps, & Meyer, 1978; Tajfel, 1969; Tajfel & Wilkes, 1963). The basic processes of categorization and category accentuation are presumed to be the same whether we are talking about individuals' partitioning of the world of physical objects and events or of the social world. Individuals learn to classify objects as functionally interchangeable and develop concepts that distinguish members of one category from those of another as a fundamental tool for negotiating the physical and social environment.

The assimilation and contrast processes underlying category formation and accentuation are independent of any self-involvement in the category system. Just as one can acquire a concept of "apple," which may include a representation of the prototypic member of the category, a theory of the "essence" of appleness, and an understanding of the variability among exemplars of the category, so one can acquire similar conceptualizations of social objects such as "librarian" or "African American." Stereotypic representations (prototypes) of social categories are a natural consequence of categorization and concept formation processes, motivated by the need for cognitive simplification and social structure. As with any other category concept, whether social category stereotypes are positive or negative (or mixed) is a function of what has been learned about the content of the category representation.

What makes social categorization different from nonsocial categorization systems, however, is the potential for self-involvement in that social perceivers are themselves members of *some* social categories (ingroups) and not others. Thus, an additional categorical distinction between ingroup and outgroups may be *superimposed* onto particular social classifications. In the absence of the engagement of this ingroup-outgroup distinction, social categories are merely cognitive concepts that help individuals to make sense of their social world and to direct their behavior toward other individuals. When social categories are also recognized as social ingroups, however, additional processes associated with *self-categorization* (Turner, Hogg, Oakes, Reicher, & Wetherell, 1987) are engaged that lay the groundwork for further social differentiation. Categorization of the self as an ingroup member entails assimilation of the self to the ingroup category prototype and enhanced similarity to other ingroup members. Self-categorization provides the cognitive substrate for attachment to ingroups and differentiation from outgroups—the first step toward ingroup bias and discrimination.

Ingroup Positivity: The Causes and Consequences of Social Identification

Differentiation between ingroups and outgroups does not necessarily carry evaluative implications, and acknowledging one's ingroup membership is not equivalent to identification with that social group. This is clear from Tajfel's (1981) definition of social identity as "that part of an individual's self-concept which derives from his knowledge of his membership of a social group . . . *together with* the value and emotional significance attached to that membership" (p. 255; emphasis added). Social identification, then, entails affective and evaluative processes that are above and beyond mere cognitive classification of the self and others into a shared social category. The affective significance of social identification arises from the felt attachment between the self and the ingroup as a whole.

Social identification represents the extent to which the ingroup has been incorporated into the sense of self, and at the same time, that the self is experienced as an integral part of the ingroup. With high levels of social identification, the group's outcomes and welfare become closely connected to one's own sense of well-being (Brewer, 1991). According to social identity theory, it is this engagement of the self that accounts for the positive valuation of the ingroup and positive orientations toward fellow ingroup members. Self-worth is both projected onto and derived from positive ingroup evaluation. The distinction between ingroup membership and ingroup identification implies that social identification is not an automatic by-product of categorization. Identification implies some *motivation* to define oneself in terms of that group membership and to achieve and maintain inclusion in the ingroup category. Since identification entails some sacrifice of an autonomous self-concept, the question arises as to why individuals would attach some measure of their self-worth and well-being to the fate of a collective.

One explanation that has been offered is that social identity and ingroup positivity are engaged in the interests of enhanced self-esteem (Turner, 1975; Tajfel, 1978). But group outcomes are not always positive or self-aggrandizing, and identification often entails assimilation of group failures as well as successes (Brewer & Weber, 1994; Crocker & Major, 1989; Hirt, Zillmann, Erickson, & Kennedy, 1992; Turner, Hogg, Turner, & Smith, 1984). Overall, results of research on the causal role of self-esteem in social identification are far from convincing (Abrams & Hogg, 1988; Rubin & Hewstone, 1998). In fact, there is good reason to believe that attachment of the self to the group (or other objects) leads to positive valuation of the group, rather than vice versa (Greenwald & Banaji, 1995).

If strength of ingroup identification is largely independent of ingroup status, then motives other than self-enhancement must be implicated in selecting and maintaining social identities. An alternative motivational explanation is provided by optimal distinctiveness theory (Brewer, 1991). The theory postulates that human beings have two powerful social motives: a need for *inclusion* that motivates assimilation of the self into large, impersonal social collectives, and an opposing need for *differentiation* that is satisfied by distinguishing the self from others. As opposing motives, the two needs hold each other in check. When a person feels isolated or detached from any larger social collective, the drive for inclusion is aroused; on the other hand, immersion in an excessively large or undefined social collective activates the search for differentiation and distinctiveness.

Identification with distinctive social groups emerges from the processes involved in satisfying both needs simultaneously. Groups that are exclusive rather than inclusive, groups that have clear categorical boundaries—satisfy the need for inclusion (intragroup assimilation) at the same time that they provide a basis for satisfying the need for differentiation (intergroup contrast). Clear ingroup boundaries serve to secure both inclusion and exclusion. According to optimal distinctiveness theory, ingroups that meet these simultaneous conditions become an integral part of the individual's sense of self and the basis for a secure and stable self-concept. Group identification in this sense involves "transformations in the definition of self and the basis for self-evaluation. When the definition of self changes, the meaning of self-interest and self-serving motivation also changes accordingly" (Brewer, 1991, p. 476).

Optimal distinctiveness theory proposes that social identification is the product of the search for inclusion and differentiation, rather than a consequence of the search for self-esteem. Nonetheless, although the desire for self-enhancement may not be a primary cause of ingroup identification, identification may well lead to a motivation to view the ingroup in the most favorable possible terms. Drawing on Heider's (1958) principles of cognitive balance, the connection between self and ingroup constitutes a *unit* relationship. Assuming that affect toward the self is primarily one of positive regard, positive attitudes toward the group creates balance between unit and sentiment relations. There is empirical evidence that positivity biases associated with ingroup identification arise automatically and without awareness. Perdue, Dovidio, Gurtman, and Tyler (1990), for instance, demonstrated that ingroup signifiers (terms such as "we," "us," and "our") automatically activate positive evaluative responses, as indicated by differential reaction time to recognize subsequent words as "good" (vs. "bad").

Consistency motives are also implicated in relationships between attitudes and behavior; positive evaluations and expectations give rise to trust and cooperative behavior that in turn justify positive feelings and future expectancies. Thus, the process of assimilation between self and others that underlies ingroup formation instigates a "benign cycle" of positive affect and behavior.

The emphasis at this stage on positive affect and evaluations directed toward the ingroup is not devoid of implications for *inter*group relations. Positive attitudes and expectations about ingroup members, perceived similarity, and cooperative orientation are all *limited* to those who share membership in the common ingroup. The extension of positive self-regard to others stops at the boundary between ingroup and outgroups; attitudes toward those outside the boundary are, at best, characterized by indifference. Differential indifference is not without its consequences. When positive regard, empathy, and cooperation are extended to some individuals but not others on the basis of category membership, an initial form of intergroup discrimination is evident (Brewer, 1979, 1996). Compared to ingroupers, outgroupers are less likely to be helped in ambiguous circumstances (Frey & Gaertner, 1986; Gaertner & Dovidio, 1977; Gaertner, Dovidio, & Johnson, 1982), more likely to be seen as provoking aggression (Baron, 1979; Rogers & Prentice-Dunn, 1981), less likely to receive the benefit of the doubt in attributions for negative behaviors (Weber, 1994), and likely to be seen as less deserving of public welfare (Pettigrew & Meertens, 1995).

Studies of ethnic and racial prejudice in the United States and Europe confirm that the essence of "subtle racism" is not the presence of strong negative attitudes toward minority outgroups but the *absence* of positive sentiments toward those groups (e.g., Dovidio & Gaertner, 1993; Pettigrew & Meertens, 1995; Stangor, Sullivan, & Ford, 1991, Study 1). As Gaertner, Dovidio, Anastasio, Bachmann, & Rust. (1993) put it, "Initially it was assumed that in situations in which blacks were treated differently than whites, whites discriminated *against* blacks, and thus reflected subtle, indirectly expressed *negative* racial attitudes. Alternatively, it is possible that, at some fundamental level, aversive racism reflects a pro-white (i.e., pro-ingroup) rather than the solely anti-black bias that was originally proposed" (p. 4).

If social groups differ in access to resources and power, the benefits of ingroup favoritism accrue to members of some groups more than others and contribute to substantial differences in outcomes between the groups as a whole. Ultimately, many forms of discrimination may develop not because outgroups are hated, but because positive affects such as admiration, sympathy, and trust are reserved for the ingroup and withheld from outgroups (Pettigrew & Meertens, 1995). Differential positivity toward ingroups over outgroups also sets the stage for more pernicious forms of intergroup discrimination.

Intergroup Comparison: Social Competition for Positive Distinctiveness

Ingroup positivity implies a sort of self-absorption whereby group members attend to the concerns and welfare of their own group with disregard for the status or outcomes of those outside the ingroup boundary. The orientation is simply "us" versus "not us," with little need to differentiate among outgroups or to take outgroup outcomes into account while pursuing ingroup goals. Satisfaction with the ingroup's well-being is evaluated against internal standards and expectations, independent of the status of those outside the group.

The idea that assessments of goodness and satisfaction can be made in an absolute sense against clear internal standards may hold true for some dimensions of evaluation or some conditions of group living. In studies of the individual self-concept, Neidenthal and Beike (1997) demonstrated that some self-evaluations are affected by comparative context, but others remain stable and independent of comparative information. A parallel distinction may hold for ingroup self-evaluations. Groups that are physically or psychologically isolated from outsiders, for instance, may measure success in terms of basic sustenance or survival in the face of environmental hardships, or in terms of adherence to dogma or beliefs and practices that are not shared by those outside the group.

In most cases, however, standards of evaluation are not so clear-cut, and knowledge of the status of outgroups becomes relevant to assessing the state of welfare of the ingroup. The conditions of social comparison at the intergroup level are parallel to those for interpersonal comparison in the pursuit of self-evaluation as outlined by Festinger (1954). The need for social comparison is aroused when there is uncertainty about one's standing on some dimension of self-evaluation, uncertainty that can be resolved by comparing one's own position to that of *relevant others*. The relevance requirement is particularly interesting because it implies that the self and other (or ingroup and outgroup) must be perceived as similar in some sense (i.e, as subject to the same values or sharing a common frame of reference for evaluation) in order to be useful targets for comparative appraisal. Thus, when ingroup evaluation is dependent upon intergroup comparison, it is necessary to identify specific outgroups for comparison and to distinguish between outgroups that are relevant to ingroup self-regard and those that are not.

Comparison (whether interpersonal or intergroup) is not inherently competitive. This depends on what motives social comparison is serving (Wood, 1989). Comparison can be undertaken for purposes of objective self-appraisal or to motivate self-correction and improvement. When assessments are relative *and* evaluative, however, the better the other is judged to be, the worse the self-evaluation. In this case, ingroup favoritism takes a subtle shift from motivated perceptions that "we are good" to perceptions that "we are *better*." When all of the groups in a social milieu are jockeying for this type of ingroup advantage, ingroup-outgroup relations are characterized by what Turner (1975) referred to as "social competition" for positive identity. Combined with motivations for self-enhancement, then, social comparison becomes social competition and the pursuit of positive self-regard can be achieved only at the expense of the other.

In this case, competition is not necessarily inherent in the availability of positive outcomes but is *created* by the evaluation that is attached to outcomes for the ingroup and outgroup. If resources (economic and social benefits) are valued in an absolute sense, increases in ingroup welfare can be achieved even if the outgroup is also benefitting. However, when valuation (e.g., subjective states such as status) is relative, the welfare of the ingroup and the outgroup is psychologically a *zero-sum* distribution. We cannot improve our position or sense of well-being unless the outgroup is doing *less* well than we are. When resources are also attached to intergroup differences in status and power, this zero-sum mentality is exacerbated. Ingroup bias motivated by a desire to establish or maintain positive distinctiveness of the ingroup relative to the outgroup is a second form of intergroup discrimination that can be differentiated, at least conceptually, from simple ingroup favoritism (Brewer, 1996).

Interestingly, the more similar groups are in their values and aspirations, the more acute the intergroup social competition. When the ingroup and outgroup are arrayed along a single dimension of evaluation that all groups regard as important and relevant to collective self-esteem, comparative appraisals are inevitably competitive. In a context of self-enhancement motives, outgroup achievements are threatening to ingroup position and the closer the outgroup, the greater the threat (Tesser, 1988). Social competition and intergroup threat are diluted when the outgroup is very remote or distant from the ingroup on the dimension of evaluation. Ingroups that enjoy very high status often display largess or magnanimity, rather than ingroup discrimination, toward outgroups that are much lower down on the status ladder. Conversely, low-status groups often exhibit outgroup positivity in evaluations that are related to the status distinction, conceding outgroup superiority on dimensions where the status difference is clear and large (Hinkle & Brown, 1990; Mullen, Brown, & Smith, 1992).

Either of these forms of outgroup favoritism, however, is qualified by strategies that serve ingroup positivity overall. Whereas low-status groups exhibit outgroup positivity on status-relevant evaluations, they generally display greater ingroup bias (compared to their high-status counterparts) on dimensions unrelated to the status differential (Brewer & Campbell, 1976; Brewer, Manzi, & Shaw, 1993; Mullen, Brown, & Smith, 1992). Similarly, outgroup largess on the part of high-status groups quickly reverts to ingroup favoritism when the status gap between ingroup and outgroup is perceived to be closing (Sachdev & Bourhis, 1991; Sidanius, 1993).

In a pluralistic context where multiple dimensions of evaluation are possible, social competition for positive distinctiveness may be more diffused and less intense. In research on individual self-evaluation maintenance it has been demonstrated that individuals feel threatened by a friend's achievements when the domain of performance is highly important and relevant to their own self-evaluation, but a friend's accomplishments are celebrated when the domain is not self-important (Tesser, 1988). Similar effects have been observed in research on ingroup bias and intergroup discrimination. Mummendey and Schreiber (1983) found that when individuals are given the opportunity to choose dimensions of evaluation, they evaluate ingroup products more favorably than outgroups on dimensions chosen by the ingroup but rate the outgroup positively on other dimensions. In general, in-group favoritism is highest on dimensions of evaluation that are important to the ingroup, but is mitigated for dimensions that are important to the outgroup but relatively unimportant to the ingroup (Mummendey & Schreiber, 1984; Mummendey & Simon, 1989).

In interpreting these findings, Mummendey and Schreiber (1983) suggest that social competition occurs only when there is no alternative for establishing one's own positive identity than at the expense of the outgroup. When positive identity is possible for both groups at the same time, judgments are more influenced by fairness than by ingroup bias. Thus, positive distinctiveness does not necessitate across-the-board favoritism of ingroup over outgroups. Ingroup distinctiveness at the expense of outgroups obtains only when valuation is relative and on dimensions that are particularly important to the group's collective self-worth.

Outgroup Antagonism and Intergroup Aggression

Intergroup comparison and social competition provide an initial connection between valuing the ingroup and devaluing relevant outgroups. In the literature on social motives (McClintock, 1972), however, a clear distinction is made between *competition*—the motivation to seek relative gain for the ingroup over others—and *aggression*—the motivation to harm the other as an end in itself. Following this distinction, we can distinguish between intergroup discrimination that is based solely on ingroup favoritism, and discrimination or prejudice that entails an active component of outgroup derogation and aggression (Levin & Sidanius, 1999; Struch & Schwartz, 1989). Aggression directed against an outgroup may originate in the service of protection or enhancement of the ingroup, but it may also become an end in itself—outgroup hate that has become dissociated from ingroup enhancement or desire to benefit the ingroup.[1]

When outcomes are objectively (or perceived to be) zero-sum, it becomes difficult to pin down the locus of bias (Brewer, 1979). If ingroup outcomes improve only as outgroup benefits decrease, it is not clear whether the motivation for discriminatory behavior is to benefit the ingroup (i.e., discrimination *for* us) or to disadvantage the outgroup (discrimination *against* them). Still, the experimental literature on intergroup discrimination provides evidence that the primary motivation is to benefit the ingroup rather than harm the outgroup. In studies where evaluations of the ingroup can be assessed independently of evaluations of the outgroup, conditions that increase ingroup identification and favoritism generally involve enhancement of ingroup evaluations rather than decreased evaluation or derogation of outgroups (e.g., Bettencourt & Dorr, 1998; Brewer, 1979; Brewer, Manzi, & Shaw, 1993).

More direct evidence is provided by research on the asymmetry of positive and negative ingroup bias (Mummendey & Otten, 1998). Although the initial experiments by Tajfel et al. (1971) claimed that ingroup bias in the minimal intergroup situation occurred for allocations of both positive and negative outcomes, subsequent research suggests that when the outcomes to be distributed are negative or harmful, the usual intergroup discrimination may be lessened or may disappear all together. Hewstone, Fincham, and Jaspars (1981) modified the normal paradigm by asking group members to subtract money from ingroup and outgroup recipients. Although some ingroup bias was observed in this context, the levels were lower than those obtained with the standard allocation matrices. Mummendey et al. (1992) extended this finding by asking participants to distribute different durations of an unpleasantly high-pitched tone to ingroup and outgroup members. With harm as an outcome, ingroup bias was generally eliminated and strategies to equalize or minimize the amount of aversive stimulation were observed.

Mummendey and Otten (1998) have suggested that the positive-negative asymmetry in intergroup discrimination is explained by normative con- staints that make it more difficult to *justify* differential allocations that harm others directly than just benefit some more than others. As long as everyone obtains some benefit, it is relatively easy to find justification for why the in- group might be entitled to benefit more than the outgroup. There is even evidence that such ingroup benefiting is considered normative in its own right (Blanz, Mummendey, & Otten, 1997; Platow, O'Connell, Shave, & Hanning, 1995). Thus, allocations that favor the ingroup over the outgroup may be motivated primarily by intentions to be a "good" ingroup member, rather than by any sentiments against the outgroup.

Inflicting harm, however, is not sanctioned so directly. It is more difficult to justify protecting the ingroup if it comes at the expense of inflicting harm on others (Mummendey & Otten, 1998). Thus, even when the ingroup may be disadvantaged, intergroup discrimination is constrained when there is no direct motivation to harm or derogate the outgroup. These are the constraints that are lifted when outgroups are viewed with hatred or con- tempt—emotions that justify outgroup harm above and beyond ingroup benefit. Yet outside of the laboratory, the world is full of evidence of the existence of such self-justified harm toward outgroups, even at great costs to the ingroup. A desire for positive distinctiveness can account for prefer- ential hiring of ingroup members over outgroup members and for selective investment in projects that benefit one's own group over others. But wars of conquest, pograms, and ethnic cleansing require explanation that goes beyond that of achieving positive distinctiveness for the ingroup.

Social identity theory provides an adequate framework for understand- ing ingroup bias and intergroup discrimination of the positive types de- scribed earlier. Assimilation of the self to the ingroup accounts for ingroup positivity, and from there, the extension to relative enhancement of the in- group over outgroups under conditions of intergroup comparison is not a big motivational leap. The story becomes more complicated, however, when one tries to use the same framework to account for more virulent out- group hate and intergroup hostility. To justify aggression against outgroups in the interest of the ingroup, the very existence of the outgroup, or its goals and values, must be seen as a threat to the maintenance of the ingroup and to one's own social identity. Thus, understanding the relationship be- tween ingroup identification and outgroup hostility requires understanding how the interests of the ingroup and those of the outgroup come to be perceived as in conflict. For that purpose, we need to reconsider the fundamental motivations underlying ingroup attachment and the path from ingroup identity to outgroup threat.

From Ingroup Formation to Intergroup Conflict: Another Look

Realistic competition over scarce vital resources provides one explanation for perceived conflict of interests. When resources for survival or flourishing are scarce and groups are locked into negative interdependence (competing for the same resources), the link between ingroup survival and destruction of the outgroup is direct. But analyses of warfare and intergroup violence call into question the necessary role of realistic, objective conflicts of interest in many cases of intergroup conflict (e.g., Sears & Funk, 1991). Perceived threat is often subjective and symbolic, and overt conflict often appears to be the product of prior intergroup antagonism rather than its cause.

The thesis that is being developed here gives prior status to ingroup categorization and identification for understanding the origins of intergroup behavior. This view assumes that ingroups are formed for reasons independent of intergroup conflict and competition over resources. The social and psychological functions served by ingroup formation and identification provide the necessary conditions for collective action—either intragroup or intergroup. Hence, ingroup attachment and loyalty lay the groundwork for intergroup conflict, but outgroup antagonism is not a necessary extension of ingroup positivity and enhancement. Explicating the relationship between social identity and intergroup conflict requires a fuller understanding, first, of the functions of ingroup identification and, then, of the additional conditions that lead to a connection between ingroup attachment and outgroup hostility.

Ingroup Formation: The Boundaries of Cooperation and Trust

If ingroup-outgroup distinctions do not always involve intense (or even mild) competition or conflict over scarce resources, there is need for a theory of the evolution of social groups that does not depend on intergroup conflict per se. Such a theory starts from the recognition that group living represents the fundamental survival strategy that characterizes the human species. In the course of our evolutionary history, humans abandoned most of the physical characteristics and instincts that make possible survival and reproduction as isolated individuals or pairs of individuals in favor of other advantages that require cooperative interdependence with others in order to survive in a broad range of physical environments. In other words, as a species we have evolved cooperation rather than strength and social learning rather than instinct as basic adaptations.

The result is that, as a species, human beings are characterized by *obligatory interdependence* (Brewer, 1997; Caporael, 1997). For long-term survival, we must be willing to rely on others for information, aid, and shared resources, and we must be willing to give information and aid and to share resources with others. At the individual level, the potential benefits (receiving resources from others) and costs (giving resources to others) of mutual cooperation go hand-in-hand and set natural limits on cooperative interdependence. The decision to cooperate (to expend resources to another's benefit) is a dilemma of trust since the ultimate benefits depend on everyone else's willingness to do the same (Brewer, 1981). A cooperative system requires that trust dominate over distrust. But indiscriminate trust (or indiscriminate altruism) is not an effective individual strategy; cooperation must be contingent on the probability that others will cooperate as well.

Social categorization and clear group boundaries provide one mechanism for achieving the benefits of cooperative interdependence without the risk of excessive costs. Ingroup membership is a form of contingent altruism. By limiting aid to mutually acknowledged ingroup members, total costs and risks of nonreciprocation can be contained (see Takagi, 1996, for a related argument). Thus, ingroups can be defined as bounded communities of mutual trust and obligation that delimit mutual interdependence and cooperation.

An important aspect of this mutual trust is that it is *depersonalized* (Brewer, 1981), extended to any member of the ingroup whether personally related or not. Psychologically, expectations of cooperation and security promote positive attraction toward other ingroup members and motivate adherence to ingroup norms of appearance and behavior that ensure one will be recognized as a good or legitimate ingroup member. Symbols and behaviors that differentiate the ingroup from local outgroups become particularly important here, to reduce the risk that ingroup benefits will be inadvertently extended to outgroup members, and to assure that oneself is recognized as a member of the ingroup and entitled to those benefits. Assimilation within and differentiation between groups is thus mutually reinforcing, along with ethnocentric preference for ingroup interactions and institutions.

The optimal distinctiveness model of social identity (Brewer, 1991) was based on this evolutionary perspective on the functions of ingroup formation and differentiation. The theory assumes that psychological mechanisms at the individual level (opposing needs for differentiation and inclusion) co-evolved with structural requirements at the group level for successful group functioning and coordination (size and boundedness). The relative strength of inclusion and differentiation needs at the individual level interacts with group properties such as size and permeability to determine social identification and ingroup attachment and loyalty. The psychology of assimilation and differentiation limits the extent to which strong social identification can be indefinitely extended to highly inclusive, superordinate social groups or categories.

Thus, one implication of optimal distinctiveness theory is that ingroup loyalty, and its concomitant depersonalized trust and cooperation, is most effectively engaged by relatively small, distinctive groups or social categories. Groups that satisfy these needs are those that provide the necessary boundaries on mutual obligation and trust. Optimal group identities become essential to a secure self-concept. Once group identification has been achieved, maintaining a secure sense of inclusion and boundedness becomes tantamount to protecting one's own existence. When optimal inclusion within a distinctive ingroup is not achieved, the sense of self is threatened and vulnerable.

Intergroup Differentiation and Outgroup Stereotypes

A consequence of ingroup identification and intergroup boundaries is that individuals modify their social behavior depending on whether they are interacting with ingroup or outgroup members. Ingroup behavior is governed by norms and sanctions that reinforce expectations of mutual cooperation and trustworthiness. Depersonalized trust is supported by implicit understandings that ingroup members will monitor the behavior and interactions of other group members, sanctioning deviations from group expectations about appropriate ingroup attitudes and behavior. Thus, shared ingroup membership may be taken as *prima facie* evidence that other members of the group will live by the codes of conduct that bind them as a group (Kramer, Brewer, & Hanna, 1996).

Just as there is a realistic basis for ethnocentric trust of ingroups, differences in norms and sanctions applied to ingroup behavior compared to behavior in interactions with outgroup members provide a realistic basis for outgroup distrust and negative stereotypes. At the same time that groups promote trust and cooporation within, they caution wariness and constraint in intergroup interactions. Thus, even in the absence of overt conflict between groups, the differentiation between ingroup and outgroup behavior creates a kind of self-fulfilling prophecy in the realm of intergroup perceptions. As LeVine and Campbell (1972) put it, "if most or all groups are, in fact, ethnocentric, then it becomes an 'accurate' stereotype to accuse an outgroup of some aspect of ethnocentrism" (p. 173).

Combined with the accentuation principle that exaggerates perceived differences between social categories, this leads to a set of "universal stereotypes" to characterize ingroup-outgroup differences. Whereas "we" are trustworthy, peaceful, moral, loyal, and reliable, "they" are clannish, exclusive, and potentially treacherous. What is particularly interesting about this pattern of stereotypes is that the same behaviors that are interpreted as reasonable caution on the part of the ingroup in dealings with outgroup members become interpreted as "clannishness" and indicators of potential treachery when exhibited by outgroupers toward the ingroup.

Evidence for this hypothesized universal difference in ingroup versus outgroup stereotypes was provided by data from our survey of intergroup perceptions in East Africa (Brewer & Campbell, 1976). Respondents in the survey were presented with a lengthy list of character traits (both positive and negative) and asked to indicate which groups were most likely to exhibit each trait. When responses to this trait list were factor analyzed, the first factor that emerged was a bipolar evaluative factor interpretable as trustworthiness versus untrustworthiness. Positive loadings on this factor were associated with traits such as "peaceful," "obedient," "honest," "gentle," and "friendly." Negative loadings were obtained for traits such as "quarrelsome," "disobedient," "dishonest with others," "cruel," and "hot-tempered." An index of positive regard was constructed by taking the frequency with which a group was mentioned in connection with positive traits on this factor and subtracting the frequency of mentions in connection with the negative traits. Comparing ingroup and outgroup ratings on this index revealed that all 30 groups in the survey rated their own group more positively than the average rating given to outgroups. Further, 27 of the groups rated the ingroup higher than *any* outgroup in the sample (Brewer & Campbell, 1976, p. 79). Although the assignment of negative traits such as "quarrelsome," "dishonest," and "cruel" varied considerably across outgroups, attributions of positive traits such as "peaceful," "honest," and "friendly" were almost universally reserved for the ingroup.

The socialization experiences that lead to differential expectations and comfort in ingroup dealings compared to dealings with outgroups may be generalized in the form of a generic schema that is brought to all intergroup contexts. Whenever ingroup-outgroup distinctions become salient, the intergroup schema is activated. Just such a generic schema was suggested by Tajfel in his initial explanations for the minimal intergroup discrimination findings (Tajfel et al., 1971). At that time, Tajfel (1970) speculated about a "generic norm" of intergroup behavior that prescribed outgroup competition. More recently, Insko and Schopler (1987) also postulated such a group schema as one explanation for their robust finding that in interdependent situations, people are consistently more competitive in intergroup exchanges than when facing the same situation in an interpersonal context—a finding that is known as the "individual-group discontinuity effect" (Insko et al., 1987, 1990). A primary component of the group schema, as developed by Insko and his colleagues, is schema-based distrust—the learned belief or expectation that intergroup relations are inherently competitive and therefore the outgroup cannot be trusted and the ingroup's welfare must be protected (see also Fiske & Ruscher, 1993). In an experimental test of the schema-based mistrust hypothesis, Insko et al. (1990) found that group discussion preceding an intergroup prisoner's dilemma game was characterized by frequent references to the potential untrustworthiness of the other group, and there was a strong negative correlation between the amount of recorded distrust during discussion and later cooperation in the PDG play. Further, groups more than individuals chose to withdraw from play when that option was made available, where withdrawal serves as an indicator of fear that the other player will prefer competition to cooperation.

The Role of Emotions in Intergroup Contexts

When distrust leads groups to compete in an effort to protect themselves from anticipated outgroup defection, a self-fulfilling cycle of competitiveness is set in motion (Kelley & Stahelski, 1970). What is of importance here is the idea that this cycle is the product of a misattribution process whereby universal ethnocentric behavior (intragroup trust and lack of trust in intergroup encounters) is used to infer malevolent intent on the part of outgroups. Similar misattribution processes may be at work in interpreting and evaluating intergroup differences more generally. If individuals feel discomfort and unease in interactions with outgroups, those feelings may well be attributed to intergroup differences in values, attitudes, and cultural practices. Hence, negative affect becomes associated with intergroup differences and, through a process of misattribution of arousal, intergroup anxiety is transformed into more virulent intergroup emotions of fear, hatred, or disgust (Smith, 1993; Stephan & Stephan, 2000). It is this emotional component that is postulated here to be the critical ingredient that turns intergroup comparison into intergroup antagonism.

One perspective on the etiology of intergroup emotions can be derived from the theory of optimal distinctiveness (Brewer, 1991) described earlier. The theory holds that strong ingroup identification is associated with meeting needs for secure inclusion (though similarity to the ingroup) and secure differentiation (through intergroup distinctions). From this perspective, there are two fundamental sources of potential threat to a person's social identity. One threat comes from feelings of marginalization from the desired ingroup—loss of a secure sense of inclusion and fit. One way of coping with this type of threat is to reaffirm support for ingroup positivity and moral superiority. However, hypervaluation of the ingroup alone may actually increase the distance between the self and the ingroup ideal. Derogation of outgroups, however, increases the contrast between ingroup and outgroup and, indirectly, the relatively similarity between the self and the ingroup by comparison. Thus, threats to inclusion are predicted to heighten feelings of moral superiority, intolerance of difference, and concomitant emotions of contempt and disgust toward relevant outgroups.

The emotions associated with moral superiority may justify some negative discrimination against outgroups, but do not necessarily lead directly to hostility or conflict. In various contexts, groups have managed to live in a state of mutual contempt over long periods without going to war over their differences. The emotions of contempt and disgust are associated with avoidance rather than attack, so intergroup peace may be maintained through segregation and mutual avoidance. However, social changes that give rise to the prospect of close contact, integration, or influence from the outgroup engage the second form of threat to social identity—the threat of loss of distinctiveness, accompanied by feelings of invasion. The emotions engendered by this form of threat are fear and anger—emotions that propel action against the outgroup rather than mere avoidance. This analysis suggests that the combined emotions of contempt (engendered by moral superiority in the service of insecure identity) and anger (engendered by fear of invasion and loss of distinctiveness) provide the potent ingredients that are sufficient to kindle hatred, expulsion, and even ethnic cleansing.

Some Moderating Conditions

The preceding analysis indicates that there are a number of steps by which the effects of social categorization and ingroup-outgroup differentiation may provide a fertile ground for conflict and hate. As the steps progress, the line is crossed between the absence of trust and the presence of active distrust, or between noncooperation and overt conflict. In this final section I consider a few of the conditions that may exacerbate or moderate the process whereby maintaining ingroup integrity and loyalty paves the way to outgroup hate and hostility.

Common Goals.   The presence of superordinate goals or common threat is widely believed to provide the conditions necessary for intergroup cooperation and reduction of conflict (e.g., Sherif, 1966). This belief is an extrapolation of the general finding that *intragroup* solidarity is increased in the face of shared threat or common challenge. It may be true that loosely knit ingroups become more cohesive and less subject to internal factioning when they can be rallied to the demands of achieving a common goal. The dynamics of interdependence are quite different, however, in the case of highly differentiated social groups. Among members of the same ingroup, engaging the sense of trust necessary for cooperative collective action is essentially nonproblematic. In an intergroup context, however, perceived interdependence and the need for cooperative interaction make salient the absence of mutual trust. Without the mechanism of depersonalized trust based on common identity, the risk of exploited cooperation looms large and distrust dominates over trust in the decision structure. It is for this reason that I have argued elsewhere (Brewer, 2000) that the *anticipation* of positive interdependence with an outgroup, brought on by perceptions of common goals or common threat, actually promotes intergroup conflict and hostility. When negative evaluations of the outgroup such as contempt are also already present, common threat in particular may promote scapegoating and blame rather than mutual cooperation.

Perceived positive interdependence with the outgroup also threatens intergroup differentiation. To the extent that feelings of secure inclusion, ingroup loyalty, and optimal identity are dependent upon the clarity of ingroup boundaries and intergroup distinctions, shared experiences and cooperation with the outgroup threaten the basis for social identification. Particularly for individuals who are exclusively vested in a single group identity, the threat of lost distinctiveness may override the pursuit of superordinate goals and lead to resistance to cooperation (collaboration) even at the cost of ingroup self-interest.

Power Politics. Moral superiority, distrust of outgroups, and social comparison are all processes that emerge from ingroup maintenance and favoritism and can lead to hostility and conflict between groups even in the absence of realistic conflict over material resources or power. When groups are political entities, however, these processes may be exacerbated through deliberate manipulation by group leaders in the interests of mobilizing collective action to secure or maintain political power. Social category differentiation provides the fault lines in any social system that can be exploited for political purposes. When trust is ingroup-based, it is easy to fear control by outsiders; perceived common threat from outgroups increases ingroup cohesion and loyalty; appeals to ingroup interests have greater legitimacy than appeals to personal self-interest. Thus politicization—an important mechanism of social change—can be added to the factors that may contribute to a correlation between ingroup love and outgroup hate.

Culture. In addition to psychological needs, there are social structural and cultural factors that may promote the intensity of ingroup attachment and loyalty and enhance the distance between ingroup and outgroups. When the salience and strength of intragroup interdependence and mutual obligation is increased, the importance of maintaining group boundaries is also increased. Hence we might expect that in collectivist societies ingroup-outgroup distinctions and distrust of outgroups would be higher than in individualistic societies where social interdependence is less emphasized. Indeed, findings from cross-cultural studies of ingroup bias in collectivist and individualist societies supports this prediction (Triandis, 1995).

Social Structural Complexity. A strong relationship between intense ingroup favoritism and outgroup antagonism might also be expected in highly segmented societies that are differentiated along a single primary categorization, such as ethnicity or religion. And this would be especially true if the categorization is dichotomous, dividing the society into two significant subgroups. Such segmentation promotes social comparison and perceptions of conflict of interest that give rise to negative attitudes toward outgroups and high potential for conflict. By contrast, the potential for intergroup conflict may be reduced in societies that are more complex and differentiated along multiple dimensions that are not perfectly correlated. Such a complex social structure gives rise to cross-cutting category distinctions that mean that, at the individual level, a person may be attached to one ingroup by virtue of ethnic heritage, to another by religion, to yet another based on occupation, or region of residence, and so forth. With this profusion of social identities some individuals will be fellow ingroup members on one category distinction but outgroupers on another. Such cross-cutting ingroup-outgroup distinctions reduce the intensity of the individual's dependence on any particular ingroup for meeting psychological needs for inclusion, thereby reducing the potential for polarizing loyalties along any single cleavage or group distinction and perhaps increasing tolerance for outgroups in general.

Summary and Concluding Perspectives

The main point of this chapter has been to argue that any relationship between ingroup identification and outgroup hostility is progressive and contingent rather than necessary or inevitable. Ingroup formation arises from processes of social categorization and the need for cooperative interdependence within groups. At the individual level, identification with ingroups is motivated by the need to belong and to participate in bounded cooperative social units. The bounded nature of ingroup attachment means that trust and cooperation are limited to ingroup relations and withheld from outgroups.

Once the self is attached to a distinctive ingroup, additional motives to achieve positive valuation, maintain secure inclusion, and protect ingroup boundaries are engaged. It is at this point that outgroups may become relevant to the maintenance or enhancement of ingroup identity. Social competition for positive valuation shifts initial indifference about outgroup outcomes to concern for the relative position of the ingroup over outgroups. Under these conditions, benefiting the ingroup comes at the expense of outgroup benefits, and positive outcomes for the outgroup may arouse resentment and antagonism if the comparison threatens important bases of ingroup evaluation. This is the first step in connecting ingroup identity to negative outgroup attitudes and underlies many forms of social discrimination and intergroup competition for social status.

At a more extreme point in the progression from ingroup identity to intergroup conflict, perceived threats to ingroup inclusion or differentiation from outgroups promote perceived conflict between ingroup identity and the very existence of the outgroup or its goals and values. This is the point at which preservation of the ingroup justifies direct aggression against the outgroup and underlies conflicts over political control, dominance, and wars of annihilation. Such intense outgroup hostility is not a necessary or inevitable concomitant of strong ingroup identity, but the basic processes of social categorization that give rise to differential treatment of ingroup and outgroup lay the groundwork for distrust and vulnerability that make this escalation possible.

This analysis of the relationship between ingroup identity and outgroup attitudes has a number of implications for research on intergroup relations and the prevention of the more virulent forms of intergroup conflict. First, it implies that the study of ingroup bias, prejudice, and discrimination should make a clearer distinction between discriminatory attitudes and behavior that are based on ingroup preference and positivity and discrimination that is based on antagonism and hostility toward outgroups. This is not to suggest that ingroup-based prejudices are entirely benign or acceptable. Indeed, these are the prejudices that are most likely to be subtle, unconscious, and pervasive and thus more difficult to detect and address than "old-fashioned" outgroup hatred. But understanding the motives underlying discrimination based on group membership leads to different prescriptions for preventing or reducing the discriminatory outcomes.

When differential cooperation, positivity, and trust toward others is based on shared ingroup membership, discrimination can best be reduced by conditions that foster greater inclusiveness, extending the boundaries of the ingroup to include former outgroup members. This is the basic rationale for the common ingroup identity model for reducing intergroup bias through recategorization of ingroup and outgroup into a superordinate category identity (Gaertner et al., 1993). This is most likely to be successful when symbols of superordinate category membership are highly salient and individual needs for differentiation are not aroused.

When intergroup attitudes and relations have moved into the realm of outgroup hate or overt conflict, however, the prospect of superordinate common group identity may constitute a threat rather than a solution (Brewer, 2000). When outgroup attitudes are characterized simply by lack of trust rather than active distrust, there is opportunity for capitalizing on common interests and shared identities. But when intense distrust has already developed, common group identities are likely to be seen as threats (or opportunities) for domination and absorption. In this case, the prescription for conflict reduction may first require protection of intergroup boundaries and distinctive identities.

From this analysis there is an inevitable tension between promoting cooperative interdependence and shared interests at high levels of inclusiveness and the need to maintain and recognize intergroup differentiation and distinctiveness. The negative effects of divisiveness will be most virulent when individuals have very limited options for meeting their needs for secure, optimal group identification. When social cleavages are defined along a single dimension of differentiation, vulnerability to threats to inclusion and differentiation is very high, and maintenance of ingroup identity is most likely to be achieved at the cost of high levels of distrust and antagonism toward outgroups. When societies are more complex, when individuals have multiple avenues for meeting needs for inclusion and distinctiveness, intergroup comparisons along any particular division are likely to be less competitive or critical to member identities. Under these conditions, the positive benefits of distinctive ingroup identities may be attained without the costs of intergroup hostility and conflict.

Note

1. Note, we are dealing here with prejudice and hostility at the collective level. The hatred that a specific individual bears toward a particular type of people is not at issue unless that hatred is grounded in norms and attitudes shared by the ingroup as a whole.

References

Abrams, D., & Hogg, M. A. (1988). Comments on the motivational status of self-esteem in social identity and intergroup discrimination. *European Journal of Social Psychology, 18*, 317–334.

Allport, G. W. (1954). *The nature of prejudice*. Cambridge, MA: Addison-Wesley.

Baron, R. A. (1979). Effects of victim pain cues, victim's race, and level of prior instigations upon physical aggression. *Journal of Applied Social Psychology, 9*, 110–114.

Bettencourt, B. A., & Dorr, N. (1998). Cooperative interaction and intergroup bias: Effects of numerical representation and cross-cut role assignment. *Personality and Social Psychology Bulletin, 24*, 1276–1293.

Blanz, M., Mummendey, A., & Otten, S. (1997). Normative evaluations and frequency expectations regarding positive and negative outcome alloctions between groups. *European Journal of Social Psychology, 27*, 165–176.

Brewer, M. B. (1972). (Series editor). HRAFLEX Ethnocentrism Interview Series. New Haven, CN: Human Relations Area Files.

Brewer, M. B. (1979). In-group bias in the minimal intergroup situation: A cognitive motivational analysis. *Psychological Bulletin, 86*, 307–324.

Brewer, M. B. (1981). Ethnocentrism and its role in intergroup trust. In M. Brewer & B. Collins (Eds.), *Scientific inquiry in the social sciences* (pp. 214–231). San Francisco: Jossey-Bass.

Brewer, M. B. (1991). The social self: On being the same and different at the same time. *Personality and Social Psychology Bulletin, 17*, 475–482.

Brewer, M. B. (1996). In-group favoritism: The subtle side of intergroup discrimination. In D. Messick & A. Tenbrunsel (Eds.), *Codes of conduct: Behavioral research into business ethics* (pp. 160–170). New York: Russell Sage Foundation.

Brewer, M. B. (1997). On the social origins of human nature. In C. McGarty & S. A. Haslam (Eds.), *The message of social psychology* (pp. 54–62). Oxford: Blackwell.

Brewer, M. B. (2000). Superordinate goals versus superordinate identity as bases of intergroup cooperation. In D.Capozza & R. Brown (Eds.), *Social identity processes: Trends in theory and research* (pp. 117–132). London. Sage.

Brewer, M. B., & Brown, R. (1998). Intergroup relations. In D. Gilbert, S. Fiske, & D. Lindzey (Eds.), *The handbook of social psychology. Fourth Edition* (Vol. 1, pp. 99–142). Boston: McGraw-Hill.

Brewer, M. B., & Campbell, D. T. (1976). *Ethnocentrism and intergroup attitudes: East African evidence*. Beverly Hills, CA: Sage.

Brewer, M. B., Manzi, J., & Shaw, J. S. (1993). In-group identification as a function of depersonalization, distinctiveness, and status. *Psychological Science, 4*, 88–92.

Brewer, M. B., & Weber, J. G. (1994). Self-evaluation effects of interpersonal versus intergroup social comparison. *Journal of Personality and Social Psychology, 66*, 268–275.

Caporael, L. R. (1997). The evolution of truly social cognition: The core configurations model. *Personality and Social Psychology Review, 1*, 276–298.

Crocker, J., & Major, B. (1989). Social stigma and self-esteem: The self-protective properties of stigma. *Psychological Review, 96*, 608–630.

Deschamps, J-C., & Brown, R. (1983). Superordinate goals and intergroup conflict. *British Journal of Social Psychology, 22*, 189–195.

Diehl, M. (1990). The minimal group paradigm: Theoretical explanations and empirical findings. In W. Stroebe & M. Hewstone (Eds.), *European review of social psychology* (Vol. 1, pp. 263–292). Chichester, England: Wiley.

Doise, W., Deschamps, J-C., & Meyer, G. (1978). The accentuation of intra-category similarities. In H. Tajfel (Ed.), *Differentiation between social groups* (pp. 159–170). London: Academic Press.

Dovidio, J. F., & Gaertner, S. L. (1993). Stereotypes and evaluative intergroup bias. In D. Mackie & D. Hamilton (Eds.), *Affect, cognition, and stereotyping* (pp. 167–193). San Diego, CA: Academic Press.

Festinger, L. (1954). A theory of social comparison proccesses. *Human Relations, 7*, 271–282.

Fiske, S. T., & Ruscher, J. (1993). Negative interdependence and prejudcie: Whence the affect? In D. Mackie & D. Hamilton (Eds.), *Affect, cognition, and stereotyping* (pp. 239–268). San Diego, CA: Academic Press.

Frey, D., & Gaertner, S. L. (1986). Helping and the avoidance of inappropriate interracial behavior: A strategy than can perpetuate a non-prejudiced self-image. *Journal of Personality and Social Psychology, 50*, 1083–1090.

Gaertner, S. L., & Dovidio, J. F. (1977). The subtlety of white racism, arousal, and helping behavior. *Journal of Personality and Social Psychology, 35*, 691–707.

Gaertner, S. L., Dovidio, J. F., & Johnson, G. (1982). Race of victim, non-responsive bystanders, and helping behavior. *Journal of Social Psychology, 117*, 69–77.

Gaertner, S. L. , Dovidio, J. F., Anastasio, P., Bachman, B., & Rust, M. (1993). The common ingroup identity model: Recategorization and the reduction of intergroup bias. In W. Stroebe & M. Hewstone (Eds.), *European review of social psychology* (Vol. 4, pp. 1–26). Chichester, England: Wiley.

Greenwald, A. G., & Banaji, M. R. (1995). Implicit social cognition: Attitudes, self-esteem, and stereotypes. *Psychological Review, 102*, 4–27.

Heider, F. (1958). *The psychology of interpersonal relations.* New York: Wiley.

Hewstone, M., Fincham, F., & Jaspars, J. (1981). Social categorization and similarity in intergroup behaviour: A replication with "penalties." *European Journal of Social Psychology, 11*, 101–107.

Hinkle, S., & Brown, R. (1990). Intergroup comparisons and social identity: Some links and lacunae. In D. Abrams & M. Hogg (Eds.), *Social identity theory: Construction and critical advances* (pp. 48–70). London: Harvester Wheatsheaf.

Hirt, E. R., Zillmann, D., Erickson, G., & Kennedy, C. (1992). Costs and benefits of allegiance: Changes in fans' self-ascribed competencies after team victory versus defeat. *Journal of Personality and Social Psychology, 63*, 724–738.

Insko, C. A., & Schopler, J. (1987). Categorization, competition and collectivity. In C. Hendrick (Ed.), *Personality and Social Psychology Review. Vol. 8: Group Processes* (pp. 213–251). Beverly Hills, CA: Sage.

Insko, C. A., Pinkley, R., Hoyle, R., Dalton, B., Hong, G., Slim, R., Landry, P., Holton, B., Ruffin, P., & Thibaut, J. (1987). Individual versus group discontinuity: The role of intergroup contact. *Journal of Experimental Social Psychology,* *23,* 250–267.

Insko, C. A., Schopler, J., Hoyle, R., Dardis, G., & Graetz, K. (1990). Individual-group discontinuity as a function of fear and greed. *Journal of Personality and Social Psychology, 58,* 68–79.

Kelley, H. H., & Stahelski, A. J. (1970). The social interaction basis of cooperators' and competitors' beliefs about others. *Journal of Personality and Social Psychology, 16,* 66–91.

Kramer, R. M., Brewer, M. B., & Hanna, B. A. (1996). Collective trust and collective action: The decision to trust as a social decision. In R. Kramer & T. Tyler (Eds.), *Trust in organizations* (pp. 357–389). Thousand Oaks, CA: Sage.

Levin, S., & Sidanius, J. (1999). Social dominance and social identity in the United States and Israel: Ingroup favoritism or outgroup derogation? *Political Psychology, 20,* 99–126.

LeVine, R. A. & Campbell, D. T. (1972). *Ethnocentrism: Theories of conflict, ethnic attitudes and group behavior.* New York: Wiley.

McClintock, C. (1972). Social motivation: A set of propositions. *Behavioral Science, 17,* 438–454.

Mullen, B., Brown, R., & Smith, C. (1992). Ingroup bias as a function of salience, relevance, and status: An integration. *European Journal of Social Psychology, 22,* 103–122.

Mummendey, A., & Otten, S. (1998). Positive-negative asymmetry in social discrimination. In W. Stroebe & M. Hewstone (Eds.), *European review of social psychology* (Vol. 9, pp. 107–143). Chichester, England: Wiley.

Mummendey, A., & Schreiber, H. (1983). Better or just different? Positive social identity by discrimination against or by differentiation from outgroups. *European Journal of Social Psychology, 13,* 389–397.

Mummendey A., & Schreiber, H. (1984). 'Different' just means 'better': Some obvious and some hidden pathways to in-group favoritism. *British Journal of Social Psychology, 23,* 363–368.

Mummendey, A., & Simon, B. (1989). Better or different? III: The impact of importance of comparison dimension and relative ingroup size upon intergroup discrimination. *British Journal of Social Psychology, 28,* 1–16.

Mummendey, A., Simon, B., Dietze, C., Grunert., M., Haeger, G., Kessler, S., Lettgen, S., & Schaferhoff, S. (1992). Categorization is not enough: Intergroup discrimination in negative outcome allocations. *Journal of Experimental Social Psychology, 28,* 125–144.

Neidenthal, P. M., & Beike, D. (1997). Interrelated and isolated self-concepts. *Personality and Social Psychology Review, 1,* 106–128.

Perdue, C. W., Dovidio, J. F., Gurtman, M. B., & Tyler, R. B. (1990). "Us" and "Them": Social categorization and the process of intergroup bias. *Journal of Personality and Social Psychology, 59,* 475–486.

Pettigrew, T. F., & Meertens, R. W. (1995). Subtle and blatant prejudice in Western Europe. *European Journal of Social Psychology, 25,* 57–75.

Platow, M., O'Connell, A., Shave, R., & Hanning, P. (1995). Social evaluations of fair and unfair allocations in interpersonal and intergroup situations. *British Journal of Social Psychology, 34,* 363–381.

Rogers, R. W., & Prentice-Dunn, S. (1981). Deindividuation and anger-mediated interracial aggression: Unmasking regressive racism. *Journal of Personality and Social Psychology, 41*, 63–73.

Rubin, M., & Hewstone, M. (1998). Social identity theory's self-esteem hypothesis: A review and some suggestions for clarification. *Personality and Social Psychology Review, 2*, 40–62.

Sachdev, I., & Bourhis, R. (1991). Power and status differentials in minority and majority group relations. *European Journal of Social Psychology, 21*, 1–24.

Sears, D. O., & Funk, C. L. (1991). The role of self-interest in social and political attitudes. In M. Zanna (Ed.), *Advances in experimental social psychology* (Vol. 24, pp. 2–92). New York: Academic Press.

Sherif, M. (1966). *In common predicament: Social psychology of intergroup conflict and cooperation.* New York: Houghton Mifflin.

Sidanius, J. (1993). The psychology of group conflict and the dynamics of oppression: A social dominance perspective. In S. Iyengar & W. McGuire (Eds.), *Explorations in political psychology* (pp. 183–219). Durham, NC: Duke University Press.

Smith, E. R. (1993). Social identity and social emotions: Toward new conceptualizations of prejudice. In D. Mackie & D. Hamilton (Eds.), *Affect, cognition, and stereotyping* (pp. 297–315). San Diego, CA: Academic Press.

Stangor, C., Sullivan, & Ford, T. E. (1991). Affective and cognitive determinants of prejudice. *Social Cognition, 9*, 359–380.

Stephan, W., & Stephan, C. (2000). An integrated threat theory of prejudice. In S. Oskamp (Ed.), *Reducing prejudice and discrimination* (pp. 23–45). Mahwah, NJ: Lawrence Erlbaum.

Struch, N., & Schwartz, S. H. (1989). Intergroup aggression: Its predictors and distinctness from in-group bias. *Journal of Personality and Social Psychology, 56*, 364–373.

Sumner, W. G. (1906). *Folkways.* New York: Ginn.

Tajfel, H. (1969). Cognitive aspects of prejudice. *Journal of Social Issues, 25*, 79–97.

Tajfel, H. (1970). Experiments in intergroup discrimination. *Scientific American, 223*(2), 96–102.

Tajfel, H. (1978). *Differentiation between social groups: Studies in the social psychology of intergroup relations.* London: Academic Press.

Tajfel, H. (1981). *Human groups and social categories.* Cambridge: Cambridge University Press.

Tajfel, H., Billig, M., Bundy, R., & Flament, C. (1971). Social categorization and intergroup behaviour. *European Journal of Social Psychology, 1*, 149–178.

Tajfel, H., & Turner, J. C. (1986). The social identity theory of intergroup behavior. In S. Worchel & W. Austin (Eds.), *Psychology of intergroup relations* (pp. 7–24). Chicago: Nelson-Hall.

Tajfel, H., & Wilkes (1963). Classification and quantitative judgement. *British Journal of Psychology, 54*, 101–114.

Takagi, E. (1996). The generalized exchange perspective on the evolution of altruism. In W. Liebrand & D. Messick (Eds.), *Frontiers in social dilemma research* (pp. 311–336). Berlin: Springer-Verlag.

Tesser, A. (1988). Toward a self-evaluation maintenance model of social behavior. In L. Berkowitz (Ed.), *Advances in experimental social psychology* (Vol. 21, pp. 181–227). San Diego, CA: Academic Press.

Triandis, H. C. (1995). *Individualism and collectivism.* Boulder, CO: Westview Press.

Turner, J. C. (1975). Social comparison and social identity: Some prospects for intergroup behaviour. *European Journal of Social Psychology, 5*, 5–34.

Turner, J. C. (1978). Social categorization and social discrimination in the minimal group paradigm. In H. Tajfel (Ed.), *Differentiation between social groups* (pp. 101–140). London: Academic Press.

Turner, J. C. , Hogg, M., Turner, P., & Smith, P. (1984). Failure and defeat as determinants of group cohesiveness. *British Journal of Social Psychology, 23*, 97–111.

Turner, J. C. , Hogg, M., Oakes, P., Reicher, S., & Wetherell, M. (1987). *Rediscovering the social group: A self-categorization theory*. Oxford: Blackwell.

Weber, J. G. (1994). The nature of ethnocentric attribution bias: Ingroup protection or enhancement? *Journal of Experimental Social Psychology, 30*, 482–504.

Wood, J. V. (1989). Theory and research concerning social comparisons of personal attributes. *Psychological Bulletin, 106*, 231–248.

Ethnic Identity, National Identity, and Intergroup Conflict

The Significance of Personal Experiences

There exists by now an enormous literature on contemporary ethnicity and nationalism in its various forms. It deals with a wide range of phenomena—North American multiculturalism and indigenous rights movements, post-Soviet ethnonationalism in Central and Eastern Europe, urban minority dilemmas and Islamic revivalism in Western Europe, *indigenista* movements in Latin America, and processes of political fission and fusion in contemporary Africa. The analytical focus of this chapter will be on the concept of identity. The naïve question to be asked at the outset is: what is it about identity politics that makes it such a formidable force in the contemporary world? Some important issues will have to be omitted—notably the relationships among identity politics, globalization, and reflexive modernity (e.g., Bauman, 1993; Friedman, 1994; Giddens, 1994). Instead, what is offered amounts to an anthropological perspective on the relationship between personal identity and political identity, using conflicts based on identity politics as empirical examples.

This chapter sets out to do three things. First, a brief overview of the standard social anthropological perspective on the politics of identity is provided. Identity politics should be taken to mean political ideology, organization, and action that openly represents the interests of designated groups based on "essential" characteristics such as ethnic origin or religion, and whose legitimacy lies in the support of important segments of such groups. Membership in such groups is generally ascribed, unlike membership in other political groups (socialists, liberals, trade unions, etc.). Second, by way of examples from India, Fiji, and Yugoslavia, parallels and differences between some such conflicts are highlighted. The examples are chosen mainly for their differences: what they have in common is, apart from their temporal location in the 1990s, apparently only that they are based on ideologies of culture and identity. The Yugoslav conflict has been extremely brutal and tragic; the Fijian one has involved only a few casualties, but has led to important constitutional changes; while the Indian conflict, although occasionally bursting into violence, is largely contained within the framework of institutional Indian politics. If it can persuasively be argued that these conflicts have important features in common, it is likely that those features will also be present in other settings where identity politics has a major impact. The third and final part of the chapter draws on classic political anthropology in order to suggest some general features of the relationship between personal identity and politics.

The Anthropology of Identity

The last decades of the 20th century saw a dramatic reconceptualization of core concepts, including culture and society, within the social sciences. Until the 1960s, the close overlap between culture and ethnicity, or even culture and nationhood, was generally taken for granted in the scholarly community. During the past 30 years, however, hardly a single serious contribution to the field has failed to point out that there is no one-to-one relationship between culture and ethnicity (the seminal text here is Barth, 1969); that cultural differences cut across ethnic boundaries; and that ethnic identity is based on *socially sanctioned notions* of cultural differences, not "real" ones. While ethnic identity should be taken to refer to a notion of shared ancestry (a kind of fictive kinship), culture refers to shared representations, norms, and practices. One can have deep ethnic differences without correspondingly important cultural differences (as in the Bosnian example below); and one can have cultural variation without ethnic boundaries (as, for example, between the English middle class and the English working class).

Several recent debates in anthropology and neighboring disciplines pull in the same direction: away from notions of integrated societies or cultures toward a vision of a more fragmented, paradoxical, and ambiguous world. The currently bustling academic industry around the notion of globalization (see Featherstone, 1990, for an early, influential contribution) represents an empirically oriented take on these issues, focusing on the largely technology-driven processes that contribute to increasing contact across boundaries and diminished importance of space. This focus on unbounded processes rather than isolated communities has contributed to a reconceptualization of the social, which is radically opposed to that of classic Durkheimian sociology and anthropology; where flux, movement, and change become the rule and not the exception in social life (Strathern, 1991; Hannerz, 1992; Lash & Urry, 1994).

Particularly in North America, the classic concept of culture has been used for what it is worth in domestic identity politics, leading in some cases to controversial policies of multiculturalism, where individuals have been endowed with special rights in accordance with their ethnic origins. Critics might point out that multiculturalism in some of its versions resembles apartheid; also, that by positing a simple one-to-one relationship between ethnic origin and culture, it not only encouraged a "disuniting of America" (Schlesinger, 1992) but also contributed to reifying misleading notions of culture seen as the commonalities of a bounded set of individuals, like so many nationalisms writ small.

A further disruptive tendency has been the so-called postcolonial movement in literary studies, spilling into anthropology and other disciplines, that has raised the question of who has the right to identify whom; a standard text in this field of discourse is Edward Said's *Orientalism* (1978), although Frantz Fanon developed similar insights two decades earlier. Said and others argued, briefly, that ethnocentrism was deeply embedded in Western scholarship dealing with non-Western peoples. Postcolonial critics also tend to call attention to the multiplicity of voices (an academic cliché by the late 1990s) present in any society and the general unwillingness of academic researchers to give all of them the attention they deserve.

Two related debates defined the field for many years. First, there was the controversy over primordialism and instrumentalism. Was ethnic identity "primordial"—that is, profoundly rooted in, and generative of, collective experiences; or did it arise as an ad hoc supplement to political strategies? An early, powerful defense of the instrumentalist view was represented in Abner Cohen's work on urban ethnicity in Africa (1969, 1974), showing the conscious manipulation of kinship and cultural symbols by political entrepreneurs seeking political gain. This perspective is still used with considerable success in studies of identity politics. Who, then, were (or are) the primordialists? Clifford Geertz is often associated with this view, arguing as he does along hermeneutic lines that cultural systems are more or less self-sustaining and are thus not subject to the willful manipulation of individuals (Geertz, 1973), a perspective he retained when writing about nationhood in the Third World (Geertz, 1967). Typically, however, ethnicity studies were—and are—instrumentalist in their basic orientation (Rex, 1997).

The second debate, usually framed as the opposition between constructivism and essentialism, concerns the question of whether ethnic or national communities are created more or less consciously, or whether they grow organically, as it were, out of preexisting cultural communities. In nationalism studies the most highly profiled antagonists regarding this issue have been the late Ernest Gellner (1983, 1997) and Anthony D. Smith. Smith (1986, 1991) has developed an intermediate position in arguing the importance of preexisting *ethnies* for the development of nationalism while acknowledging its essential modernity. Gellner, on the other hand, champions the view that nations are entirely modern creations—the progeny of industrialism and the state—that more or less fraudulently invent their past to gain a semblance of antiquity and deep roots; his final statement on the issue is reproduced in the posthumously published *Nationalism* (Gellner, 1997) under the heading "Do Nations Have Navels?", a pun on the biblical enigma relating to Adam's navel. Regarding definitions, there are also important differences between theorists. While Gellner holds nations to be ethnic groups who either control a state or who have leaders who wish to do so, Anderson (1983) sees no necessary link between the abstract "imagined community" of the nation and particular ethnic groups; indeed, several of the main examples in his famous book on "imagined communities," including the Philippines and Indonesia, are multiethnic countries. Yet others have distinguished between ethnic nations and "civic" ones (Smith, 1991). There is nonetheless general agreement that nations are by definition linked with states, whether they are based on a common ethnic identity or not.

In anthropology at least, the recent shift toward the study of identities rather than cultures has entailed an intense focus on conscious agency and reflexivity; and for many anthropologists, essentialism and primordialism appear as dated as pre-Darwinian biology. In addition, there seems to be good political sense in discarding the old, static view of culture, which is being used for many political purposes that are difficult to endorse by academics committed to democratic values, ranging from the Balkan war to discrimination against ethnic minorities in Western Europe. Further, this is an age when the informants talk back. It could, perhaps, be said that a main purpose of an earlier anthropology consisted of identifying other cultures. Representatives of these so-called other cultures are now perfectly able to identify themselves, which leaves the scholars either out of a job or with a new mission—that is, to identify their identifications—in other words, to study reflexive identity politics.

Not so many years ago, anthropology was still a discipline fueled by a programmatic love of cultural variation for its own sake, and anthropologists involved in advocacy tended to defend indigenous peoples' or other minorities' traditional ways of life against the onslaught of modernity. A main tendency in recent years has, on the contrary, consisted of deconstructing instrumentalist uses of notions of authenticity and tradition, and showing not only that the internal variation within a group is much greater than one would expect but also that traditionalist ideologies are, paradoxically, direct results of modernization (e.g., Roosens, 1989). This theoretical shift is a very significant one. It offers a method for investigating extremely well the strategic action, politics of symbols, and contemporary processes of identity politics within a uniform comparative framework.

In other words, cracks in the edifice of mainstream social and cultural anthropology, some of them directly inspired by events well beyond the confines of academia, have led to a widespread reconceptualization of society and culture. Reification and essentialism have become central terms of denunciation; multiple voices, situational identification, and cultural flows are some of the key words delineating the current intellectual agenda. It has become difficult if not impossible to talk of, say, Nuer culture, Hopi culture, Dutch culture, and so on, since such terms immediately invite critical questions of *whose* Nuer culture, Hopi culture, and so on, intimating that there are an infinite number of versions of each culture, none of which is more "true" than the others (Holland, 1997). Ethnicity and nationalism, then, become the political reifications or constructions of a particular authorized version of a culture, freezing that which naturally flows, erecting artificial boundaries where they did not exist before, trimming and shaping the past to fit present needs, and inventing traditions where no organic traditions exist, or are not adequate, to ensure a sense of continuity with the past.

A new kind of political responsibility has entered academia in acute ways during the last decades. Academic or semiacademic statements about nations, ethnic groups, or cultures may now immediately be picked up, or assimilated more or less subconsciously, by ideologists and politicians wishing to build their reputation on national chauvinism, ethnic antagonism, enemy images, and so on. The liberal academic establishment thus wags a warning finger at those who dare to talk of culture as the *cause* of conflicts, shaking their heads sadly over those lost souls who have not yet heeded the words of leading theorists such as Barth (1969) and Gellner (1983), criticizing those who do not realize that culture is chimerical and fleeting, and that reified culture is a dangerous tool. It is, thus, not only intellectually correct but also politically correct to reject all forms of essentialism.

The current scholarly orthodoxy on ethnicity and the politics of identity can be summed up as follows:

- Although ethnicity is widely believed to express cultural differences, there is a variable and complex relationship between ethnicity and culture; and there is certainly no one-to-one relationship between ethnic differences and cultural ones.
- Ethnicity is a property of a relationship between two or several groups, not a property of a group; it exists *between* and not *within* groups.
- Ethnicity is the enduring and systematic communication of cultural differences between groups considering themselves to be distinct. It appears whenever cultural differences are made relevant in social interaction, and it should thus be studied at the level of social life, not at the level of symbolic culture.
- Ethnicity is thus relational and also situational: the ethnic character of a social encounter is contingent on the situation. It is not, in other words, inherent.

This instrumentalist framing of ethnicity, which may appear simply as a set of methodological guidelines, has firm, although usually untheorized, philosophical foundations and is, as I have tried to show elsewhere (Eriksen,

1998b), deeply embedded in empiricist thought. I shall argue that this approach, notwithstanding its strengths, is limited in overemphasising choice and strategy (instrumental aspects) when analyzing identity politics. As a result, the self is taken for granted (A.P. Cohen, 1994), and it is therefore not shown how it can be possible to mobilize particular aspects of personal identity for antagonistic identity politics. Yet, anthropology as a discipline is in a privileged situation to study the dynamics of identity politics, precisely because of its focus on the ongoing flow of social interaction.

Although an enormous amount of anthropological research has been carried out on ethnicity and nationalism since around 1970, surprisingly few studies have dealt with violent conflicts and conflict resolution (see, however, Tambiah, 1994; Turton, 1997). The dominant approaches to ethnicity have been instrumentalist (with a focus on politics) or constructivist (with a focus on ideology), and research questions have concentrated on the establishment and reproduction of ethnically incorporated groups, not on the circumstances under which ethnicity may become politically less important. While my examples (below) and the ensuing discussion will indicate the fruitfulness of these approaches, it is also necessary to point out the need for a phenomenological understanding of social identity, which sees it as emerging from experiences, not as a mere construct of ideology. In this, I follow scholars such as A. P. Cohen (1994) and Jenkins (1996), who have called for an anthropology of identity that does not concentrate exclusively on its political and ideological aspects, but also strives to understand the self.

As noted by Holland (1997), anthropologists are generally associated with a culturalist view of the self, arguing its cultural specificity as against psychologists, who have been more prone to a universalist view—the self as something proper not to particular cultures but to humanity, with universal characteristics lurking below a thin veneer of culture. For the purposes of the present argument, it is not necessary to take a stance on this controversy, partly since it can be presupposed that modernity creates a particular kind of selves with important shared characteristics everywhere (Giddens, 1991), but also because this chapter restricts its scope to the relationships among personal experiences, ideology, and political mobilization. As the examples will, it is hoped, show, the similarities are more striking than the differences here.

Culture and the Breakup of Yugoslavia

No other recent ethnic conflict has been more intensely studied, discussed, and moralized over than the breakup of Yugoslavia in 1991. This was followed by three major wars and a number of smaller skirmishes, and the situation in many parts of ex-Yugoslavia remains unstable and tense. In Europe, the outbreak of war in Yugoslavia has been interpreted by hundreds of commentators. In the press, it was occasionally argued, along sociobiological or Hobbesian lines, that humans are driven by aggressive instincts that emerge when the social fabric falls apart, in this case organized as factions ultimately based on kinship. Another view, popular in the European nationalist right, implied that ethnic conflict was inevitable when different groups are forcibly integrated into one state. Most scholars have, on the contrary, tended to focus on the cultural logic of feuding in Balkan society, the deep economic crisis underlying the conflict, or the rise of Serbian supremacy during the 1980s, looking for contradictions within Yugoslav society rather than into human nature for an explanation of the conflict. A widespread view nevertheless sees the cultural differences between the constituent groups as a basic cause of the conflict (cf., the influential analysis by Ignatieff, 1994, or Huntington's controversial model, 1996).

Yugoslavia was a state that came into being twice: after the First World War and after the Second World War. The first Yugoslav republic (1918–41) was for all practical purposes the Serb monarchy writ large, and was riddled with continuous internal tension. Croats and Slovenes reluctantly supported King Alexander's regime, seeing it as a possible defense against Italian, Austrian, and Hungarian aggressors. It was a precarious state, periodically dictatorial, that had been on the verge of collapse several times before it fell apart as Germany invaded the country in 1941. While Serbs generally resisted the Germans, Croats collaborated and saw the German intervention as an opportunity to create their own state.

Before the formation of the second Yugoslav republic in 1945, both of the largest constituent groups suffered large-scale massacres—Serbs at the hands of Croatian fascists (Ustasa) in 1941 and Croats killed by Serbian communists (Partisans) in 1945. The new Yugoslav state (1945–91) was a nonaligned socialist federation led by a pro-Serbian Croat, Josip Broz Tito, until his death in 1980. Ethnicity was officially declared a nonissue in socialist Yugoslavia. This official blindness stems from the Marxist view that class is a more objective and more authentic vessel of social identity than ethnicity or nationality, which were officially seen as expressions of false consciousness. This does not, however, imply that Yugoslav policies were particularly repressive regarding expressions of cultural distinctiveness symbolizing ethnic identity; on the contrary, in this area Yugoslavia was more liberal than many Western European countries whose leadership feared separatism and social fission. Ethnic identity was seen as politically irrelevant, and partly for this reason, the use of various languages and the practice of different religions were tolerated in civil society. It is true that the merging of Serbian and Croatian into one language, Serbo-Croatian, in the 1950s signaled an attempt at building a unitary Yugoslav identity, but the two languages were so closely related that few, except Croat intellectuals reacting against the relegation of specific Croat variants as "dialect," seem to have taken offense (Schöpflin, 1993). Albanian remained an official language in Kosovo, as did Slovene in Slovenia.

There were nearly twice as many Serbs as Croats in Yugoslavia, and twice as many Croats as Slovenes or Muslims. Regarding the territorial dimension, Slovenes were—and are—largely confined to the nearly monoethnic republic of Slovenia. Both Croatia and Serbia had large minorities of Serbs and Croats, respectively, as well as Gypsies, while Serbia also included nearly a million Albanians (in Kosovo) and smaller numbers of Hungarians and others. In Macedonia, most of the population were (and are) Slav-speaking Macedonians, while the Montenegrins of Montenegro are culturally close to the Serbs. Bosnia-Herzegovina was the most throroughly mixed republic, with roughly equal numbers of Serbs, Croats, and Bosnian Muslims, often living in mixed areas. As is well known, the conflicts of the 1990s have modified this picture somewhat, creating large monoethnic territories in formerly mixed areas.

Although the ruling Communist party seems to have believed that a common Yugoslav identity would eventually supersede the national identities based on ethnic membership, ethnic identity remained strong in most parts of the country throughout the postwar era. There were nevertheless important exceptions, particularly in cities such as Belgrade, Sarajevo, and Zagreb, where many people increasingly identified themselves primarily as Yugoslavs and where mixed marriages were common.

Ethnic identities did, in other words, not disappear during the existence of Yugoslavia. In some urban areas they were arguably weakened, but it could be—and has been—argued that the nonethnic character of Yugoslav politics actually led to its strengthening as a vehicle for the political opposition *and* made it possible for Serbs to gain control over the armed forces and state bureaucracy: since political ethnicity officially did not exist (only cultural ethnicity did), there were no institutionalized ways of preventing one group from dominating the public sector.

The wars in the former Yugoslavia have bequeathed to the world the neologism *ethnic cleansing*. It is nevertheless easy to show that the conflicts involving Serbs, Croats, Bosnian Muslims, Slovenes, and Albanians were never conflicts over the right to assert one's ethnic or cultural identity, but were based on competing claims to rights such as employment, welfare, and political influence. What needs to be explained is the fact that the conflicts over these resources were framed in ethnic terms rather than being seen as, say, regional, class-based, or even ideological.

The relevant questions are therefore: what is the stuff of ethnic identity in the former Yugoslavia; in which ways do the groups differ from one another, and why did group allegiances turn out to be so strong? Bosnia-Herzegovina may be considered as an example. There are three large ethnic groups inhabiting Bosnia: Serbs, Croats, and Muslims. The main difference between the groups is religion—Serbs are Orthodox and Croats are Catholics. (Ironically, religious fervor was not particularly widespread in prewar Bosnia.) They all have common origins: Slav immigration into Illyria from the north took place between c. A.D. 400 and 700, and the cultural differences between Croats and Serbs are perhaps comparable to those between Norwegians and Swedes. The "objective" difference between Bosnian Christians and Bosnian Muslims, further, has been compared to the difference between English Protestants and English Catholics (Cornell & Hartmann, 1998). Unlike the impression sometimes given in Serbian and Croatian propaganda, Bosnian Muslims are not the descendants of alien invaders, but of locally residing converts. Although each group has its numerical stronghold, many Bosnian regions and villages were mixed before the war. This implies, among other things, that they went to school together, worked together, and took part in various leisure activities together. A Serbian villager in Bosnia had more in common, culturally speaking, with a Muslim co-villager than with a Serb from Belgrade. This would hold true of both dialect spoken and way of life in general. However, since religion turned out to be the central marker of collective identity in the Bosnian conflict, the effective boundary was drawn not between villagers and city-dwellers, but between religious categories.

The boundaries between the groups may seem arbitrary. However, the large, "national" groups are clearly embedded in smaller, local networks based on kinship and informal interaction, as well as being culturally founded in religious schisms, collective myths or memories of treason and resistance under Ottoman rule, massacres, deception, and humiliations. Although it is tempting to argue that any so-called cultural trait can be exploited in the formation of national or ethnic groups, it is obvious that not just anything will do. Nothing comes out of nothing, and strong collective identities—such as the ones revealed during the war in Bosnia—are always embedded in personal experiences. In one of the most detailed accounts of ethnicity at the village level in prewar Bosnia, Bringa (1996) shows that although cultural differences between the groups were perhaps negligible, and although relations among Serbs, Muslims, and Croats might be cordial at the local level, there were nevertheless important social practices of affiliation that created boundaries between them—not in the cosmopolitan Sarajevo middle class embraced by Western commentators, perhaps, but elsewhere. Intermarriage was rare, the close informal networks of friends tended to be monoethnic, and the discrete groups maintained different, sometimes conflicting myths of origin. The intimate sphere, in other words, seems to have been largely monoethnic and by this token, Bosnia was a plural society in the classic sense (Furnivall, 1948); the public arenas were shared, but the private ones were discrete.

One may choose not to speak of such features of social reality and everyday life in terms of "culture," but they are no more "invented" than any other social fact. People do not choose their relatives, they cannot choose to do away with their childhood and everything they learned at a tender age. These are aspects of identity that are not chosen, that are incorporated and implicit. People relate to them as reflexive agents, but they do so within limitations that are not chosen. Such limitations form the objective foundations of social identification. When analysts such as Cornell and Hartmann (1998) argue that ethnic identities before the war were weak, sometimes socially irrelevant, and in many cases ambiguous (many had parents from different groups), they refer to particular segments of society—a main example is the Yugoslav basketball team—whose members were active participants in pan-Yugoslav contexts.

The maintenance of ethnic boundaries in socialization and the private sphere reveals a main cause of the failure of Yugoslav social engineering in doing away with ethnic identification. It does not explain the outbreak of war in the early 1990s, but it indicates why the groups that emerged were so strong, and why they were based on ethnicity (seen as fictive kinship) instead of, say, class or region. Their foundation must be sought not in the biology of kinship, as some might want to argue, but in the phenomenology of social experience, the raw material of personal identity. This argument will be elaborated after an examination of two very different examples of intergroup conflict in polyethnic societies.

The Fijian Coup-D'etat

The Pacific island-state of Fiji, located at the ethnographic crossroads of Melanesia and Polynesia, is perhaps less heterogenous than Yugoslavia, but it is scarcely less ethnically divided. Its population of about 800,000 is largely composed of two ethnic categories: Fijians and Indians. The Fijians are indigenous, largely Christian, speak a Polynesian language, and make up slightly less than half the population. The Indians are uprooted "overseas Indians" whose ancestors were brought to Fiji during colonialism under the British indentureship system described, probably a trifle too grimly, as "a new system of slavery" by Tinker (1974). They are overwhelmingly Hindus (with a Muslim minority), speak a locally modified dialect of Hindi, and were slightly more numerous than the indigenous Fijians until the political changes in the late 1980s leading to mass migration of Indo-Fijians. The small minorities of Europeans and Chinese are politically insignificant, but the economically powerful Europeans, representing the former colonial regime, have in no small measure shaped the Fijian public sphere, notably through establishing English as the national lingua franca.

The relatively brief history of democratic Fijian politics up to 1987 has been described with the metaphors of balance and power sharing (Premdas, 1993; Kelly, 1998). While Indians in practice wielded disproportionate economic power, it was tacitly agreed that Fijians should be politically paramount. However, there were indications that the "equilibrium" model was under severe stress in the early- to mid-1980s, and in the 1987 elections, a coalition supported by most Indians and only a few Fijians won. Although the new prime minister was a Fijian, many saw his government as a vehicle for Indian communal politics. In May and September 1987, the military seized power through two successive coups-d'etat, explicitly doing so to protect "native" Fijian interests. In the period following the coups, thousands of Indians emigrated.

The tension between Fijians and Indians had been evident throughout Fijian history. Unlike the situation in Yugoslavia and especially Bosnia, nobody would question the view that there are deep cultural differences between Indians and Fijians. Their languages, cultural traditions, religions, and gender relations differ markedly—indeed, one of their recent ethnographers has poetically described striking, and culturally potent, differences in body language between Fijians and Indians (Williksen-Bakker, 1991). There seems to be little informal interaction between the groups, most rural areas are dominated by one or the other, and intermarriage has always been nearly nonexistent. The effective separation of Fijians from Indians has always been much deeper than that obtaining between the major groups (or "nationalities") in rural Bosnia after the Second World War. Until 1987, policies of compromise had nonetheless ensured political stability and had made Fiji a remarkably liberal and relaxed society.

Invoking the slogan "Fiji for Fijians" (which had been launched before the 1977 elections), the writers of the new constitution, promulgated in 1990, ensured continued indigenous Fijian dominance of the political sphere, by according that group disproportionate representation in parliament, ruling that only Fijians can become prime ministers, and giving Fijians preferential treatment in other areas as well, such as religion. In addition, Fijians are guaranteed control over most of the arable land, about 82 percent of which has been communally owned by Fijian kin groups since the beginning of colonialism in the 19th century.

The conflict culminating in the military coups can, at one level of analysis, be seen as a clear case of group competition. Indians have done better economically than Fijians. Ironically, this may partly be explained through the British colonial policy of indirect rule relating to Fijians, who were allowed to retain important traditional institutions, such as chieftainship and the rudiments of a caste system, making them in consequence unprepared to compete with Europeans and Indians in a capitalist economy later. The Indians, by contrast, had shed important aspects of their traditional social organization in the process of migration, and were accustomed to economic individualism through the indentureship system whereby they were made to work on the European-owned plantations.

The demographic growth rate among Indians has been higher than among Fijians (just as the Muslims in Bosnia were more prolific than the other groups), and there was generally a growing sentiment among Fijian leaders that they were becoming a minority in the land of their ancestors. The inegalitarian measures introduced by the military regime, discriminating between categories of citizens on ethnic grounds, were condemned by the international community, but less strongly than one might have expected in a different setting. What is remarkable about the Fijian case is the nativist quality of the supremacist rhetoric—how they brought "sons-of-the-soil" arguments to bear on a national legislation, creating, in effect, a two-tier society where non-Fijians were relegated to the status of second-class citizens. They argued that their culture, like that of Maoris in New Zealand and Aborigines in Australia, was threatened with marginalization from outside forces. In contrast, nobody in countries like Mauritius, Trinidad and Tobago, and Guyana—which are in many ways similar to Fiji but lack substantial indigenous populations—would have been able to invoke arguments of cultural authenticity and preservation of traditional cultures in a bid to introduce differential treatment for different ethnic groups (see Eriksen, 1992, 1998a, for details on Trinidad and Mauritius).

It may well be asked whether contemporary Fijians, being Methodists and proficient English speakers, are any less culturally uprooted than, say, Trinidadians of African descent or, for that matter, Fijians of Indian descent. The question of cultural authenticity is outside the scope of this chapter; let me now make a few more pertinent points relating to this example.

Fiji had developed an informal formula for interethnic accommodation where the largest ethnic groups divided societal sectors between them. In addition there were—and still are, at least to some extent—developing fields of shared meaning and cross-cutting alignments, such as the common use of English as a national language and a shared educational system. Nevertheless the segregation between the groups in both social and cultural domains is more striking to the outside observer than tendencies toward assimilation. Conflict avoidance would thus have to rely chiefly on group compromise rather than the development of a hybridized, shared identity—an option that has occasionally been proposed by politicians and intellectuals in other insular, postcolonial plantation societies such as Mauritius and Trinidad. Finally, owing to historical circumstances and cultural differences, Indians and Fijians have participated in different ways and have succeeded to varying degrees in the modern sectors of politics and the economy. It could indeed be argued that processes of modernization in Fiji, far from reducing cultural differences, have deepened them, at least at the socially operational level. Unlike in Bosnia, it is possible to refer to differences in local organization, cosmology, and traditional economical practices when accounting for the ethnic conflict in Fiji, which is nevertheless much less violent than the Bosnian one. This is a reminder, against cultural determinists à la Huntington (1996), of the relative unimportance of cultural differences for ethnic conflict—and it also indicates one of the main strengths of the constructivist-instrumentalist perspective on identity politics: cultural differences do not in themselves lead to intergroup conflict, but are invoked strategically to mobilize support. At the same time, it must be conceded that the differences in life-worlds and personal identities in Fiji, as in Bosnia, explain why the political cleavages were given ethnic expression. The differences were already there before they were exploited for particular political ends.

Hindutva: An Apparent Anomaly in Contemporary Indian Society

My third and final example differs from the two previous ones in significant ways. India is a tough case for any scholar trying to develop a general theory of ethnicity or nationalism, and with few exceptions, it does not figure in general introductory texts on the field. India is hardly a state based on cultural similarity or even equality in the Western sense; it is a country with deeply embedded hierarchies and a very considerable degree of internal cultural variation. Its population of nearly a billion is divided by language, religion, caste, and culture, and it has often been argued that India is culturally more complex than continents such as sub-Saharan Africa or Europe. Although 80 percent of the population are Hindus in one meaning of the word or another, India also has the second-largest Muslim population in the world (after Indonesia) and more Christians than all the Scandinavian countries put together. Since independence (and partition) in 1947, India has been defined in Gandhian-Nehruvian terms as a secular, federal country using English and Hindi as national languages, but with another dozen or so official regional languages.

Since the early 1980s—but particularly forcefully during the 1990s—a formerly marginal political movement has steadily increased its influence in India, culminating in its victories in the successive general elections of 1998 and 1999. This is the movement often referred to as *hindutva,* meaning roughly "Hindu-ness," which rallies behind slogans to the effect that India should be redefined as a Hindu country. The *hindutva* movement, led by an organization called the RSS (Rashtriya Swayamsevak Sangh) began modestly in the interwar years, and its more recent parliamentary wing, the BJP (Bharatiya Janata Party, "The Indian People's Party") is now in power not only federally, in New Delhi, but in several of the states as well.

The rhetoric of *hindutva* is strongly reminiscent of European ethnic nationalism. It invokes ancient myths of bitter defeats and noble sacrifices, reframing them to fit a contemporary political scene. It quotes liberally from 19th-century poets and sacred texts, and it redefines history to make the past conform to a redefined present. It advocates a return to the roots, condemns Westernization and its adverse moral effects on the young, praises the family as the key institution of society, and seeks to promote the vision of India as a *hindu rashtra*—a Hindu nation. While the late Rajiv Gandhi allowed himself to be photographed wearing a Lacoste shirt and khaki shorts, BJP leaders always wear traditional Indian clothes. The main enemy image is nevertheless not the West but Islam, which is depicted as a martial and cruel religion alien to the subcontinent, and Indian Muslims (the descendants of converts, like Bosnian Muslims) are represented partly as traitors to Hinduism, partly as foreign invaders. The demolition of a mosque in the northern town of Ayodhya in December 1992, the ensuing riots in several Indian cities, and the call for the rebuilding of a Hindu temple allegedly destroyed by a Mughal ruler four centuries ago marked a climax of sorts in this respect (see van der Veer, 1994, for details).

The phenomenal rise of this traditionalist movement is a result of several connected processes of sociocultural change or modernization. First, the very notion of *hindutva*, Hindu-ness, is a modern one. Hinduism is not a "religion of the Book." It is an noncentralized religion with scores of holy scriptures, thousands of *avatars* (incarnations of divinities), and very many ways of worshiping them. The idea of the Hindu identity as an imagined community based on cultural similarity is alien to Hinduism as such, which is a religion based on complementarity, difference, and hierarchy. Regarding political Hinduism, some Indian commentators actually speak of a *Semitization* of Hinduism whereby it takes on structural characteristics from the great religions of West Asia.

Second, the *hindutva* movement is explicitly modeled on European nationalism—some early *hindutva* ideologists were even warm admirers of Hitler—which has been, for 150 years, an attempt to reconcile change and continuity by talking of roots and traditions in a situation of industrialization and urbanization. This is obvious in *hindutva* practice, whereby issues regarding national anthems, dress, and foreign foods are given prominence, while profound social changes continue to affect everyday life as before. There is a clear connection between the rise of the BJP and the liberalization of the Indian economy, the rise of a substantial new middle class with a strong consumerist orientation and the rapid spread of new mass media including the Rupert Murdoch-controlled Star TV network. While liberalization of this kind stimulates consumerism (perceived as Westernization), it also indirectly boosts traditionalism since the new patterns of consumption and the new media scene may indicate that cherished traditions are under threat.

Third, the "contagious" influence from political Islam is obvious; *hindutva* is the assertion of Hindu identity *as opposed to* Muslim identity both in Pakistan and in India itself. Doubly ironic, *hindutva* has double origins in European romanticism and West Asian political Islam. When its first ideologist, Dr. Veer Savarkar, wrote in the 1920s that "*Hindutva* is not the same thing as Hinduism," he was therefore right, but not for the reasons he believed. Savarkar saw *hindutva* as a wide-ranging social movement emanating from Hindu faith and practices, while a more historically correct account sees it as the result of cultural diffusion from Europe and West Asia.

Fourth, and perhaps most important, the *hindutva* movement can be seen as a reaction against a growing egalitarianism in Indian society. Already in the 1950s, policies attempting to improve the conditions of the "Untouchables," the lowest castes, were introduced, and during the 1990s, very radical measures have been proposed to this effect—and in some cases carried out. About half of India's population are now defined as being either *Dalits* ("Untouchables"), tribals, low-caste people, or "OBCs" (Other Backward Classes), and in theory, all of 49.5 percent of jobs in the public sectors should be reserved for these groups, following the recommendations of the government-appointed Mandal commission. Since the early 1990s, this principle has been enforced in many areas. Naturally, many members of the "twice-born," upper castes feel their inherited privileges eroding away, and *hindutva* is largely a movement representing the interests of the disenchanted upper castes. It is for the most part a reaction against the movement toward greater equality in Indian society. Although *hindutva* seems to promote equality among Hindus, an implication of its traditionalist Hinduism is the reinvigoration of the caste system, which in effect benefits only the "twice-born" castes.

This analysis of *hindutva* must by necessity be a superficial one (see Hansen, 1999, for a full treatment). It must be remarked, however, that interreligious marriages (and, indeed, intercaste marriages) are rare outside certain elite groups. Casual interaction between Hindus and Muslims is far from unusual, but as in the Bosnian and Fijian cases, the intimate (family) spheres, as well as personal networks of close friends, rarely cross religious boundaries. Social classification in India is nonetheless complex, and as will be indicated later, the Hindu-Muslim divide is only one of several possible social dichotomies—unlike in Bosnia and Fiji, where religious or ethnic contrasts tend to be paramount.

Some Comparisons

Previous sections have outlined three contemporary conflicts involving collective identity as a political resource. The differences are obvious; the focus here will therefore be on the similarities.

The conflicts have three important sociological features in common. First, there is in all three cases *competition over scarce resources*. As Horowitz (1985) and many others writing about group conflict in contemporary societies have shown, such conflicts invariably involve perceptions of scarcity and struggles to retain or attain hegemony or equality. Successful mobilization on the basis of collective identities presupposes a widespread belief that resources are unequally distributed along group lines. "Resources" should be interpreted in the widest sense possible, and could in principle be taken to mean economic wealth or political power, recognition, or symbolic power—although what is usually at stake is either economic or political resources. This feature is easy to identify in all three examples described above: Fijians and Indians compete over relative political and economic power; the constituent groups of Bosnia compete over political power and/or sovereignty; *hindutva* is an attempt to defend the political and economic interests of "Hindus" in secular India.

Second, *modernization actualizes differences and triggers conflict*. With the integration of formerly discrete groups into shared economic and political systems, inequalities are made visible, as comparison between the groups becomes possible. In a certain sense, ethnicity can be described as the process of making cultural differences comparable, and to that extent, it is a modern phenomenon. The Fijian example, where the increasing integration of Fijians into the modern sphere made it apparent that Indians were doing better economically, illustrates this point. In India, the rise of the *Dalit* movement struggling for recognition and equal rights on behalf of "Untouchable" groups is an expression of the modern value of equality, and the counterreaction from the Hindu right is an attempt to stop egalitarianism from spreading, as well as reflecting—almost with the accuracy of a mirror image—symbolic competition with Muslims within and (especially) outside India. The Bosnian example, admittedly, seems less straightforward, as socialist Yugoslavia was in many ways no less modern than its successor countries (some would indeed argue that at least at the level of ideology, it was infinitely more modern than them). What is clear, and which also holds true for other Eastern and Central European countries, is that the sudden introduction of liberal political rights and a capitalist economy around 1990—core characteristics of non-socialist modernization—created a new dimension of comparison between individuals and new arenas of competition.

Third, *the groups are largely self-recruiting*. Intermarriage is rare in all three cases (excepting urban Yugoslavia). Although biological self-reproduction is by no means necessary for a strong collective identity to come about, it should be kept in mind that kinship remains an important organizing principle for most societies in the world, and a lot of what passes for ethnicity at the local level is really kinship. Kinship has an important social dimension in addition to its symbolic side, which is highlighted in ideologies of fictive or metaphoric kinship. Symbolic boundaries are never effective unless underpinned by social organization.

Further, there are several important ideological similarities. First, at the level of ideology, *cultural similarity overrules social equality*. Ethnic nationalism in Yugoslavia, political Hinduism in India, and the "sons-of-the-soil" rhetoric of Fiji all depict the ingroup as homogeneous, as people "of the same kind." Internal differences are undercommunicated, and moreover, in the wider political context, equality values are discarded for ostensible cultural reasons. (Although it could be argued that *hindutva* is a Trojan horse concealing upper-caste interests with all-Hindu rhetoric, the point is that it stresses the commonalities of all Hindus irrespective of caste or language.)

Second, *images of past suffering and injustice are invoked*. Serbs bemoan the defeat at the hands of the Turks in Kosovo in 1389; Hindu leaders have taken great pains to depict Mughal (Muslim) rule in India from the 1500s as bloody and authoritarian; and indigenous Fijian leaders compare their plight to that of other indigenous peoples who have suffered foreign invasions. Violence targeting the descendants of the invaders can therefore be framed as legitimate revenge. Even *hindutva* leaders, who claim to represent 80 percent of India's population, complain that Hinduism is under siege and needs to defend itself with all means available.

Third, *the political symbolism and rhetoric evokes personal experiences*. This is perhaps the most important ideological feature of identity politics in general. Using myths, cultural symbols, and kinship terminology in addressing their supporters, promoters of identity politics try to downplay the difference between personal experiences and group history. In this way, it becomes perfectly sensible for a Serb to talk about the legendary battle of Kosovo in the first person ("*We* lost in 1389"), and the logic of revenge is extended to include metaphorical kin, in many cases millions of people. The intimate experiences associated with locality and family are thereby projected onto a national screen. This general feature of social integration has been noted by Handelman (1990), analyzing national rituals, and much earlier in Turner's (1967) studies of ritual among the Ndembu of Zambia. In showing that rituals have both an instrumental and an emotional (or sensory) dimension—one socially integrating, the other metaphorical and personally meaningful—Turner actually made a point crucial to the present analysis—namely, that loyalty to a larger collectivity (such as a tribe or a nation) is contingent on its imagery being personally meaningful.

Fourth, *first-comers are contrasted with invaders*. Although this ideological feature is by no means universal in identity politics, it tends to be invoked whenever possible, and in the process, historical facts are frequently stretched. In Fiji, the Fijian population—although genetically a Polynesian-Melanesian mix—has a strong case here, although it is less obvious that Indo-Fijians can be immigrants to a country in which they were born, and therefore legitimately deprived of equal rights. Regarding Bosnia and India, as mentioned above, there is nothing to suggest that the ancestors of Muslims in the respective countries were more recent arrivals than the ancestors of Christians or Hindus, although Islam is a relatively recent import. What is interesting here is how the varying depth of cultural genealogies ("roots") is used to justify differential treatment. The historical location of the self along the dimensions of descent and place is thereby invested with political significance.

Fifth and finally, *the actual social complexity in society is reduced to a set of simple contrasts*. As Adolf Hitler wrote in *Mein Kampf*, the truly national leader concentrates the attention of his people on one enemy at the time. Since cross-cutting ties reduce the chances of violent conflict, the collective identity must be based on relatively unambiguous criteria (such as place, religion, mother-tongue, kinship). Again, internal differences are undercommunicated in the act of delineating boundaries toward the demonized Other. This mechanism is familiar from a wide range of interethnic situations, from social classification in Zambian mining towns (Epstein, 1992) to Norwegian–Sami relations in sub-Arctic Scandinavia (Eidheim, 1971), the Sinhalese–Tamil conflict (Kapferer, 1988) and Quebecois nationalism (Handler, 1988): the Other is reduced to a minimal set of "traits," and so is the collective Self.

These similarities do not necessarily indicate that there are universal mechanisms linking personal selves and larger collectivities, but they do suggest that there is a universal "grammar" common to contemporary identity politics everywhere. In the final sections of this chapter this argument will be pursued slightly further, and it will be suggested that universal connections between the self and the collective exist, which must be understood not only to account for traditional societies but to make sense of the present. Far from being an "atavistic" or "primitive" counterreaction to globalization or modernization, identity politics is a special case of something more general—namely, collective identity anchored in personal experiences.

Where Is the Identity of Identity Politics?

Social scientists have proposed many typologies of ethnic conflict, dividing the groups involved into categories such as majority, minority, irridentist, and separatist, using variables such as division of labor, relative political power, and historical intergroup relations as criteria of classification. In my view, this kind of exercise can at best generate a limited understanding of the dynamics of group conflict. To begin with, the very adjective "ethnic" is hardly appropriate to describe all conflicts based on identity politics. Indian Hindus are not an ethnic group in any meaningful sense, and it is a matter of definition whether Serbs, Croats, and Muslims in Bosnia should be considered ethnic groups (they have shared origins only a few centuries back). Many contemporary conflicts displaying some or all of the features listed above cannot be seen as ethnic. I note a few African examples: The Sudanese civil war is partly fought over religion (northerners are Muslims trying to Islamicize the south), partly over culture and language—neither northern nor southern Sudanese are ethnic groups. Hutus and Tutsis in Rwanda and Burundi, like the constituent groups of Bosnia, are culturally very close; they speak the same language and have the same religion. The Somali civil war presents an even more puzzling case, as Somalia is one of the few sub-Saharan states that are truly ethnically homogeneous and so far the only one that seems to have relinquished the trappings of statehood completely, having dissolved into warring clans (an intermediate level of social organization, between the family and the ethnic group) since the early 1990s. To the northwest of Somalia, one of the great forgotten wars of Africa is being fought over a contested border area between Eritrea and Ethiopia. Eritrea, which seceded from Ethiopia in 1991, has never been based on religion or ethnic identity, but has a vague legitimacy as a historical nation in the brief period of Italian colonialism before the Second World War. The current war is being fought between Tigrinya speakers on both sides of the borders, who are united through religion, language, customs, history, and even kinship ties, but they are no less bitterly divided politically. This conflict in turn creates its strange bedfellows in the alliance between Ethiopian Tigrinyas and Amhara speakers from the highlands, who are traditional enemies.

In other words, the concept "ethnic conflict" is misleading, whether it is used to classify phenomena or to explain hostilities. Several of the alternative terms one might consider are, however, no less misleading: "Cultural conflict" will clearly not do, as it is obviously not what is usually thought of as cultural differences that lie at the heart of the conflicts. At the village level, even Hindus and Muslims in India hold many of the same beliefs and worship in similar ways. The low-intensity conflict in Fiji involves groups that are by any criterion more culturally different than, say, the Bosnian groups. All the conflicts considered here are over resources perceived as scarce: territory, political power, economic gain, employment, recognition—rights in a wide sense. What they have in common is their successful appeal to collective identities perceived locally as imperative and primordial, identities associated with a deep moral commitment, whether ethnic (based on notions of kinship and descent), regional (based on place), or religious (based on beliefs and forms of worship). For these reasons, the term "identity politics" is preferable as a generic term for all such political movements, whether nonviolent or violent.

This final section will therefore amount to an attempt to unravel the identity of identity politics. What is it that makes it so powerful? What is the "identity" that such political movements can draw upon?

Benedict Anderson proposes an answer in the introduction to his seminal *Imagined Communities* (1983), where he points out that nationalism has more in common with phenomena such as religion and kinship than with ideologies like liberalism and socialism. He argues that nationalism (and, one might add, any form of identity politics) expropriates personal identity, transforming intimate experiences into the raw material of politics. I owe my existence to my parents, and by metonymical extension they represent the larger, abstract collective. I harbor tender feelings for my childhood, which by extension becomes my group's glorious and tragic history. I feel attached to the place where I grew up, which was not just any arbitrary place but the nation (or, as the case might be, the sacred land of Hinduism, the traditional territory of the Fijians, the tormented country of the brave, but sadly misunderstood Serbs). Indeed, this argument can profitably be seen as echoing Turner's aforementioned argument on the instrumental and emotional dimensions (or "poles") of ritual. In both cases, the integrative strength of the imagined community (be it a tribe or a nation) depends on its ability to mobilize emotions proper to the intimate sphere of kinship and personal experience.

The conditions for this transformation to take place—the move from an interpersonally anchored identity to an abstract national, ethnic, or religious identity—are usually tantamount to certain general conditions of modernity (cf. Gellner, 1997). It is through school and mass media that people are taught to identify with an abstract, mythically rooted community of people "of the same kind." Through the replacement of traditional economies with an abstract labor market, they become participants in a large-scale system of subsistence. Through the implementation of a bureaucratic system of political management, their allegiances are at least partly moved from the concrete to the abstract community.

It is important to remember, as theorists of nationalism and ethnicity have pointed out time and again, that identification is relational, situational, and flexible, and that each person carries a number of potential identities, only a few of which become socially significant, making a difference in everyday life. Even fewer gain political importance, forming the basis of power struggles and group competition. This is not, however, to say that collective identities can be created out of thin air. They have to be connected, in credible ways, to people's personal experiences. These experiences in turn are flexible—not only historians but everybody else as well selects and interprets events to make a particular kind of sense of the past— but not indefinitely so. Regarding our main examples, in Fiji virtually nobody doubts whether he or she is Indian or Fijian, and politics—whether based on compromise or conflict—will have to take this into account for the foreseeable future. In Yugoslavia after the breakup, cross-cutting ties and cultural hybridity were undercommunicated. Cosmopolitanism was increasingly seen as a suspect, unpatriotic attitude, and people of mixed ancestry were forced to choose a bounded, unambiguous identity: they had to select past experiences that made them either Serbian, Croatian, or Muslim—more or less like the proverbial North African mule, who speaks incessantly about his uncle, the horse, but never mentions his father, the donkey. In India, finally, some of the strongest scholarly arguments against the lasting influence of *hindutva* have actually pointed toward people's personal experiences (Frøystad, 1999). Since Indian everyday life is still permeated by caste distinctions, and caste continues to define the very fabric of social integration, these scholars argue that *hindutva*—the idea that all Hindus have something profound in common—is so counterintuitive to most Indians that it can unite Hindus only as long as the enemy image of Muslims can be kept ablaze.

All the basic components of political identity familiar from classic political anthropology can be identified in contemporary identity politics: it is based on a sometimes ambiguous mix of kinship and locality; it has well developed myths of origin and myths of past suffering; and it distinguishes clearly between "us" and "them." The main difference between, say, the nomadic Nuer society studied by E. E. Evans-Pritchard (1940) in the 1930s and Serbian (or Croatian) nationalism today is probably that of scale: while the Nuer rarely imagined themselves as members of larger groups than the clan, a Serb in Vojvodina can readily identify him or herself with a Serb in

Kosovo. The act of transformation from personal, concrete social experiences to the abstract community is naturally much more demanding in a large-scale society than in a village-based one, hence the importance of modern institutions of communication, economic transactions, and political rule for the growth of abstract communities.

Some Final Lessons from Political Anthropology

Having long ago abandoned the early ambition of becoming "a natural science of society," social and cultural anthropology has for decades been reluctant to formulate lawlike propositions about the functioning of society. The constructivist turn of recent years seems to confirm that contemporary anthropology is less concerned with absolute truths than with the analysis of local cultural constructions. This need not be so, and the study of current identity politics may illustrate the power of comparative anthropology in generating general hypotheses.

Early instrumentalist research on ethnic groups, particularly in Africa (as in A. Cohen, 1974), searched for the logic of group cohesion, which they assumed to be roughly the same everywhere. The related, actor-based perspective developed by Barth (1969) and his colleagues assumed the logic of action to be quite universal—people act to maximize benefits. Later analyses of the constructedness of ethnic and national ideologies (the seminal text is Hobsbawm and Ranger, 1983; see Chapman, Malcolm, McDonald, & Tonkin, 1989, for an overview) also emphasize universal characteristics of a particular kind of societal formation (the modern state) and its relationship to group identities based on notions of culture. The canonical texts on nationalism (such as Gellner, 1983; Anderson, 1983; Smith, 1991) also have clear universalist ambitions. As this chapter has made clear, these approaches have obvious strengths, but they need to be supplemented by detailed research on the experiential world of the everyday—the *Lebenswelt* (life-world) of the actors. A renewed focus on the informal, intimate, and often noninstrumental dimensions of everyday life reveals that terms such as "ethnicity" by themselves explain little. The parallels between a supporter of the BJP and a supporter of Serbian supremacists should not be located to their respective "ethnic" identities or "civilizational" membership, but to the fact that their everyday life, social networks, and personal obligations connect them to particular groups that may be exploited politically, given the right circumstances. It should also be kept in mind that class politics can sometimes be a form of identity politics (Shore, 1993), which can profitably be understood along the same lines as ethnic or religious identity politics. The cause of group allegiance lies in the everyday, not in the overarching ideology.

In order to complete this analysis, it is necessary to go a few decades back, to classic political anthropology, in order to see how the perspectives developed earlier in the chapter can be enriched by the work of previous generations.

The integration of persons into groups can be described as the work of an inverted refrigerator: the function of a refrigerator is to generate inward coldness, but in order to do so more or less inadvertently, as a side effect, creates outward warmth. Conversely, groups form to create warmth for their members, but they necessarily create some outward coldness in order to be able to do so. Under particular circumstances, the outward coldness is more readily perceptible than the inward warmth. A sociological principle originally formulated by Georg Simmel, known as "Simmel's Rule," simply states that the *internal cohesion of a group is contingent on the strength of external pressure*. This principle may explain why group integration generally is so much stronger in small groups, especially if they are oppressed, than in large ones—why, for example, Scots seem to have fewer difficulties defining who they are than do the English.

An interesting corollary of Simmel's Rule is the fact that what *kind* of group emerges depends on where the perceived pressure comes from. Both gender-based and class-based social movements have periodically been successful, given that the perceived threat was seen, not as alien religion or foreign ethnic groups, but as male supremacy and ruling classes, respectively. In accordance with this, some inhabitants of Sarajevo during the war felt that the conflict was really an urban–rural one, since city-dwellers had a lot in common, irrespective of religion, that they did not share with rural people. Strong opposition groups in India, similarly, argue against a view of Indian politics as divided between Hindu communalists and liberals because they see the main problem of Indian society as one of poverty and distribution of resources, to which neither of the parties seems to give priority. In Fiji, finally, the immediate reason for the 1987 coup was the establishment of a government of national unity promising to address issues of social welfare and economic development rather than intergroup issues. In other words, redefinitions of societal cleavages are entirely possible insofar as they do not contradict people's everyday experiences too obviously.

In the course of this chapter, cross-cutting ties and conflicting loyalties have already been mentioned as mitigating forces in situations of intergroup conflict. Phrased within the terminology used here, one might say that shared experiences across boundaries reduce the risk of conflict. In Max Gluckman's reinterpretation of Evans-Pritchard's Nuer material from the 1930s (Gluckman, 1956–1982), this point was made forcefully. The Nuer were organized along kinship lines across villages, but they were also locally integrated in villages. The women married out of the village and the lineage, so that everybody had affines (in-laws) in other villages. Furthermore, men were tied to nonrelatives through trade, initiation rituals, and friendship. All of these factors led to a reduction in the incidence of violence among the Nuer. In contemporary identity politics, it can easily be seen—and has been remarked above—how political leaders emphasize inward similarity and outward boundaries in order to reduce the potentially mitigating impact of cross-cutting ties. They are true to people's everyday life, but try to emphasize certain experiences at the expense of others (inward solidarity and similarity, outward conflict and difference).

Another, even more time-honored principle from political anthropology is the twin notions of fusion and fission in tribal societies. When the sole organizing principle for a group lacking hierarchies and formal political office is kinship, there are limits to the group's growth; at a certain point, it splits into two. Without such a fission, internal conflicts would soon become overwhelming given the simple social organization of such societies, and the effects would be destructive. Fusion of discrete groups has also been studied extensively, but in many acephalous societies it is seasonal (nomadic groups fuse in the dry season or in winter) and fragile.

A more dynamic view of contraction and expansion of tribal groups was developed, especially by Africanists, from the 1940s (Fortes & Evans-Pritchard, 1940). In studies of feuding and political competition, they showed how two or several local groups that might be periodically involved in mutual feuding united temporarily when faced with an external enemy. This form of organization, described as *segmentary* by Evans-Pritchard, follows the proverb often cited in recent years to explain the logic of the Somali civil war: "It's me against my brother, my brother and I against our cousins, and our cousins, my brother and I against everybody else." A form of segmentary logic is apparent in politics nearly everywhere; a distinguishing mark of modern nation-building has nevertheless been its attempt to channel loyalties away from various subnational levels of identity in order to monopolize the political loyalty of individual citizens.

The segmentary logic creates a fluid, relational political organization that, in its pure form, is impracticable in modern state societies given their requirements for stability, centralized power, and reified systems of political representation. This does not, however, mean that segmentary identification does not continue to exist, and one of the causes of oppositional identity politics in modern nation-states is their not providing subnational identity groups appropriate political arenas, thereby encouraging counter-reactions in the form of identity politics directed against the state.

The formation of identity-based political groups generally entails both an expansion and a contraction of the focus for identification. At the time of the breakout of conflict in Bosnia, the federal or even state level was increasingly seen as irrelevant—the process was one of fission. At the same time, internal conflicts and schisms within each constituent group were minimized, and as a result each group became more coherent and united than before. In the cases of Fiji and India, this is even more obvious: among Fijians, rivalry between chiefs and clans has diminished in importance as Fijian politics has grown increasingly ethnic; similarly, rifts within the Indian population on the basis of regional origin, which could formerly lead to Indian subgroups supporting Fijian-dominated governments, have become much less important since the military coup. In the Indian case, the very idea of *hindutva* implies an enormous expansion of the ingroup for Hindus. Trying to bridge differences based on language, caste, region, and culture, *hindutva* tries to create a morally committing all-Indian Hindu identity based on symbolic equality. This is, in the Indian context, a very radical move. Simultaneously, Indian citizenship and (overarching, supra-religious) national identity become less important since the federal Indian state includes millions of non-Hindus, who are depicted as internal enemies by *hindutva* spokespersons.

In all the examples considered here, group segmentation at a higher level, and the ensuing formation of imagined communities larger than the locality but smaller than the state, is immediately related to the need for a firm boundary in a situation of conflict within the state. The alternative identity of national citizenship, which encompasses the other as well, no longer functions. Interestingly, contemporary identity politics is very similar to nationalism—for example, in its appeal to mythical foundations, its abstract postulation of similarity and equality, its rejection of segmentary identity formation, and its attempt to reduce a world of many small differences to a world of only a few, major ones. In many cases, it is more successful than nationalism, particularly in postcolonial, multiethnic states. This is not only because identity politicians promise its adherents that they will win zero-sum games against political competitors, but also because they are able to represent themselves as natural extensions of people's personal, experience-based identities.

A challenge for modern states, thus, consists in coping with the fact that personal identity can be exploited politically not only by the state itself but by others as well, not because the self is infinitely multifaceted (it is not), but because the experiences and relationships that make up the self can be expanded symbolically in several, often conflicting ways. Processes of segmentary fusion and fission, the formation of different kinds of groups involving overlapping personnel owing to the functioning of Simmel's Rule, group-based antagonism, and competition: these ways of expressing political interests, underpinned by shared meaning within the ingroup, are no more eradicated by modernity than is personal identity. The challenge thus consists in laying the foundations for "a sense of belonging to a community larger than each of the particular groups in question" (Laclau, 1995, p. 105), and this can be done only by first acknowledging both the richness and the variability of personal identities.

In the face of violent identity politics, "ethnic cleansing," and the strong attention to "roots" and historically based identities (ungenerously described as "the narcissism of small differences" by Michael Ignatieff) characterizing many societies in recent years, it is not surprising that intellectuals have recently tried to think essentialism away, emphasising the endlessly flexible and fluid character of human identification. A typical expression of this position can be found in a recent text by the influential sociologist

Zygmunt Bauman, where he states: "If the *modern* 'problem of identity' is how to construct an identity and keep it solid and stable, the *postmodern* 'problem of identity' is primarily how to avoid fixation and keep the options open" (Bauman, 1996, p. 18).

In today's world it may be ethically imperative to endorse Bauman's position, but it is equally important to keep in mind that humans are not free-floating signifiers, and no amount of benevolent intentions will be able to change people's life-worlds overnight. Rather than trying to think them away, it is necessary to understand them and come to terms with their enduring power. Notwithstanding globalization and the universalization of modernity, cultural differences continue to exist, within and between places, within and between nations and ethnic groups. It is also, however, doubtlessly true that carbon can be turned into graphite as well as diamonds, and the ways in which cultural differences become socially relevant vary importantly. But to pretend they do not exist outside ethnic and nationalist ideologies would be intellectually indefensible; people's personal experiences are the very raw material of such ideologies. Here lies an important limitation in constructivist models of identity. Collective identities are constructed, consciously or not, but nothing comes out of nothing. In locating the universal not in the workings of identity politics (it changes historically and varies geographically), nor in the eternal sovereignty of the state (the same objection applies), but rather in the social life-worlds in that individuals make sense of the world, we may have found a basis for comparison that will outlive academic fads and contemporary politics.

Acknowledgments

The author would like to express his thanks to the editors and three anonymous readers for their critical readings and useful comments on an earlier version of the chapter.

References

Anderson, B. (1983). *Imagined communities: Reflections on the origin and spread of nationalism*. London: Verso.

Barth, F. (Ed) (1969). *Ethnic groups and boundaries*. Oslo: Scandinavian University Press.

Bauman, Z. (1993). *Postmodern ethics*. Cambridge: Polity.

Bauman, Z. (1996) From pilgrim to tourist; or a short history of identity. In S. Hall & P. Du Gay (Eds.), *Questions of cultural identity* (pp. 18–36). London: Sage.

Bringa, T. (1996). *Being Muslim the Bosnian way: Identity and community in a central Bosnian village*. Princeton, NJ: Princeton University Press.

Chapman, M., McDonald, M., & Tonkin, E. (1989). Introduction—history and social anthropology. In E. Tonkin, M. McDonald, & M. Chapman (Eds.), *History and ethnicity* (pp. 1–21). London: Routledge.

Cohen, A. (1969). *Custom and politics in urban Africa: A study of Hausa migrants in a Yoruba town*. London: Routledge & Kegan Paul.

Cohen, A. (1974). *Two-dimensional man: An essay on power and symbolism in complex society*. London: Routledge & Kegan Paul.

Cohen, A. P. (1994). *Self consciousness: An alternative anthropology of identity*. London: Routledge.

Cornell, S., & Hartmann, D. (1998). *Ethnicity and race: Making identities in a changing world*. London: Pine Forge Press.

Eidheim, H. (1971). *Aspects of the Lappish minority situation*. Oslo: Scandinavian University Press.

Epstein, A. L. (1992). *Scenes from African urban life: Collected Copperbelt essays*. Edinburgh: Edinburgh University Press.

Eriksen, T. H. (1992). *Us and them in modern societies: Ethnicity and nationalism in Trinidad, Mauritius and beyond*. Oslo: Scandinavian University Press.

Eriksen, T. H. (1998a). *Common denominators: Ethnicity, nationalism and compromise in Mauritius*. Oxford: Berg.

Eriksen, T. H. (1998b). Culture and ethnicity: A second look. Lecture at 6th SIEF conference, Amsterdam, 21 April 1998.

Evans-Pritchard, E. E. (1940). *The Nuer*. Oxford: Clarendon.

Featherstone, M. (Ed). (1990). *Global culture*. London: Sage.

Fortes, M., & Evans-Pritchard, E. E. (Eds.). (1940). *African political systems*. London: Oxford University Press.

Friedman, J. (1994). *Global culture and local process*. London: Sage.

Frøystad, K. (1999). Personal communication.

Furnivall, J. S. (1948). *Colonial policy and practice: A comparative study of Burma and Netherlands India*. New York: New York University Press.

Geertz, C. (Ed.). (1967). *Old societies and new states: The quest for modernity in Africa and Asia*. New York: The Free Press.

Geertz, C. (1973). *The interpretation of cultures*. New York: Basic Books.

Gellner, E. (1983). *Nations and nationalism*. Oxford: Blackwell.

Gellner, E. (1997). *Nationalism*. London: Weidenfeld & Nicolson.

Giddens, A. (1991). *Modernity and self-identity*. Cambridge: Polity.

Giddens, A. (1994). *Beyond left and right*. Cambridge: Polity.

Gluckman, M. (1956/1982). *Custom and conflict in Africa*. Oxford: Blackwell.

Handelman, D. (1990). *Models and mirrors: Towards an anthropology of public events*. Cambridge: Cambridge University Press.

Handler, R. (1988). *Nationalism and the politics of culture in Quebec*. Madison: Wisconsin University Press.

Hannerz, U. (1992). *Cultural complexity: Studies in the social organization of meaning*. New York: Columbia University Press.

Hansen, T. B. (1999). *The saffron wave: Democracy and Hindu nationalism in modern India*. Princeton, NJ: Princeton University Press.

Hobsbawm, E., & Ranger, T. (Eds.) (1983). *The invention of tradition*. Cambridge: Cambridge University Press.

Holland, D. (1997). Selves as cultured: As told by an anthropologist who lacks a soul. In R. Ashmore & L. Jussim (Eds.), *Self and identity: Fundamental issues* (pp. 160–190). Oxford: Oxford University Press.

Horowitz, D. L. (1985). *Ethnic groups in conflict*. Berkeley: University of California Press.

Huntington, S. (1996). *The clash of civilizations and the remaking of a world order*. New York: Simon and Schuster.

Ignatieff, M. (1994). *Blood and belonging: Journeys into the new nationalism*. London: Vintage.

Jenkins, R. (1996). *Social identity*. London: Routledge.

Kapferer, B. (1988). *Legends of people, myths of state*. Baltimore, MD: Smithsonian Institution Press.

Kelly, J. D. (1998). Aspiring to minority and other tactics against violence. In D. C. Gladney (Ed.), *Making majorities: Constituting the nation in Japan, Korea, China, Malaysia, Fiji, Turkey and the United States* (pp. 173–197). Stanford, CA: Stanford University Press.

Laclau, E. (1995). Universalism, particularism and the question of identity. In J. Ratchmann (Ed.), *The identity in question*. London: Routledge.

Lash, S., & Urry, J. (1994). *Economies of signs and space*. London: Sage.

Premdas, R. (1993). Balance and ethnic conflict in Fiji. In J. McGarry & B. O'Leary (Eds.), *The politics of ethnic conflict regulation* (pp. 251–274). London: Routledge.

Rex, J. (1997). The nature of ethnicity in the project of migration. In M. Guibernau & J. Rex (Eds.), *The ethnicity reader: Nationalism, multiculturalism and migration*. Cambridge: Polity.

Roosens, E. E. (1989). *Creating ethnicity*. London: Sage.

Said, E. W. (1978). *Orientalism*. New York: Pantheon.

Schlesinger, A. M. Jr. (1992). *The disuniting of America*. New York: Norton.

Schöpflin, G. (1993). The rise and fall of Yugoslavia. In J. McGarry & B. O'Leary (Eds.), *The politics of ethnic conflict regulation* (pp. 172–203). London: Routledge.

Shore, C. (1993). Ethnicity as revolutionary strategy: Communist identity construction in Italy. In S. Macdonald (Ed.), *Inside European identities* (pp. 27–53). Oxford: Berg.

Smith, A. D. (1986). *The ethnic origins of nations*. Oxford: Blackwell.

Smith, A. (1991). *National identity*. Harmondsworth: Penguin.

Strathern, M. (1991). *Partial connections*. Savage, MD: Rowman and Littlefield.

Tambiah, S. J. (1989). The politics of ethnicity. *American Ethnologist, 16*, 335–349.

Tinker, H. (1974). *A new system of slavery: The export of Indian labour overseas 1830–1920*. Oxford: Oxford University Press.

Turner, V. (1967). *The forest of symbols: Aspects of Ndembu ritual*. Ithaca, NY: Cornell University Press.

Turton, D. (Ed.) (1997). *War and ethnicity: Global connections and local violence*. Woodbridge, Suffolk: University of Rochester Press.

van der Veer, P. (1994). *Religious nationalism: Hindus and Muslims in India*. Berkeley: University of California Press.

Williksen-Bakker, S. (1991). Fijians in business: A study in the transformation of symbols. Doctoral dissertation, University of Oslo.

THE CONTRIBUTION OF ETHNIC AND NATIONAL IDENTITIES TO POLITICAL CONFLICT IN THE UNITED STATES

Jack Citrin
Cara Wong
Brian Duff

4

The Meaning of American National Identity

Patterns of Ethnic Conflict and Consensus

National identity is one among many often co-existing and overlapping social identities, including territorial, racial, religious, linguistic, and gender
identities. The psychological task for individuals is to order and integrate
their different collective "selves" (Ashmore & Jussim, 1997). The political
task for government is to balance the need for national unity with the competing claims of other group identities. In modern society, emphasizing loyalty to the "nation" and making this the essence of the individual's political
self-definition emerged as the dominant way to boost social solidarity
(Greenfield & Chirot, 1994). As an immigrant nation, the United States has
always faced the problem of coping with ethnic diversity; the motto *e
pluribus unum* expresses the desire for a strong sense of common American
identity without indicating the proper balance between the national "one"
and the ethnic "many."

The contemporary meaning of American national identity is the focus of
this chapter. Immigration and differences in fertility rates have changed the
ethnic and religious composition of the United States (Farley, 1996;
Warner, 1993). Compared to 50 years ago, the country is more diverse, with
many more people today from Latin America, Asia, and Africa. Moreover,
this demographic change has occurred in the context of technological transformations eroding national sovereignty in economic life and of the emergence of intellectual trends legitimating the primacy of ethnicity in political
life.

Scholars disagree about whether globalization and multiculturalism have
weakened Americans' sense of attachment to the "nation," particularly
among minority groups (Reich, 1992; Barber, 1995; Hollinger, 1997;

Wolfe, 1998; de la Garza, Falcon, & Garcia 1996). There also are conflicting views about the implications of a stronger sense of ethnic, as opposed to national, identity. Some scholars (Raz, 1994; Young, 1990) regard ethnic pride as a source of individual self-esteem among cultural minorities that contributes to the achievement of their group's goals. Others (Schlesinger, 1992; Miller, 1995) claim that the emphasis on ethnic distinctiveness (ingroup favoritism) inevitably weakens common bonds and intensifies group conflict (outgroup hostility), raising the specter of cultural and political Balkanization.

This chapter employs survey research to analyze the meaning and political consequences of American national identity in the context of the demographic, economic, and intellectual changes noted above. The conceptualization of national identity formulated here draws on social identity theory (Tajfel & Turner, 1986; Thoits & Virshup, 1997) to encompass both self-categorization (or identification *as*) and affect (or identification *with*). However, it goes beyond merely assessing the individual's positive (or negative) feelings about the nation to determine the normative foundations of their sense of American identity.

The content of American identity is the set of ideas and sentiments that form the conceptual framework of nationhood. At the cultural level, this refers to a particular collective representation of the nation indicating the subjective criteria for membership in the national community (Citrin, Haas, Muste, & Reingold, 1994). A given conception of national identity thus includes normative assumptions about how members of different ethnic and cultural groups *should* relate to one another. For example, *must* minority groups assimilate to a dominant language, religion, or political outlook in order to achieve full acceptance as fellow-nationals, or can a nation accommodate loyalty to a variety of cultural traditions? Historical experience suggests that there is no single answer to this question, so it is important to conceive of national identity in a way that recognizes the possibility of several conceptions of "Americanness" vying for popular support.

The next section of the chapter provides a more detailed account of the tripartite definition of national identity that distinguishes among the dimensions of self-categorization, affect, and normative content. The second section summarizes the content of competing ideological conceptions of American identity, with particular attention to their normative assumptions regarding the articulation of strong ethnic identities. The analysis of survey data, presented in the third section, addresses three main questions:

1. What is the degree of national versus ethnic identification in American public opinion, as assessed by several different measures of self-categorization and affective support?
2. What is the pattern of consensus and cleavage among white, black, Hispanic, and Asian respondents? Specifically, do minority ethnic groups have a weaker sense of national identity than whites, and

are there ethnic group differences in how people order their national and ethnic identities?

3. What is the impact of national and ethnic identities on policy preferences? Drawing on symbolic politics theory (Sears, 1993), the final section of the chapter tests hypotheses about the relative influence of these identifications on preferences regarding foreign policy, racial policies, and "multicultural" issues such as immigration and group representation.

These analyses shed light on the impact of a superordinate "American" identity on feelings about "outgroups," both domestic and foreign, and provide a basis for speculating about the implications of different patterns of national and ethnic identity for conflict and cooperation among America's racial and ethnic groups.

The Dimensions of Social Identity

Identity is a slippery concept. It is an assertion of both sameness and difference. One answers the question "What is your identity?" by naming who one is like. This entails drawing boundaries: one is the same as some others and different from everyone else. For this reason, a social identity both integrates and divides.

The first step in measuring a social identity is to determine the basis of *self-categorization*; one identifies the characteristic(s) shared by those with whom one psychologically belongs. We each possess multiple *potential* social identities whose degree of overlap and whose relative significance for our self-concept and behavior may vary (Thoits & Virshup, 1997). Moreover, while self-categorization may be the initial step in the formation of a psychologically meaningful social identity, the range of one's options is finite. Biology, the life cycle, social structure, the economy, and the government create the categories that demarcate social identities with potential political consequences. Thus, some social identities are optional and others imposed. Furthermore, the borders dividing identity groups are permeable, but not entirely open. It is easy to be a Bulls fan and then to "exit" psychologically for the Celtics when Michael Jordan retires. It is harder to shed one's nationality or ethnicity and almost impossible to change one's race or sex. Finally, even when one can adopt a particular social identity by self-categorization (Turner, Hogg, Oakes, Reicker, & Blackwell, 1987), this choice frequently must be affirmed by the agreement of others in the group that you do indeed possess the criteria for membership. The daughter of Chinese immigrants may call herself an American, yet might be told by fellow-citizens of European origin that she does not share their national identity.

Self-categorization refers to "identification *as*," connoting a perceived self-location in a group, and should be distinguished from "identification *with*," which indicates positive *affect* toward others in the group and must be measured separately. Social identity theory (Tajfel, 1978) posits that mere awareness of belonging to a group engenders positive feelings about the group and a tendency to act on behalf of other group members, even if they are unknown to one personally. In the same vein, Miller (1995) has argued that the moral value of a strong sense of national identity is that it fosters diffuse feelings of sympathy and obligation toward fellow citizens.

In addition, there is a difference between membership in a group and psychological attachment to it. One can identify with members of a minority group, agreeing that they deserve more access to jobs or political power, without categorizing oneself as a member of that group. This example underscores the potential significance of identities based on shared values rather than sociological similarities and the need to determine the conditions under which "identification *as*" and "identification *with*" are closely connected.

"Identification *with*" entails learning about a group's defining customs, expectations, and values, and making them one's own. These common values or ideas define the third component of a social (e.g., national) identity— its *content*. The specific content of a group identity is socially constructed, in the sense that consensual decisions shape and reinforce the normative criteria for membership. Since these criteria are vulnerable to challenge and subject to change, it is important to assess the extent of their legitimacy.

Still, social identities are not automatically political. They are politicized when feelings of identification with a group are combined with a belief in advancing its goals through collective action (Miller, Gurin, Gurin, & Malanchuk, 1981). During the British Raj, Indians undoubtedly differentiated themselves cognitively from the English. The emergence of an ideology and organized movement demanding change in the cultural, economic, and legal status of Indians infused this social identity with political content.

The Affective Dimension: Patriotism versus Chauvinism

A nation denotes a group of people seeking or possessing a common homeland. Nationalism as a doctrine asserts that a group of people sharing characteristics that differentiate them, *in their own minds*, from others should be politically autonomous. The affective dimension of national identity (identification *with*) refers to feelings of closeness to and pride in one's country and its symbols. Many scholars go further, however, and distinguish love of one's own country from a sense of superiority to other countries (Schaar, 1981; Staub, 1997; Kosterman & Feshbach, 1989; Sullivan, Fried, & Dietz, 1992; Connor, 1993; Taylor 1995). They invoke the concept of patriotism to refer to the positive emotion of love for one's own people and homeland

and use "nationalism" pejoratively, not technically, to designate arrogance and contempt toward other countries. Writing in this vein, for example, George Orwell described patriotism as defensive and nationalism as aggressive. For Schaar (1981, p. 285), nationalism is a perversion of patriotism, "its bloody brother." Psychologists developing separate measures for these concepts tend to give the label "nationalism" or "blind patriotism" to name disdain for other countries and a drive to dominate them (Bar-Tal, 1993; Kosterman and Feshbach, 1989; Staub, 1997).

Drawing on social identity theory's distinction between ingroup favoritism and outgroup hostility clearly is useful when studying national and ethnic identity. The emotive use of the term "nationalism," however, is unnecessarily confusing. "Chauvinism," not nationalism per se, is the term used here to refer to an extreme and bounded loyalty, the belief in one's country's superiority, whether it is right or wrong. Whether patriotism, an ideology of mutual affection among those with a common sense of national consciousness (Kelman, 1997, p. 170), and chauvinism empirically slide into each other, such that caring for one's own typically is associated with hostility toward others, is a controversial issue to be explored below (see also Brewer, this volume).

Normative Conceptions of American Identity

History shows that the attributes used to define the idea of a "people" or "nation" are numerous and malleable (Greenfield, 1992). Historians distinguish "civic" nationalism, where criteria for belonging are identical to citizenship and so, in principle at least, open to all, from "ethnic" nationalism, where membership is based on a sense of shared blood (Connor, 1993). There is a modern tendency to endorse the principle of ethnicity as the legitimate basis for political autonomy, but there are prominent counterexamples of multiethnic states such as the United States (Greenfield, 1992). As Max Weber put it, nationality ultimately is based on the principle of territory, ethnicity on lineage.

Whatever the specific foundations of a sense of national identity, nationalism, in its neutral, technical meaning, implies that membership in the nation is the citizen's overriding group loyalty, taking precedence over other available foci of affiliation, including ethnicity, in circumstances where they conflict. If a strong national identity means consciousness of special bonds to one's fellow-nationals, so that they become, at least symbolically, a large extended family, then constructing a nation may involve psychological losses as well as gains. The development of a national identity may require diminishing or abandoning one's attachment to other groups, including one's ethnic group.

The third dimension of our conception of national identity refers to its normative content. This means the particular set of ideas about what makes the nation distinctive—ideas about its members, its core values and goals, the territory it ought to occupy, and its relations to other nations (Citrin et al., 1994). In a multiethnic society, these ideas lay down the nature of legitimate commitments to subnational communities of descent. In contemporary American politics, liberalism, nativism, and multiculturalism are alternative political theories about how society should be organized and how national identity should be defined. Each proposes a different solution for how properly to balance national and ethnic identities, with conflicting implications for policymakers. The analysis below therefore assesses the degree of popular support for these competing ideas.

The liberal conception of American identity is "civic," not "ethnic." Commitment to the national "creed" of democracy and individualism (Huntington, 1981; Gleason, 1980) is what makes one an American. Since belonging to the nation is equated not with shared blood but with common beliefs and customs (Gleason, 1980; Lind, 1995), anyone, regardless of ancestry, can become American through adherence to the dominant set of ideals, which include equality of opportunity and respect. The liberal image of nationality is ethnically inclusive, in principle, if not always in practice (Smith, 1997).

When it comes to ethnic diversity, the liberal conception of national identity is optimistic about the ability of contemporary American society to assimilate newcomers. This means that ethnic Balkanization is not a serious threat, so there is no reason to extirpate the traditions of new immigrants as attempted by the Americanization program in the 1920s. Over time, the largely Asian and Hispanic newcomers will blend into the cultural mainstream, just like their European predecessors. Thus, people are free to honor their ethnic heritage if they wish, without undermining America's ability to create one people out of many. Still, according to the liberal conception of national identity, when the claims of nationality and ethnicity conflict, the former should take precedence. In psychological terms, liberalism rejects the notion of primordial identities, the idea that differences among communities of descent are *fundamental* and *enduring*, exercising an inherent dominion over the individual's political conduct.

Rogers Smith (1997) documents the persistent gap between the liberal theory of national identity and more nativist political practices. From the beginning of the United States, the official definition of "Americanness" excluded blacks and Native Americans and consigned women to a lesser role. Then, in the 19th and 20th centuries, restrictive immigration and naturalization laws discriminated on a racialist basis. Asians were denied citizenship, Mexicans were repatriated, and in 1924, immigration was limited to a small number of people of Northern European origin.

The nativist response to ethnic diversity (Higham, 1988) is to insist on cultural conformity. If there is to be immigration, the nation's policy should favor the admission of people who already are familiar with American political culture (Brimelow, 1995). Once here, newcomers should undergo a program of indoctrination that cleanses them of their traditional loyalties and imparts knowledge of cultural practices. Nativism thus gives an ethnocentric cast to American national identity. Here, nationality does not simply trump one's ethnicity; rather, nationality fuses with a particular Anglo-Saxon ethnicity.

Scholars disagree about the extent and the voluntary nature of cultural assimilation of immigrants to America (Gerstle, 1997; Hollinger, 1997; Gordon, 1964; Glazer & Moynihan, 1959). While the passage of the 1964 Civil Rights Act and the 1965 Immigration and Nationality Act marked the ascendancy of the liberal conception of citizenship, in previous decades nativism and racism strongly influenced public policy. Gerstle (1997, p. 556) argues that government support for nativism and the end of mass immigration suppressed the hyphenated American identities that had thrived earlier and narrowed the range of acceptable cultural behavior. Even so, nativism never entirely succeeded (Glazer & Moynihan, 1959); every immigrant did not truly "melt" into a single, unchanging political culture.

Multiculturalism is an alternative ideological response to the presence of ethnic diversity in America. The "soft" or "liberal" version of this conception of national identity emphasizes the virtues of cultural pluralism and calls on the government to help ensure tolerance toward minorities (Miller, 1995; Appiah, 1994; Raz, 1994). "Hard" or "radical" multiculturalism goes further, conceiving of the nation as a confederation of ethnic groups with equal rights and construing ethnicity as the *preferred* basis of one's political identity (Citrin, Sears, Muste, & Wong, forthcoming; Sears, Citrin, Cheleden, & van Laar, 1999).

Unlike liberalism, then, multiculturalism assumes that one's ethnic identity is essential to one's personal dignity and self-realization (Raz, 1994). This conception of national identity does hold that differences among communities of descent are basic and persisting. Since no culture is superior to any other, none should be privileged in a multiethnic polity (Young, 1990; Goldberg, 1994). To assure that minority cultures survive and flourish— something that is viewed as indispensable for the well-being of their members—"hard" multiculturalism therefore demands *group* rights and government efforts to preserve minority cultures (Okin, 1997). Without such support, it is argued, the standing of minority ethnic groups inevitably will decline in the face of the cultural and economic power of the numerical majority, and members of minority ethnic groups will lose the core of their social identity.

Multiculturalism emphasizes ethnic consciousness and pride, but provides no apparent basis for social solidarity among America's ethnic groups save the principle of mutual tolerance (Raz, 1994). Because of this, critics (Schlesinger, 1992; Kateb, 1994) warn that elevating the psychological salience of ethnic identity, as Yugoslavia's tragic recent history illustrates, will increase group conflict or make it difficult to mobilize citizens on behalf of national goals. In the vocabulary of social identity theory, they claim that legitimating ingroup favoritism will lead inexorably to hostility and aggression toward outgroups, including other ethnic groups within the American national community.

Research Questions and Method

Discussion about the consequences of changing the balance between national and ethnic identities often proceeds in an empirical vacuum, without much reference to the prevailing attitudes and beliefs of the American public. This chapter employs survey data to present evidence about the following questions: What is the level of patriotism in the United States, and does it differ substantially across ethnic groups? Do white, black, Hispanic, and Asian Americans differ in how they order their national and ethnic identities or in how they conceive of membership in the national community? And does one's particular conception of national identity influence opinions about government policies?

Psychological theories regarding intergroup relations differ in their predictions about the preeminence of ethnicity in how people define themselves politically (Sidanius, Levin, Rabinowitz, & Frederico, 1999; Sears et al., 1999). Our own expectations are guided by symbolic politics theory (Sears, 1993; Sears et al., 1999). This approach assumes that individuals possess stable predispositions established in early socialization (e.g., through parents or mass media) and reinforced by later experience (e.g., through education or work). Ethnicity has no inherent priority in identify formation. Ethnic identification is one potentially significant predisposition, national attachment is another. The relative strength of these identities varies according to one's socialization experiences, and their influence on current behavior depends upon the nature of environmental cues. For example, feelings of national identity are likely to be evoked by international terrorist activities because these raise the salience of one's status as an American, but not by proposals to increase the tax on tobacco.

By emphasizing the role of social learning, the symbolic politics perspective is compatible with either ethnic antagonism or harmony in multiethnic societies. In the American context, it appears that national pride and a sense of the country's exceptionalism are strongly socialized attitudes, and this socialization may mitigate ethnic conflict by integrating diverse groups in an overarching identity (Horowitz, 1985). All the country's ethnic groups are exposed to patriotic norms and the country's liberal political tradition (Hartz, 1955; Lipset, 1996) that transmits belief in individual rights, not group rights. The potency of these cultural messages would predict only minor ethnic differences in national identity and support for multiculturalism.

Symbolic politics theory conceives of national and ethnic identities as structures of valenced beliefs stored in memory (Lau & Sears, 1986). Which of a person's political predispositions influences her political choices partly

depends on the nature of the stimuli she encounters, such as events, policies, and candidates' messages (Zaller, 1992). When a particular attitude
such as national pride is evoked, the theoretically predicted response is to
act in a way that reinforces one's preexisting orientation. Accordingly, subjective conceptions of national identity are hypothesized to govern opinions
about specific issues, such as foreign policy, immigration, or teaching
American history, which evoke symbols of nationhood, but not about "neutral" issues, such as protecting endangered species.

The survey method relies on self-reports as the basis for classifying social
identities. The main body of evidence here comes from the 1996 General
Social Survey (GSS) of the American public aged 18 and older conducted
by the National Opinion Research Center (Davis & Smith, 1997). This survey employed a split-sample design and the results are based on the 1,367
respondents of the total sample of 2,094 who were asked questions about
national identity. In part because the 1996 GSS national survey included
very few Hispanic and Asian respondents, comparable evidence from the
1994 and 1995 Los Angeles County Social Surveys (LACSS), conducted by
UCLA's Institute for Social Science Research (Sears et al., 1999) also is reported. The Los Angeles data have special interest since they delineate the
degree of ethnic consensus and conflict in an extraordinarily diverse local
community where the salience of multiculturalism is a political constant.
The 1994 LACSS sample included 279 whites, 231 blacks, 264 Latinos, and
47 Asian respondents, and the corresponding numbers in the 1995 sample
were 259, 71, 202, and 47.

The 1996 GSS included a variety of items regarding beliefs and feelings
about America. From this set the analyses in this chapter use items covering
the different aspects of patriotism and chauvinism, as well as other questions assessing subjective beliefs about the normative criteria for American
nationality. Other questions about the respondent's level of pride in distinct
features of American society and history were used to provide convergent
evidence regarding national attachment. In addition, questions concerning
one's political self-categorization and one's level of identification with one's
ethnic group provided evidence about the balance between national and
ethnic identities.

Public Attachment to America

The present survey evidence shows clearly that most Americans retain a
strong, positive sense of national identity. Table 4.1 presents the responses
of the 1996 GSS national sample, broken down by ethnicity, to an array of
relevant items, with the relatively few "don't know" answers excluded. (For
the full wording of the questions, see Davis & Smith, 1997). Table 4.1
groups these questions to reflect the tripartite definition of national identity
outlined above and to indicate the composition of multi-item attitude

TABLE 4.1 Beliefs about American National Identity (1996 GSS)

	Total (1367)	Whites (1018)	Blacks (156)	Hispanics (61)
Political Self-Categorization				
Think of self mainly as "just American" in social and political issues*	90%	96%	66%	79%
Affective Attachment to America				
*Patriotism scale items:***				
How important is being an American to you? (% saying 'most important thing in their life')	46	47	49	26
How close do you feel to America? (% saying 'close' or 'very close')	81	83	69	83
Agree 'I would rather be a citizen of America than any other country'	91	92	89	79
Pride in Aspects of America				
% saying 'very proud' or 'somewhat proud'				
The way democracy works	83	85	77	81
Its political influence in the world	80	81	77	75
Its history	88	92	69	81
Its fair and equal treatment of all groups in society	57	60	42	51
Chauvinism scale items:				
Agree 'World would be a better place if people from other countries were more like Americans'	40	40	47	47
Agree 'America is a better country than most other countries'	81	83	74	73
Agree 'America should follow its own interests, even if this leads to conflicts with other nations'	44	44	50	39
Agree 'People should support their country even when it's in the wrong'	32	30	41	33
Normative Conceptions of American Identity				
% Saying very or fairly important for a True American:				
Nativism scale items:				
To have been born in America	69	67	82	42
To be a Christian	54	50	77	50
To have lived in America for most of one's life	73	71	84	77
Assimilationism scale items:				
To be able to speak English	93	94	91	85
To feel American	87	89	81	72
To have American citizenship	93	92	93	93
Multiculturalism				
Agree 'It is impossible for people who do not share American customs and traditions to become fully American'	35	34	47	34
Agree 'Ethnic minorities should be given govt assistance to preserve their customs and traditions'	17	11	44	45
Think it is better if groups adapt and blend into larger society rather than maintain their distinct customs and traditions	58	61	56	50

*This question was not asked in the 1996 GSS. The data we report is from the 1994 GSS.
**The items listed under Patriotism, as well as those under the headings Chauvinism, Assimilationism, and Nativism, are the items that were used in constructing these scales for the analyses appearing in other tables.

scales. The Political Self-Categorization item asks respondents to consider which identity is primary to them when they think about political and social issues. The Patriotism and Chauvinism items assess the affective dimension of national identity. These items are similar in content to other measures of psychological attachment to the nation (Kosterman & Feshbach, 1989; Staub, 1997). Another set of "pride" questions taps the respondent's sense of pride in regards to specific aspects of American society. The "true American" questions capture normative conceptions of national identity and are modeled on an earlier Traditional Americanism scale (Citrin, Reingold, & Green, 1990). In addition, several items assess support for the maintenance of diverse cultures within the political community, a core principle of the multiculturalist conception of American identity.

Clearly, table 4.1 shows that patriotic sentiment remains pervasive in the American public. One poll is just a snapshot in time, of course, and the level of positive affect one records will vary with the response categories used to measure the underlying attitude. Nevertheless, the consistency in expressions of pride and belonging is impressive. When asked to rate the importance of being an American on a 10-point scale, fully 46 percent of the 1996 GSS sample said it was "the most important thing in their life." In response to similar questions, 81 percent said they felt "close to America" and 91 percent agreed that they would "rather be a citizen of America than any other country." Responses to the items in the "Pride" subheading in table 4.1 show that this generalized feeling of attachment carries over to judgments about most specific features of national experience. For example, 83 percent of the 1996 GSS sample expressed pride in "the way democracy works in America." However, many fewer, 57 percent, said they were proud of the country's record in treating all groups in society equally. Clearly, one can have a strong sense of patriotism without believing that the nation is perfect.

Nor does everyone extend pride in America to a conviction in the country's superiority. While 81 percent of the 1996 national sample did agree that America is a better country than most others, just 40 percent thought the world would be a better place if people from other nations were more like Americans. Only 32 percent agreed that one should support their country "even when it is wrong," compared to 50 percent who disagreed. Chauvinism, in the sense of a latent hostility toward other nations, is present, but the dominant outlook seems to be just a preference for one's own people and place.

The pattern of answers to the questions about what is important for being "truly American" reinforces this conclusion. Each of the attributes listed was deemed either "very" or "fairly" important, suggesting that most Americans believe that there is a distinct national identity. The more inclusive political criteria—American citizenship (87 percent) and simply feeling American (93 percent)—were chosen more often than the ascriptive qualities of being native born (69 percent) or Christian (54 percent). The ability to speak English (93 percent) might appear as an ethnocentric criterion, but this is an achieved rather than an ascribed trait and research indicates that within two generations most immigrants do learn the country's common language (Portes, 1996). In fact, language minorities and foreign-born residents are as likely as white or black Americans to emphasize the linguistic criterion for national identity (Citrin et al., 1990).

Multiculturalism asserts the need to maintain minority cultures within America and regards the symbols of assimilation with suspicion, if not outright hostility. The 1996 GSS asked respondents whether they believed it is "better for a country if different racial or ethnic groups maintain their distinct customs and traditions" or if they "adapt and blend into the larger society." Of those who expressed a definite opinion, 58 percent said that "blending in" would be better. (In the case of this question, however, fully 27 percent of the respondents did not express a definite opinion, suggesting substantial ambivalence about the choice as posed. When the respondents without a definite opinion are included, 43 percent of the total sample are in favor of "blending in," while 31 percent favor the maintenance of cultural diversity). Even fewer, only 17 percent of the GSS sample, agreed with the position of many advocates of multiculturalism that ethnic minorities should receive government support to preserve their traditions.

At the same time, there was considerable confidence about the possibility of assimilation. More respondents (42 percent) disagreed than concurred (35 percent) with the proposition that "it is impossible for people who do not share American customs and traditions to become fully American." Perhaps because of this optimism, many Americans may seem to feel that assimilation and maintaining connections to one's ethnic heritage are mutually compatible. Public opinion endorses the importance of a common national identity without insisting on a forced march to cultural conformity. For example, a 1994 GSS poll found that only 26 percent of the public said that "ethnic history is getting too much attention in the public schools," another indication of the tendency to view the existence of a unifying American culture as compatible with respect for pluralism (Merelman, Streich, & Martin, 1998).

Using exploratory and confirmatory factor analysis, we combined the items listed in table 4.1 to construct Patriotism (alpha = .64) and Chauvinism (alpha = .66) indices and summary measures of Nativist (alpha = .79) and Assimilationist (alpha = .64) conceptions of Americanism. Although there is statistical evidence for treating these dimensions as distinct, clearly they are interrelated. Nativism and Assimilationism correlate .58 (Pearson's r) in the 1996 GSS sample, and Patriotism and Chauvinism also are associated (r = .37). An interesting note is that Assimilationism was more strongly related to Patriotism (r = .47) than to Chauvinism (r = .38), whereas the obverse was true for Nativism (r = .29 and .45, respectively), a pattern pointing to a "psycho-logical" bond between an exclusionary definition of American identity and a sense of superiority to other peoples. However, beliefs about the value of cultural diversity are not strongly related to these variants of positive attachment to the nation. Responses to the question about whether or not groups should blend into the mainstream culture correlated positively, but weakly, with the Patriotism (.13), Chauvinism (.13), Nativism (.07), and Assimilationism (.13) scales. Admittedly, these correlations may be attenuated owing to the use of just a single-item to measure support for assimilation into the mainstream culture and due to the low variance on the scales.

Normative Consensus or Ethnic Conflict?

Although strong feelings of national attachment are the norm, the possibility of ethnic conflict in outlook remains. The nativist prediction that diversity erodes national unity assumes that minority groups are less committed to the idea of a common American identity. The multiculturalist perspective yields a similar expectation. If ethnicity is the dominant criterion of one's social identity, then minority group members should be less likely than those in the dominant ethnic group to view the entire nation as "theirs" and, therefore, to be less likely to express the usual forms of pride and affection.

Despite frequent claims that there is a vast racial divide in American opinion (Kinder & Sanders, 1996), our surveys indicate that ethnic differences are slight when it comes to patriotic sentiment (table 4.1). There is a strong similarity in the outlook of blacks and whites regarding the personal importance of American citizenship. Blacks (69 percent) are somewhat less likely to say they feel "very close" or "close" to America than whites (83 percent) or Hispanics (83 percent), but, again, the overwhelming majority of all three groups express a strong sense of attachment to the nation. In the 1994 LACSS, 79 percent of the whites and 73 percent of the black respondents said they were "extremely" or "very" proud to be an American.

The opinions of Hispanics point to a continuing connection to their countries of origin among recent immigrants. As table 4.1 shows, they are less likely than either blacks or whites to say being an American is important to them, more willing to say they would move to another country, and less likely to say that being born in America or feeling American is an important characteristic of being a true American. The same general pattern exists among the Hispanic and Asian respondents in the Los Angeles data (reported in full in Sears et al., 1999). Only 44 percent of the Hispanic respondents and 58 percent of the Asians in the Los Angeles study felt "extremely" or "very" proud to be an American, but these differences from white opinion are largely because many of these respondents are recent arrivals in the country and are not yet citizens. The findings of the Latino National Political Survey (de la Garza, Falcon, & Garcia, 1996, p. 346) also indicate that after controlling for demographic characteristics, including length of time in the United States, Mexican Americans "express patriotism at levels equal to or higher than do Anglos." Somewhat surprisingly, the Los Angeles survey found virtually no ethnic differences on the question of whether "it is better if groups change so they blend into the larger society rather than maintain their distinct cultures."

The pervasive patriotic and assimilative tendencies among all ethnic groups frays, however, when one moves from the realm of ideals to judging historical experience. In the 1996 GSS survey, as reported in table 4.1, blacks and, to a lesser extent, Hispanics were less likely than whites to express pride in America's history, in the way its democracy works, and in the treatment of all social groups. Members of minority groups also are less likely than whites to agree that America has provided "people of my ethnic group a fair opportunity to get ahead in life" (LACSS) and more likely to agree that the government should give special assistance to ethnic minorities (GSS). Minority groups, then, clearly display a heightened sensitivity to their collective status, largely agreeing with whites about the goal of *e pluribus unum*, but, as previous research also found (Hochschild, 1995), asserting more often that discrimination and unequal opportunities for minority groups are ongoing problems in the United States.

The normative conceptions of what it means to be a "true American" also are very similar in all ethnic groups. In this regard, blacks are somewhat more likely to endorse what we have termed ascriptive or nativist criteria of identity. They are significantly more likely (by the chi-square test) than either white or Hispanic respondents in the 1996 GSS to agree that being born in America, living in America for most of one's life, and being a Christian are "very important" qualities of national identity. In an important sense, these opinions express the visceral quality of their American roots for the black respondents. African Americans constitute the oldest group of nonwhite immigrants in the country, despite the forcible nature of their arrival. Thus, the symbolic meaning of their invocation of nativist criteria for national identity might well be a positive statement about their own "true American-ness" rather than prejudice toward outsiders.

Symbolic politics theory emphasizes the role of socialization in the formation of social identities and would predict that common exposure to the patriotic themes so dominant in American life would engender high levels of national attachment across all ethnic groups over time. Of course, socialization is ongoing and multifaceted, and there generally are group differences in prior learning and current experience that have an impact on political predispositions (Kinder & Sears, 1985). Table 4.2 summarizes the ethnic group differences in feelings of national identity by comparing their mean scores on the multi-item measures of Patriotism, Chauvinism, Nativism, and Assimilationism Indices, with each variable scored from 0 (low) to 1 (high). The results show that in all three ethnic groups, positive attachment to American nationality prevails. Nevertheless, ANOVA indicates that several of the ethnic differences that do appear around the highly favorable norm are statistically significant. Blacks do have lower mean scores than

TABLE 4.2 Ethnic Differences in National Identity[1] (1996 GSS)

	Mean Score on a 0 to 1 Scale			
	Total	Whites	Blacks	Hispanics
Affective attachment to America				
Patriotism	.80	.81	.76	.75
Chauvinism	.59	.59	.62	.56
Normative conceptions of American identity				
Assimilationism	.86	.86	.85	.79
Nativism	.64	.62	.79	.60

1. The four attitude measures are additive indices created by summing responses to the several groups of items designated in table 4.1. The response options for each item were first recoded to range from zero to one. After summation, index scores were also recoded to range from zero to one with higher scores indicating higher levels of patriotism, chauvinism, etc. Reliabilities (Chronbach's alpha) for the respective scales are patriotism (.64), chauvinism (.66), assimilationism (.64), and nativism (.79).

whites on Patriotism, though higher scores on Nativism. Hispanics also have lower Patriotism scores than whites, as well as less support for the Assimilationist conception of national identity. Whether one should emphasize the element of consensus or these minor and spotty differences is a matter of debate (compare Sidanius, this volume). But whatever one makes of the divergences among whites, blacks, and Hispanics, clearly the glass of patriotism is much more than half full in every group. The real ethnic divide in American politics emerges on specific policies bearing directly on the status of minority groups, not on conceptions of national identity.

The results of a multiple regression analysis in which race, ethnicity, gender, age, income, education, region, and immigrant generation were employed as predictors of the Patriotism, Chauvinism, Nativism, and Assimilationism scales, respectively, confirm this conclusion. (For space reasons, the full results are not reported here, but will be provided on request.) With the imposition of statistical controls, there is no "race effect" on Patriotism or Chauvinism scores. Blacks remain significantly *more* likely than whites to endorse the nativist conception of American identity, largely because of their greater support for Christianity as a legitimate defining criterion of nationality. This suggests that another social identity, religion, is important to understanding ethnicity, national identity, and intergroup conflict in America.

More generally, there is a striking similarity in the demographic underpinnings of the four measures of national attachment: the elderly, those with lower levels of education, and those residing in the South were significantly more likely to have high, "pro-America" scale scores. Finally, first-generation immigrants were significantly less likely to have high scores on the Patriotism, Nativism, and Assimilationism indices. However, neither second- nor third-generation Americans differ from those with an even longer family history in the country, once again suggesting that socialization into a sense of national pride and belief in a distinctive American identity does not take long.

National, Hyphenated, and Ethnic Identities

Since citizens can have multiple loyalties (or identities), it is important to assess the intensity of ethnic and national identifications separately. Whether these attachments are complementary or competitive is an empirical matter. The 1996 GSS asked respondents separate questions about how close they felt to the United States and to their own racial or ethnic group. A cross-tabulation of answers to these items show that 63 percent of the white, 65 percent of the black, and 66 percent of the Hispanic respondents expressed feelings of closeness to *both* the nation and their own ethnic group. Among whites, only 11 percent felt close attachment to their own ethnic group, but not to the country as a whole, whereas 24 percent of the black and 14 percent of the Hispanic respondents fell into this category. This suggests a stronger salience of an ethnic identity among blacks, with the possible implication that they would be more likely than whites to privilege ethnicity over nationality when trade-offs must be made. Still, the dominant result is that a large majority among both races expresses affinity to both identity groups. Subjectively, national and ethnic identities in the United States tend to be experienced as complementary rather than competing.

Table 4.1 reports the responses to the political self-categorization question: "When you think of social and political issues, do you think of yourself mainly as a particular ethnic, racial, or nationality group, or do you think of yourself mainly as just an American?" (The data come from the 1994, not the 1996 GSS poll, which did not include the item). This question wording calls for a ranking of identities and explicitly places the choice in a political context. Of the white respondents, 96 percent answered "just an American," compared to 66 percent of the black and 79 percent of the Hispanic respondents (see table 4.1). The uniformity of opinion among whites is consistent with the view of the various groups of European immigrants having "melted," so that their most salient political identity is no longer cultural or religious, but simply a superordinate identity as Americans (Alba, 1990; Waters, 1990; Roediger, 1994).

The 1994 and 1995 LACSS studies asked a similar self-categorization question with equivalent results. In the pooled samples, 93 percent of the white respondents gave the overarching "just an American" self-designation. Blacks (69 percent), Hispanics (70 percent), and Asians (71 percent) were significantly less likely (by the chi-square test) than whites to say they thought of themselves as just Americans. When forced to choose, however, a large majority in all three minority ethnic groups opted for a common national identity, not ethnic particularity, as their first choice. Moreover, among Hispanics and Asians, those who categorized themselves in terms of ethnicity tended to be first-generation immigrants, suggesting, once again, that the absorption of a sense of national identity is the normal outcome of socialization in this country.

The 1995 LACSS allowed respondents to say whether they identified as *just* Americans or as *both* Americans and as members of an ethnic, racial, or nationality group. As reported in table 4.3, only 17 percent of the whites opted for a dual or hyphenated identity. But, when given this opportunity to choose, a majority in all three minority groups preferred to categorize themselves as *both* Americans and members of an ethnic group and not as exclusively "American." Unfortunately, there are no national data to replicate this result, but it is consistent with other small-scale studies testing social identity theory that suggest the relatively greater salience of an ethnic identity for members of smaller, easily demarcated, homogeneous, and disadvantaged groups (Prentice & Miller, 1999; Brewer, this volume). The historically dominant group in a multiethnic state often fuses rather than hyphenates their ethnic and national identities (Connor, 1993). It is beyond the scope of this chapter to explore the antecedents of these alternative self-categorizations by minority group members. Among immigrant groups, it appears that length of residence in the United States and speaking English diminish the likelihood of identifying oneself primarily in ethnic terms (de la Garza et al., 1996), but these factors could not account for the varied responses of blacks.

Identities and Policy Preferences

The political relevance of social identities rests partly on how they influence attitudes and behavior toward one's own and other groups. A strong sense of group identity is expected to promote conduct that favors one's fellow group members, even in a "minimal group" (Tajfel, 1978). But since there are multiple dimensions of self-identification, how one defines the "I" as "we" when a political decision arises is likely to be significant. Symbolic politics theory holds that broad attitudes, including feelings of national and ethnic identity, are more likely to determine preferences on specific issues when those predispositions are central to an individual's self-definition *and* when they are cued by stimuli associated with the objects of these attitudes (Sears, 1993; Zaller, 1992). For example, a strong sense of Jewish identity is more likely to govern opinions about American policy toward Israel or a mandatory school prayer than the future of the spotted owl. In addition, as shown above, ethnic identity may indeed be more significant for the construction of the social self among some groups than others.

Nationalism is an integrating ideology that overrides the claims of less comprehensive group loyalties. In fact, liberal theorists (Tamir, 1997;

TABLE 4.3 Political Self-Categorization: American, Dual, or Ethnic Identity (1995 LACSS)

	Whites (n = 254)	Blacks (70)	Hispanics (174)	Asians (46)
Just an American Identity	78%	16%	11%	4%
Both American and ethnic identity	17	54	59	59
Ethnic identity	5	30	31	37

	Whites		Blacks		Hispanics		Asians	
	US born (n = 223)	Not US born (31)	US born (68)	Not US born	US born (59)	Not US born (115)	US born (8)	Not US born (38)
Just an American identity	80%	65%	16%	na	24%	4%	13%	3%
Both American & ethnic identity	17	16	54	na	53	62	63	58
Ethnic identity	3	19	29	na	24	34	25	40

Hollinger, 1997; Miller, 1995) justify holding on to a national identity on the grounds that this sentiment generates feelings of special obligation to and responsibility for the other members of one's national community. If this surmise is correct, then people should be less likely to feel a sense of duty to members of groups who define themselves as somehow outside or different from the national "family." Accordingly, since multiculturalism validates the maintenance of group differences, the stronger one's attachment to an overarching American national identity, the more likely one should be to oppose recognition and support for groups emphasizing their cultural distinctiveness. Alternatively, if the majority group views ethnic minorities as disadvantaged members of a community with a *shared* identity, feelings of national attachment could accommodate, even facilitate, support for policies aimed at helping them.

In considering the political implications of ethnic consciousness, Tyler, Lind, Ohbuchi, and Sugawara (1998) found that assimilated and "biculturalist" members of minority groups (that is, those who emphasize their American identity and dual identity, respectively) were equally likely to express trust in government, to regard existing institutions as fair, and to comply with government policy. Both groups were significantly more likely than "separatist" respondents from the same ethnic group (those emphasizing their ethnic identity) to express these attitudes. The present data show that the relative salience of an ethnic as opposed to national self-identification affects how people evaluate multiculturalist principles (see table 4.4). Minority group members for whom ethnic identification takes priority over national identity generally are *less* likely than those who say they view politics mainly as an American to express pride in America and to agree that their group has had a fair chance to get ahead, and are *more* likely to believe that groups should maintain their own distinct cultures, to deny that political organizations based on ethnicity promote separatism, and to think that people are best represented by leaders with the same ethnic background. (See table 4.4 for results of chi-square tests for statistical significance.)

Table 4.4 also suggests that the association between an ethnic self-identification and support for multiculturalism is stronger and more systematic among blacks than among either Hispanics or Asians. For example, among blacks, 61 percent of those who identified themselves as "just American" felt it is better for minority groups to blend into the larger society rather than maintain their distinct cultures, compared to only 25 percent of those who defined themselves primarily as members of an ethnic group. Among Hispanics, the equivalent figures were 60 percent and 54 percent, a far smaller difference, and among Asians, they were 57 percent and 48 percent, respectively. The future trend in how the different minority groups balance their ethnic and national identities thus has clear implications for the pattern of intergroup conflict over issues of cultural recognition and representation.

Ordinary least-squared regression analysis was employed to delineate the connections between the affective and normative dimensions of national

TABLE 4.4 The Impact of Political Self-Categorization on Beliefs about the American National Community (1994 LACSS)

	Blacks		Hispanics		Asians	
	Just American ($n=156$)	Ethnic Identity (68)	Just American (182)	Ethnic Identity (66)	Just American (36)	Ethnic Identity (8)
Feel extremely or very proud to be an American	81%	54%	53%	22%	61%	33%
Agree that American society has provided people of my ethnic group a fair opportunity to get ahead in life	50	22*	70	63	69	63
Think it is better if groups change so that they blend into the larger society (as in the idea of a melting pot) rather than maintain their distinct cultures[1]	61	25	60	54	57	48#
Agree that political organizations based on race or ethnicity promote separatism and make it hard for all of us to live together	70	57#	71	52*	70	38#
Leader background doesn't matter for representation	68	40*	67	50*	60	38

Chi-square test of differences between "just American" and "ethnic identity" respondents within each racial/ethnic group:
* $p < .05$
# $p < .10$
[1]The percentages in this row represent pooled data from the 1994 and 1995 LACSS.

TABLE 4.5 The Relationship between Attitudes Toward National Identity and Policy Preferences (1996 GSS)

	Affective Attachment			Normative Conceptions		
	(1) Patriotism	(2) Chauvinism	(3) Patriotism & Chauvinism (patrsm) (chauv)	(4) Assimilationism	(5) Nativism	(6) Assimilationism & Nativism (assim) (nativ)
Policy Preferences						
Multiculturalism						
(A) Need to share American customs	.05	.38**	-.08 .42**	.17**	.27**	-.07 .29**
(B) Support melting pot as ideal	.20*	.24**	.18 .17	.25**	.01	.33** -.10
(C) Reduce immigration levels	.09	.18**	.06 .17**	.26**	.17**	.21** .09*
(D) No cultural benefit from immigrants	.04	.20**	-.01 .21**	.11**	.15**	-.01 .16**
Racial Policies						
(E) Oppose affirmative action	.02	-.01	.01 .00	-.05	-.03	-.05 -.01
(F) Oppose govt. help for blacks	.06	.14*	.03 .13	.12*	.06	.08 .04
(G) Oppose more spending on blacks	.17	.06	.14 .00	-.01	.06	.03 .05
Domestic spending						
(H) Oppose social spending	.03	.03	-.03 .05	.03	.00	.05 -.02
Foreign Policy						
(I) Support more spending on defense	.23*	.31**	.12 .25*	.19*	.13*	.10 .10
(J) Support protectionism	.18**	.42**	.06 .40**	.29**	.23**	.16** .16**

Entries are unstandardized regression coefficients for national identity variables in equations with controls for race, ethnicity, age, education, income, gender, region (South), generation, ideology, and party identification.

* $p<.05$
** $p<.01$

identity on the one hand and policy preferences on the other. The statistical model estimates the effects of the Patriotism, Chauvinism, Assimilation, and Nativism Scales, (columns 1, 2, 4, and 5 in table 4.5), respectively, on issues related to cultural diversity (rows A–D), racial issues (rows E–G), domestic spending (row H), and foreign policy (rows I–J). The equations included race, ethnicity, age, education, income, gender, region, immigrant generation, partisan affiliation, and liberal-conservative self-identification as control variables. Owing to the small number of Hispanic respondents in the 1996 GSS sample, this analysis is confined to whites and blacks. For simplicity of presentation, the table omits the effects for the control variables and reports only the unstandardized regression coefficients for the measures of national identity (Patriotism, Chauvinism, Assimilationism, and Nativism). All variables were recoded to vary between 0 and 1, and the dependent variables all are scored in the "nationalist" or "conservative" direction. Accordingly, the positive coefficient of .24 for the association between Chauvinism and the Melting Pot item (column 2, row B) indicates that believing that America is superior to other countries is strongly related to the idea that ethnic minorities in the United States should blend into the mainstream culture.

Table 4.5 also reports the results of models that simultaneously included both Patriotism and Nationalism Scales (column 3) and the Assimilationism and Nativism Scales (column 6) as predictors. These equations were designed to provide a tentative estimate of the relative degree of association between each of these affective orientations and normative conceptions of national identity. The results (which are reviewed by comparing the coefficients across columns on a row-by-row basis) do provide some evidence of tension between a strong sense of national identity and multiculturalism. Although the respondent's race has no relationship to these multiculturalist policy positions in the multivariate model, three of the four indicators of national identity predict support for the belief that it is impossible for people who do not share American customs to become fully American (row A). With regard to the question asking whether ethnic and racial groups should blend into mainstream society, Patriotism, Chauvinism, and Assimilationism had statistically significant relationships with giving the melting-pot response (row B). Immigration is the major source of ethnic diversity and new claimants for cultural recognition in America, and Chauvinism, Assimilationism, and Nativism, but not Patriotism, had statistically significant relationships with support for reducing the level of immigration (row C) and disagreement that immigrants have a positive cultural impact on America (row D).

When Patriotism and Chauvinism are included as predictors simultaneously, the more aggressive outlook tends to have the stronger association with opposition to increased cultural diversity in the United States. And when the effects of Assimilationism and Nativism are compared, it is the latter more exclusionary attitude that generally appears to have the stronger negative relationship to support for multiculturalism. An ethnocentric conception of American national identity, therefore, may intensify internal political conflict by hardening resistance to the demands of cultural minorities for recognition and support.

Table 4.5 also reports on opinions about government efforts targeted at helping blacks (rows E–G) and about spending on domestic social programs (measured by a Social Spending Index combining beliefs about whether the government should spend more on health, education, welfare, and the environment—row H). The results are a virtual mirror image of the earlier findings about the factors influencing opinions about cultural diversity and immigration. In the case of the domestic policy issues, race is strongly associated with preferences, with blacks consistently more favorable toward governmental activism. But none of the four measures of national identity has a statistically significant relationship with scores on the Social Spending Index, opinions about affirmative action, or attitudes about whether the government should spend more to help blacks. The only coefficients in the array that attain conventional levels of statistical significance are the weak associations of Chauvinism and Assimilationism with opposition to special efforts to improve the living conditions of blacks. The results of these analyses indicate that generalized feelings of national attachment neither boost support for assisting one's fellow citizens through government spending nor enhance opposition to policies, such as affirmative action, aimed at assisting blacks or other ethnic minorities.

This may not be surprising, since the controversies over domestic spending and racial policy tend not to be framed in terms that engage attitudes toward the nation's integrity or power. As hypothesized above, the impact of social identities (and other predispositions) on specific policy preferences should vary across political domains. Feelings of national attachment should be strongly engaged only when the specific issues clearly touch on the values of American power, sovereignty, or purity. The data presented in table 4.5 consistently support this proposition. In addition to their effects on beliefs about cultural diversity and immigration, all four measures of national attachment had statistically significant effects in predicting opinions about whether military spending should be increased and on scores on an American Protectionism Index (alpha = .65), constructed by summing answers to items about limiting foreign imports, prohibiting foreigners from buying land in America, and requiring television stations to give preference to American programs.

A final regression analysis, reported in table 4.6, explored potential differences in the connections of ethnic as opposed to national identities on racial policy preferences. Here, responses to both the question "How close do you feel to the United States?" and the question "How close do you feel toward your own racial or ethnic group?" were included as predictors of opinions regarding affirmative action, support for government efforts to help blacks, and government spending for blacks. In this analysis, the vari-

TABLE 4.6 National Attachment and Ethnic Identity as Predictors of Opinion on Race-Targeted Policies (1996 GSS)

	Oppose Affirmative Action	Oppose Special Govt. Help for Blacks	Oppose More Spending on Blacks
Among White Respondents			
Close to own ethnic group (close =1) (white identification)	.07**	.05*	.08*
Close to the US (national attachment)	−.02	−.02	−.03
Sample size (*n*)	543	546	347
Among Black Respondents			
Close to own ethnic group (close =1) (black identification)	.12	−.05	.09
Close to the US (national attachment)	−.11	.16	.01
Sample size (*n*)	72	74	50

Entries are unstandardized regression coefficients for national and ethnic identity variables in equations with controls for age, education, income, gender, region (South), generation, ideology, and party identification.
* $p<.05$
** $p<.01$

able coding and controls are identical to those reported for table 4.5. However, to distinguish between the impact of ethnic identifications among whites and blacks, these equations were estimated separately for whites and blacks. (Because of the paucity of Hispanic respondents, the analysis could not be replicated for that group.)

To highlight the results, table 4.6 reports only the coefficients for national attachment and ethnic closeness. Confirming the results reported above, positive affect for the nation as a whole has no impact one way or the other on the racial policies queried. There are obviously significant racial differences in policy preferences, but among blacks, feeling close to one's own ethnic group had no great additional influence on support for policies aimed at improving their collective status. The fear of some political commentators that black racial identification leads to a highly distinctive political outlook seems overstated.

Among whites, however, a stronger sense of ethnic identity does have a significant effect across the three policies; white identification seems consistently to increase opposition to government policies designed to help blacks. Given our concern about the impact of ethnic identification on intergroup conflict, these results are sobering. "Identity politics," by which we mean the tendency to judge issues and events in terms of how they affect the standing of one's own group, can juxtapose one's ethnic and national "selves." While minorities may be more likely to express a strong ethnic identity, counterintuitively, it appears that the *effects* of ethnic identification are more prominent among whites. In a disturbing way, the results in table 4.6 are a reminder that the evocation of white consciousness, whether through nativist mobilization or through reaction to the assertion of ethnic pride by other groups, can lead to divisiveness and prejudice.

Conclusion

A large body of survey evidence confirms that a positive sense of national identity is pervasive in the United States, as is the belief that there is a unique American identity. In terms of affective attachment, patriotism—the sense that America is "best for me"—was more widespread than chauvinism—the sense that this country is inherently superior to all others. Significantly, too, we found no evidence of a deep ethnic divide in feelings about American nationality. The slightly lower level of patriotism among blacks, as a group, than whites is less compelling than the fact that the large majority of all ethnic groups express pride in and closeness to their country and its symbols. In addition, there is a broad consensus among all ethnic groups regarding the main criteria for American identity.

The strong sense of attachment to an American identity among ethnic minorities should calm fears about the consequences of the nation's increased ethnic diversity. Nearly as much as whites, minority respondents in our surveys rejected the idea of organizing political life along ethnic lines. Furthermore, most of them do not express their primary political identity in purely ethnic terms.

These results do not fit easily into an image of public attitudes as driven primarily by interest-based conflict between dominant and subordinate ethnic groups. The symbolic politics perspective outlined here presumes that attitudes and values are acquired through a process of reinforcement, and that the role of purely instrumental motivation often is secondary (Sears & Funk, 1990). The survey evidence suggests that members of all ethnic groups may be attracted to an American identity because of its traditional liberal premises. In both California and national surveys (Citrin et al., 1990, 1994), the criteria of a "true American" chosen as important most often by all four major ethnic groups were egalitarianism and tolerance ("treating people of all races equally" and "respecting people's freedom to say what they want").

The staying power of this liberal conception of American identity may help explain why many minority respondents viewed attachment to the country and a sense of closeness to their own ethnic group as complementary rather than competitive. The results presented above show that minority group members frequently conceive of themselves in dual terms, defining themselves as both Americans and part of a distinctive racial or ethnic group. Whites, by contrast, generally see themselves as "just Americans"; for them, national and ethnic identities are merged. What is critical, both psychologically and politically, is how the dual identity—national and ethnic—is accommodated intrapersonally. That is, when does the consciousness of being simultaneously American and black lead to a sense of ambivalence that pits the self against either the nation or the group, and how is this conflict among loyalties resolved? The present data reinforce the familiar point that blacks identify with American ideals, not American realities. As James Jones suggests (personal communication), their dual identity reflects recognition of the persistence of what Myrdal (1944) called the "American dilemma."

In the political domain, a strong sense of national identity consistently was related to opposition to liberal immigration policies and official support for maintaining minority cultures. There is, then, an ideological tension between multiculturalism and nationalism. Strong feelings of national attachment also were associated with approval for increasing America's military strength, as well as a willingness to take quite drastic measures to reduce the potential impact of foreign interests and influences. These issues, of course, focus on the boundaries between citizens and strangers, a distinction that is less relevant for opinion formation when it comes to domestic spending or racial policies.

The strength of national attachment was unrelated to how whites felt about policies targeted at helping blacks, their fellow-citizens. However, a strong ethnic identification among whites was associated with greater antagonism to affirmative action and more government spending to assist blacks. In this instance, ingroup favoritism does seem to lead to greater inter-group conflict.

The portrait of normative consensus among the general public seems strangely discordant with the seeming prevalence of ethnic competition in American political life. The division of political offices, government contracts, and other benefits among ethnic groups is closely watched by activists. Racial issues deeply divide the country's two political parties. Given all this and more, what accounts for the failure of the surveys to detect intense disagreements between the "majority" and "minority" groups when it comes to attitudes about national identity?

One answer is that the existence of a gulf between the views of political activists and ordinary citizens is not uncommon. Another possibility is that the current approach to measuring national and ethnic identifications is inadequate. Surveys may pay too much attention to abstract norms and too little to responses to distributive conflicts or actual social encounters among members of different groups. In this regard, researchers should frame issues in a way that asks respondents to make trade-offs among their multiple identities when it comes to allocating costs and benefits. This would enable a more comprehensive assessment of intragroup, as well as intergroup, conflict in how these choices are made.

Another important issue concerns the enduring quality of the tendency of recent immigrants to prefer a dual or hyphenated political identity. The present data indicate that a developing sense of patriotism and a sense of identity as an American are part of the process of acculturation that Hispanic and Asian groups are experiencing. More generally, today's immigrants, like their predecessors, become "*desocialized* from their native customs over time, even if the emotional significance of attachment to the group persists" (Glazer & Moynihan, 1975, p. 8). Because of this continuing affective tie, appeals to ethnicity still can be an effective strategy for mobilizing political support for the pursuit of group or individual interests (Horowitz, 1985). The utility of ethnicity in political combat, then, may reinforce the tendency of political leaders to emphasize the salience of this aspect of identity and strive to sustain its psychological significance within their ethnic group.

In addressing the unresolved issue concerning the conditions under which hostility toward outgroups accompanies ingroup pride, Gaertner, Dovidio, Nier, Ward, & Banker (1999) argue for the efficacy of a superordinate common identity in mitigating intergroup conflict. Applied to the larger realm of American national politics, the question posed by social identity theory becomes whether an enhanced sense of ethnic identification among minorities leads toward satisfactory conflict resolutions or toward entrenched Balkanization. Clearly, the mobilization of group consciousness among the disadvantaged can force movement toward less inequality and more social justice. On the other hand, the enhanced expression of ethnic identification in one group tends to be emulated, often provoking resistance to change and the hardening of group boundaries. Whatever the direction of future change in public attitudes, the evidence summarized here points to the advantages of a common sense of American identity founded on the realization of equal citizenship.

References

Alba, R. D. 1990. *Ethnic identity: The transformation of white America*. New Haven: Yale University Press.

Appiah, K. A. (1994). *Identity against culture: Understandings of multiculturalism*. Berkeley, CA: Doreen B. Townsend Center for the Humanities.

Ashmore, R. D., & Jussim, L. (1997). *Self and identity: Fundamental issues*. New York: Oxford University Press.

Barber, B. (1995). *Jihad vs. McWorld*. New York: Times Books.

Bar-tal, D. (1993). Patriotism as fundamental beliefs of group members. *Politics and the Individual, 3*, 45–62.

Brimelow, P. (1995). *Alien nation*. New York: Random House.

Citrin, J., Sears D., Muste C., & Wong, C. (Forthcoming). Multiculturalism in American public opinion. *British Journal of Political Science*.

Citrin J., Haas E. B., Muste C., & Reingold B. (1994). Is American nationalism changing?: Implications for foreign policy. *International Studies Quarterly, 38,* 1–31.

Citrin J., Reingold B. & Green. D. P. (1990). American identity and the politics of ethnic change. *Journal of Politics, 52,* 1124–1154.

Connor, W. (1993). Beyond reason: The nature of the ethno-national bond. *Ethnic and Racial Studies, 163,* 373–389.

Davis J., & Smith. T. (1997). *The general social survey codebook.* Chicago: National Opinion Research Center.

de la Garza, R. O., Falcon A., Garcia C. (1996). Will the real Americans please stand up: Anglo and Mexican-American support of core American political values. *American Journal of Political Science, 40,* (2), 335–350.

Farley, R. (1996). *The new American reality : Who we are, how we got here, where we are going.* New York: Russell Sage Foundation.

Gaertner, S. L., Dovidio J.F., Nier J. A., Ward C. M., & Banker, B. S. (1999). Across cultural divides: The value of superordinate identity. In D. Prentice & D. Miller. (Eds.), *Cultural divides: The social psychology of cultural contact* (pp. 173–212). New York: Russell Sage Foundation.

Gerstle, G. (1997). Liberty, coercion, and the making of Americans." *Journal of American History,* 84, 524–558.

Glazer, N. & Moynihan D. P. (1963). *Beyond the melting pot.* Cambridge: MIT Press.

Glazer, N., & Moynihan. D. P. (1975). *Ethnicity: Theory and experience.* Cambridge, MA: Harvard University Press.

Gleason, P. (1980). American identity and Americanization. In S. Thernstrom, A. Orlov, & O. Handlin (Eds.), *Harvard Encyclopedia of American Ethnic Groups* (pp 31–58). Cambridge, MA: Harvard University Press.

Goldberg, D. T. (1994). Introduction: Multicultural conditions. In D. T. Goldberg, (Ed.), *Multiculturalism: A critical reader* (pp. 1–41). Cambridge, MA: Blackwell.

Gordon, M. (1964). *Assimilation in American life: The role of race, religion, and national origins.* New York: Oxford University Press.

Greenfeld, L. (1992). *Nationalism : Five roads to modernity.* Cambridge, MA: Harvard University Press.

Greenfield, L., & Chiriot, D. (1994). Nationalism and aggression. *Theory and Society, 23,* 79–130.

Hartz, L. (1955). *The liberal tradition in America: An interpretation of American political thought since the revolution.* New York: Harcourt, Brace.

Higham, J. (1988). *Strangers in the land: Patterns of American nativism, 1860–1925.* 2nd ed. New Brunswick, NJ: Rutgers University Press.

Hochschild, J. L. (1995). *Facing up to the American dream: Race, class, and the soul of the nation.* Princeton, NJ: Princeton University Press.

Hollinger, D. (1995). *Postethnic America.* New York: Basic Books.

Hollinger, D. A. (1997). National solidarity at the end of the twentieth century: Reflections on the United States and liberal nationalism. *Journal of American History, 84,* 559–569.

Horowitz, D. (1985). *Ethnic groups in conflict.* Berkeley: University of California Press.

Huntington, S. P. (1981). *American politics: The promise of disharmony.* Cambridge, MA: Belknap Press.

Kateb, G. (1994). Notes on pluralism. *Social Research, 61,* 511–537.

Kelman, H. (1997). Nationalism, patriotism, and national identity: Social-psychological dimensions. In D. Bar-tal & E. Staub (Eds.), *Patriotism* (pp. 165–189). Chicago: Nelson-Hall.

Kinder, D. R., & Sanders, L. M. (1996). *Divided by color: Racial politics and democratic ideals.* Chicago: University of Chicago Press.

Kinder, D., & Sears, D. O. (1985). Public opinion and political action. In G. Lindzey & E. Aronson (Eds.), *Handbook of Social Psychology.* 3rd ed., vol 2., (pp. 659-741) Reading, MA: Random House.

Kosterman, R., & Feshbach, S. (1989). Towards a measure of patriotic and nationalistic attitudes. *Political Psychology, 10,* 257–274.

Lau, R., & Sears, D. (Eds.). (1986). *Political cognition : The 19th Annual Carnegie Symposium on Cognition..* Hillsdale, NJ: Lawrence Erlbaum Associates.

Lind, M. (1995). *The new nationalism and the fourth American revolution.* New York: The Free Press.

Lipset, S. M. (1996). *American exceptionalism: A double-edged sword.* New York: W. W. Norton.

Merelman, R. M., Streich, G. & Martin, P. (1998). Unity and diversity in American political culture: An exploratory study of the national conversation on American pluralism and identity. *Political Psychology, 19,* 781–808.

Miller, A. H., Gurin, P., Gurin G., & Malanchuk O. (1981). Group consciousness and political participation. *American Journal of Political Science, 25,* 494–511.

Miller, D. (1995). *On nationality.* Oxford: Clarendon Press.

Myrdal, G. (1944). *An American dilemma: The Negro problem and modern democracy.* New York, London: Harper & Brothers.

Okin, S. M. (1997). Is multiculturalism bad for women? *Boston Review, 22,* 5.

Portes, A. (Ed.) (1996). *The new second generation.* New York: Russell Sage Foundation.

Prentice, D. A. & Miller, D. T. (Eds.) (1999). *Cultural divides: Understanding and overcoming group conflict.* New York: Russell Sage Foundation.

Raz, J. (1994). Multiculturalism: A liberal perspective. *Dissent, 41,* 67–79.

Reich, R. B. (1992). *The work of nations: Preparing ourselves for 21st century capitalism.* New York: Vintage Books.

Roediger, D. R. (1994). *Towards the abolition of whiteness: Essays on race, politics, and working class history.* London: Verso.

Schlesinger, A. M. Jr. (1992). *The disuniting of America: Reflections on a multicultural society.* New York: Norton.

Schaar, J. H. (1981). *Legitimacy in the modern state.* New Brunswick, NJ: Transaction Books.

Sears, D. O. (1993). Symbolic politics. In S. Iyengar & W. J. McGuire, (Eds.), *Explorations in political Psychology* (pp. 113–149). Durham: Duke University Press.

Sears, D. O., Citrin J., Cheleden S., & Van Laar C. (1999). Cultural diversity and multicultural politics: Is ethnic Balkanization psychologically inevitable? In D. Prentice & D. Miller, (Eds.), *Cultural divides: The social psychology of cultural contact.* (pp. 35–79) New York: Russell Sage Foundation.

Sears, D. O., & Funk, C. L. (1990). Self-interest in Americans' political opinions. In J. J. Mansbridge, (Ed.), *Beyond self-interest* (pp. 147–170) (1999). Chicago: University of Chicago Press.

Sidanius J., Levin S., Rabinowitz J. L., & Frederico C. M. (1990). Peering into the jaws of the beast: The integrative dynamics of social identity, symbolic racism and social dominiance. In D. A. Prentice & D. T. Miller, (eds.), *Cultural divides: Understanding and overcoming group conflict* (pp. 80-132) New York: Russell Sage Foundation. 1999.

Smith, R. M. (1997). *Civic ideals: Conflicting visions of citizenship in U.S. history.* New Haven: Yale University Press.

Staub, E. (1997). Blind versus constructive patriotism: Moving from embeddedness in the group to critical loyalty and action. In D. Bar-tal & E. Staub, (Eds.), *Patriotism* (pp. 213–228).Chicago: Nelson Hall.

Sullivan, J., Fried A., & Dietz M. (1992). Patriotism, politics, and the presidential election of 1988. *American Journal of Political Science, 36,* 200–234.

Tajfel, H. (1978). Social categorization, social identity and social comparison. In H. Tajfel (Ed.), *Differentiation between social groups* (pp. 61–76). London: Academic Press.

Tajfel, H., & Turner J. (1986). The social identity theory of intergroup behavior. In S. Wrochel & W. Austin, (Eds.), *Psychology of intergroup relations.* Chicago: Nelson-Hall.

Taylor, C. (1995). Cross purposes: The liberal-communitarian debate. In *Philosophical arguments.* (pp. 181–203). Cambridge, MA: Harvard University Press.

Thoits, P. A., & Virshup, L.K. (1997). Me's and we's: Forms and functions of social identities." In R. D. Ashmore & L. Jussim, (Eds.), *Self and identity: Fundamental issues.* New York: Oxford University Press.

Turner, J. C., Hogg, M.A. Oakes, P. J. Reicher, S. D. & Blackwell, M. S. (1987). *Rediscovering the social group: A self-categorization theory.* Oxford: Basil Blackwell.

Tyler, T., Lind E. A., Ohbuchi K., & Sugawara, I. (1998). Conflict with outsiders: Disputing within and across cultural boundaries. *Personality & Social Psychology Bulletin, 24,* 137–147.

Warner, R. S. (1993). Work in progress: Toward a new paradigm for the sociological study of religion in the U.S. *American Journal of Sociology, 98,* 1044–1093.

Waters, M. (1990). *Ethnic options: Choosing identities in America.* Berkeley: University of California Press.

Wolfe, A. (1998). *One nation after all.* New York: Viking.

Young, I. M. (1990). *Justice and the politics of difference.* Princeton, NJ: Princeton University Press.

Zaller, J. (1992). *The nature and origins of mass opinion.* New York: Cambridge University Press.

Jim Sidanius
John R. Petrocik

5

Communal and National Identity in a Multiethnic State

A Comparison of Three Perspectives

As recent episodes of "ethnic cleansing" in Rwanda, Bosnia, and Kosovo make painfully clear, some multiethnic states seem as inclined to interethnic violence at the dawn of the 21st century as they were at the start of the 20th. Indeed, the national mobilization of a 50-year-long cold war may have temporarily restrained hostilities that lost none of their underlying virulence. Grievances that were set aside by a need to face a common enemy have now become priority issues for organized interests, parties, and public policy. Furthermore, ethnic conflict is not peculiar to nation-states mobilized into the stand-off between the cold war alliances, but appears quite generalized across the globe (see Gurr & Harff, 1994).

In many cases, intergroup conflict within multiethnic states turns on the compatibility of subgroup identities and commitments to the nation-state. Thus, one wonders if Israel can rely only upon Jewish citizens? Can a Gypsy also be Hungarian? Are Finns of Swedish extraction loyal to Finland? Can Francophones be as interested in the welfare of Canada as English speakers? Can a Turkish immigrant (and his children) be as German as an ethnic German? Can Chinese, Filipino, and Mexican immigrants also be good Americans? The national loyalty question arises because "social homogeneity and political consensus are regarded as prerequisites for, or factors strongly conducive to, stable democracies" (Lijphart, 1977, p. 1). These questions are crucial because the modern nation-state is predominantly (if not universally) organized around ethnic definitions of citizenship (Horowitz, 1985). Yet few nations are homogeneous and, as migration increases, ethnic diversity creates more opportunities for conflict within them along ethnic, racial, religious, and linguistic divides (hereafter referred to collectively as "communal" differences). A better understanding of the manner in which people are able to negotiate loyalty to their ethnic particularisms while adopting or retaining the civic culture and loyalty demanded by the nation-state seems as worthwhile today as it ever was in the past. This is especially true given that it is the institutions of the state that provide the principal framework within which communal differences are resolved. This chapter examines the relationship between ethnic and national identities within the United States.

Diversity as a Source of Conflict

While we recognize a history of conflict among communal groups, the ethos of American society treats such behavior as aberrant, largely idiosyncratic individual choices. Communal conflict is seen as a "breakdown" of a normal condition. We argue the contrary: communal conflict is a manifestation of a systematic tendency for: (1) groups to form social identities around communal differences, (2) there to be an inverse relationship between the strength of communal and common identities, and (3) both material and symbolic differences between groups to become occasions for conflict. The thesis underlying the following analysis is that social diversity shapes social identities that provide material and symbolic reasons for communal conflict in the United States. Further, the thesis asserts that conflict is an unavoidable, systematic by-product of social diversity itself. Material interests that coincide with social identities (especially when they are redistributive) will make communal conflict more common and severe. Institutions can moderate its severity. A civic and social culture can be constructed that pronounces communal conflict illegitimate, thereby reducing it to a minimum. But it will always be present because social identities will always be salient to some fraction of the society, and any material interest that coincides with a communal distinction will insert that communal difference into the conflict because of the sensitivity of people to communal distinctions (Lijphart, 1977; Powell, 1982).

Ethnic, Racial, and National Loyalty

This chapter analyzes ethnic conflict by focusing on certain relationships between communal identity and national loyalties. We have two "nationality" groups—Hispanic Americans and Asian Americans. The first is associated with the countries of Latin America (principally Mexico), even though many are the progeny of families that have been in the United States since the early 18th century. Although some Asian Americans also come from families that are long-term residents of the United States, most are recent immigrants. Consequently both fit into the conditions that are presumed to create the "divided loyalty" often attributed to identifiable subnational communities.

African Americans have a singular history. Even though many can trace their time in the United States to the 17th century, slavery and segregation have made them strangers in the land. Africa may not exert a sense of identity for many, but the separation from the larger society that was forced on them for almost three centuries created a group experience that is, we believe, functionally equivalent to being placed on the margins of the society.

Specifically, this chapter examines the relationship between national loyalty and a preference for one's ethnic and "racial" group. Surprisingly little empirical research has been directed at this issue. Within the American context, most thinking and research directed at this question falls into two categories: the classical "melting pot" model of incorporation and an alternative "pluralist" perspective, with the latter giving rise to multicultural visions of the social order.

The rarely examined assumption of these images of American society is that there is no inherent conflict between subgroup and national identity. A few attempts to examine the relationship have usually reported a compatibility, sometimes an easy one, between these identities (de la Garza, Falcon, & Garcia, 1996). However, this assumption and the empirical evidence in favor of it flies in the face of emerging work on social dominance, which finds incompatibility between subgroup and national social identities. In general, this work suggests that national identity is generally associated with communal identity for one group and the exclusion of others (Sidanius, 1993; Sidanius, Feshbach, Levin, & Pratto, 1997; Sidanius & Pratto, 1999). The purpose of this chapter is to further examine the linkage between communal identity and national loyalties in the United States.

The United States is a hard case because disaffection is limited and disaffected groups are few in number. The extreme group cleavages that assure a negative association between commitment to common and subgroup identities are absent in the United States. Moreover, the prevailing civic culture emphasizes the compatibility of subgroup and common identities and loyalty. Yet, as the following *data* show, such negative relationships actually exist. The nuances of this relationship and their implications for multiethnic states are elaborated below.

A Thematic History of American Identity and Ethnic Diversity

The earliest comparative studies of mass politics quickly established that conflict in even the most well-ordered democratic societies closely followed communal divisions. Religious, ethnic, racial, linguistic, and regional differences shaped social and political debate more strongly than most other distinctions (class, for example; see Lipset & Rokkan, 1967; Horowitz, 1985; Lijphart, 1979; Petrocik, 1981, 1998). The history of the United States follows this pattern (see, e.g., Kleppner, 1970; Kelley, 1979). Communal conflict was fueled by cycles of immigration that transformed the nation from a population of largely English Protestants (with some dissenter religions) to one that included continental nationalities, Catholics, and Jews. Making even the most modest assumption about fertility patterns, it seems likely that immigrants and first-generation Americans (who could be expected to be more like their immigrant parents than the children of "old stock" Americans) represented upwards of a third of the population of the country by 1900.

American politics was affected by this diversity from the earliest days of the republic. The Alien Act of 1798, for example, was passed by the declining Federalists to limit the ability of immigrants to vote in the hope that the growth of the Democratic-Republicans would be slowed. Their lack of success did not forestall many further attempts to limit the impact of immigration and population diversity on an originally English, Protestant society. The Irish, and Catholics in general, were the first to redefine what America could represent; central and north Europeans came next; southern and eastern Europeans were the major group for about 60 years in the late 1800s and early 1900s; immigration from Asia during this same period was important in the west. In different ways and at different times, this population diversification led to new political parties and legislation to limit the number of immigrants and their influence on American life.

The surge in immigration in the late 1980s—the immigration rate was 2.3 per thousand in 1980 but 6.1 per thousand in 1990—reawakened latent sensitivity to the new "strangers in our midst." This reawakening has been especially pronounced in California, where the number of new immigrants with a non-European "racial" and ethnic heritage is very large. The new immigrants, like their predecessors, are perceived by the native population to be substantially different, raising familiar questions about how they fit into the society, where their loyalties and commitments lie, what changes should be made to accommodate them, and what costs they will impose on the society. School boards, zoning boards, city councils, utilities regulators, local and state elections, and presidential politics have all been forums for conflicts between Americans and the new immigrants. Some of the disputes are material, turning on taxes and social welfare costs; others are symbolic (e.g., Chinese residents of the San Gabriel Valley objected to a switch in the telephone area code from 818 to 626 because of the numerological significance of the numbers for the Chinese). Unresolved problems between white and black Americans have acquired renewed significance with the rising tide of immigration.

Americanization and the Melting Pot

Specific disputes between natives and immigrants have always been conflicts over the identity of the national community: about what values, viewpoints, and interests were compatible, and which could not be abided because they served and promoted loyalties that were hostile to a common American identity. It rested on the expectation that different groups embraced significantly different values, beliefs, and perceptions. A *de facto* policy of "Americanization" was the first way in which the nation dealt with diversity. Everybody was expected to adopt the language, dress, customs, beliefs, and loyalties of the dominant English culture that defined the United States. By the end of the 19th century, the polity replaced "Americanization" with the "melting pot."

The melting pot replaced the expectation of submersion in the preexisting English Protestant culture with a preference (not necessarily universal) for a continuous reformulation of what constituted American culture. Immigrants, in the melting pot formulation, had valuable things to offer America, and this value was to be recognized as American society incorporated the language, cuisine, social sensibilities, and economic and political values of the immigrant cultures. This reformulation of American culture, coupled with marriage across the lines of national origin and religion, became the alternative resolution of ethnic diversity and the suspicions it produced. It resolved (at least intellectually) the struggle over whether immigrants were real Americans by loosening (if not severing) the connection between WASP and American. The result was a continually changing American culture and a continually changing American ethnicity still expressing the basic theme "from many, one" (see e.g., Salins, 1997). Restrictions on European (and especially German) nationality groups during World War I, immigration limits after 1920, and "Americanization" campaigns (largely tied to learning English and shedding the most obvious habits and custom of the immigrant culture) through World War II produced substantial assimilation and largely eliminated the salience of nationality and ethnic differences by the middle 1960s (Walch, 1994; Freedman, 1996).

The Unmelted Pot of Pluralism

A more widespread recognition of the pluralism of American society is often attributed to the reemergence of a white ethnic identity in response to the civil rights movement (Greeley, 1971, 1976; Novak, 1971), but, as Milton Gordon (1964) demonstrated almost four decades ago, and others confirmed (e.g., Wolfinger, 1965; Parenti, 1967), resistance to melting-pot pressures was strong and seems to be to the present day (Alba, 1990). While the notion of the melting pot has been the popular metaphor for most of this century, it co-existed with a "pluralist" image of "salad bowls," "quilts," or "glorious mosaics" to explain how one could be an American while retaining a distinct "racial" or ethnic identity.

While there is variation in the precise manner in which the term "pluralism" is understood, the central idea is that subgroup identities are retained. In a pluralist society, communal segments defined by religion, language, national origin, or "race" remain salient to individuals. Catholics recognize Protestants; the progeny of Italian immigrants see "Yankees" and Polish Americans; blacks and whites are aware of a "racial" divide; Louisiana Cajuns recognize differences between themselves and their Protestant neighbors. While the pluralist image expects social views and policy preferences to vary by ethnic and "racial" segment, there is no notion that the differences are unbridgeable because the pluralist political culture expects individuals in the subgroups to feel an identity and loyalty to the national community, and accept a set of obligations to it. Some formulations of pluralism expect positive supra-communal effects from the communal identity. Rather than contributing to "disuniting" and fractionation (Schlesinger, 1992), these distinct ethnic loyalties are thought to co-exist and even promote a common national identity through the communal identity (Powell, 1995; de la Garza et al., 1996).

The Melting Pot, Pluralism, and Conflict

A melting-pot, immigrant society expects virtually no communal conflict because the melting pot society has virtually no communal divisions around which material or symbolic grievances can be politicized. Pluralism, although it has a strong expectation of communal conflict *and* expects groups to be sensitive to how social resources (e.g., income, education, employment opportunities, and social standing) are distributed, assumes a political framework within which affected groups have different advantages and are able to bring them to bear in ways that ensure that their core interests are promoted. (Dahl, 1961, offers the classic exposition; but also see Polsby, 1963, for a significant elaboration of the basic theory that guided virtually all research on the topic.) Every turn to government may energize intergroup conflicts because such collective action enforces contributions that some groups will not prefer to make, especially when the outcome is redistributive. In the textbook model of political pluralism, all groups participate equally and have a similar positive regard for the basic institutions that structure the political competition because no group is permanently excluded or permanent losers to any other groups.

Diversity, Social Dominance, and Communal Conflict

Central to the pluralist argument is the notion that all ethnic groups be regarded as *co-equal* partners in the pursuit of the American dream. However, in contrast to this vision, there are a cluster of theories of intergroup relations that suggest that "co-equality" never describes relationships among salient groups within multiethnic societies. These theoretical models have been referred to as group dominance models, where social dominance theory is the most explicit and recent statement of this general position (see

Sidanius & Pratt. 1999; for related models see Blumer, 1960; Jackman, 1994). These group dominance models suggest that societies tend to be organized as *group-based* hierarchies, with dominant groups enjoying disproportionate power, prestige, and privilege. This group-based hierarchy applies to both democratic and nondemocratic states, despite differing discourses concerning inclusivity or pluralism.

Social dominance theory, as it has been developed by Sidanius and Pratto and their colleagues (see, e.g., Pratto, Sidanius, Stallworth, & Malle, 1994; Sidanius, 1993; Sidanius & Pratto, 1999) shares with pluralism an expectation that communal identities will not be submerged into a larger national consciousness, but, contrary to pluralism, *it expects some groups to be relatively consistent losers in the struggle.* The foundation for this expectation is social dominance theory's assertion that social systems are structured as group-based social hierarchies with one or few groups at the top of the hierarchy, with all others—sometimes in a carefully ordered fashion—arrayed below them. The mechanisms and processes that establish and maintain the expected social hierarchy can be informal—group-based associational patterns that create and limit opportunities—or formal—political and economic institutions that promote the interest of dominant segments (see especially Sidanius & Pratto, 1999).

In time, institutions can become identified with specific groups rather than as common institutions of the society, and considerable political conflict can turn on perceptions of who is served by them. Examples of this in the United States are easy to observe. Social welfare agencies are popularly identified with minority ethnic groups. White Americans often resist financial pleas from urban school districts because the school systems in big cities are identified with minority children. And while police forces are staffed with "officer friendlies" for whites, they are commonly regarded as hostile and dangerous by African Americans and other minorities (see Sidanius & Pratto, 1999, chap. 8).

Exclusionary Patriotism

Not only do such group dominance models have much to say about how positive and negative social value will be distributed across the group-based social hierarchy, but these models also have implications for the general interface between national and group identity. Since public institutions are closely linked to dominant groups, evaluations of them should vary with the salience of an individual's identification with the dominant as compared to the subordinate groups. Specific intergroup differences in evaluations of political figures, the police, or particular government agencies are well known. The interest here is in demonstrating a more general relationship between communal identity and a common national identity. This can have several manifestations, but our data allow us to examine only one aspect: regard for the nation or patriotism.

We expect the dynamics of communal conflict in an environment of social dominance to create *exclusionary patriotism:* a situation in which communal and national identities are supportive and positively correlated among socially dominant groups, but in conflict among those in subordinate communal groups. Specifically, we expect the following:

1. The prominence of the society's public institutions in maintaining communal hierarchies will cause dominant communal groups to be more identified with the nation's symbols.
2. We expect a differential relationship between the intensity of communal identities and a common national identity across groups. Among dominate groups we expect communal and national identities to be fused and positively correlated; among subordinate groups we expect them to be at odds and negatively correlated.
3. We expect the negative relationship to be moderated by the experiences of the subordinate group. That is, those further down the communal hierarchy are likely to see more of a conflict between their communal identity and national symbols that are associated with the communal identity of the dominant group. The subjective social distance among the groups predicts some of the effect. Of course, a real history of significant conflict between the dominant and subordinate group would lead to even stronger effects.

This relationship should be observable even though "exclusionary patriotism" is specifically contrary to the American civic culture. The key variable is not the avowed norms but the actual operation of the society. Because the society functions in a way that allows and even encourages a perception that the political order is more closely identified with European-Americans than it is with other major racial and ethnic groups, the dynamics of exclusionary patriotism will shape the relationship between subgroup identities and attitudes toward American national identity.

Empirical Implications of the Interface Between National and Ethnic Attachment

The melting-pot, pluralist, and group dominance models of American society lead to a different set of expectations concerning the interface between national and communal identity. This chapter will explore three expectations for each model.

- *The Salience of Ethnic Identity.* The melting-pot model predicts that ethnic or "racial" identification will be a trivial social category for most Americans. Both the pluralist and group dominance perspectives predict that these social identities will remain important and salient social identities. The salience of ethnicity should express itself not only in terms of social identity but also in terms of a generalized ethnocentric bias against Americans from other ethnic groups.

- *Patriotism and Ethnicity.* Both the melting-pot and pluralist models predict that patriotic attachment to the United States will be essentially equal across ethnic groups. In contrast, and for reasons explained above, the group dominance model predicts that dominant European-Americans will have significantly higher levels of patriotism than will members of subordinate groups (e.g., Asian, Latino, or African Americans).

- *The Interface Between National and Communal Identity.* The melting-pot and pluralist models predict no correlation between patriotism and communal identity. The melting-pot model predicts no correlation because it expects essentially no ethnocentrism in the society. The variance in ethnocentrism is trivial and idiosyncratic. The pluralist model of the society predicts no correlation between communal identity and regard for national institutions because the wins and losses of one's ethnic group are not predetermined by an inherently subordinate position to dominant groups who use public institutions to enforce their preferences. Indeed, the results of de la Garza et al. (1996) even suggest that ethnic identity can actually promote a stronger sense of regard for the nation. However, social dominance theory (Sidanius et al., 1997) expects the correlation between national and communal identity to vary across the social status continuum. It should be positive among dominants (e.g., European-Americans) and negative among subordinates (e.g., African-Americans). Table 5.1 summarizes the expected relationships between ethnic and national attachment for each model.

Thus far, we know of only two studies that have attempted to explore the relative plausibilities of these conflicting models (but see also Citrin et al., this volume). Using a nationally representative sample of Mexican Americans, de la Garza and his colleagues (1996) found clear empirical support for the pluralist perspective. They found that Mexican Americans who were strongly attached to their ethnic heritage were no less patriotic than Mexican-Americans with weak ethnic attachments. Furthermore, their data showed virtually no relationship between the strength of this ethnic identity and core American values such as individualism. Even more striking was their finding that Mexican Americans appeared slightly *more* patriotic than native-born white Americans.

A later study by Sidanius and colleagues (1997) found only partial support for the de la Garza findings. When comparing the relationships between ethnic and national identity between European- and African-Americans, the results showed clear support for the group dominance perspective in two respects. First, European-Americans showed significantly

TABLE 5.1 Hypotheses Derivable from the Melting-Pot, Pluralism, and Group Dominance Models

	Theoretical Model		
Hypotheses	Melting-pot	Pluralism	Group Dominance
1. Ethnicity remains strong social identity	No	Yes	Yes
2. Dominants will be more patriotic than subordinates	No	No	Yes
3. There will be a correlation between ethnocentrism and patriotic attachment to the nation	No	No, or positive correlation	Yes. Positive correlation among dominant, negative correlation among subordinates

higher levels of patriotism than African-Americans. Second, there was clear evidence of asymmetry in the correlation between patriotism and communal identity across dominant and subordinate ethnic groups. Among dominants (i.e., whites), ethnocentrism was positively correlated with patriotism, while among subordinates (i.e., blacks) ethnocentrism was negatively correlated with patriotism, as the social dominance model expects. While the dominant-subordinate asymmetry was quite consistent for the contrast between European- and African Americans; it was less consistent with respect to the contrast between European and Latino Americans. Moreover, while the asymmetry held among a sample of European- and Latino-American college students, it did not hold among a national probability sample of white and Latino adults (see Sidanius et. al., 1997). In Sidanius et al.'s (1997) analysis of an American national probability sample, the results were essentially consistent with the de la Garza et al. (1996) findings.

How might we explain the somewhat conflicting findings between the de la Garza et al. (1996) and the Sidanius et al. (1997) studies? First and most obviously, the de la Garza et al. study only compared whites and Latinos, whereas the Sidanius et al. study also included blacks. Second, even the slightly different findings with respect to Latinos might have something to do with major differences in political context. In recent years, immigration from Mexico and Central America has become a salient and contentious political issue in California, where the Sidanius et al (1997) data were collected. It is quite possible that Southern California's highly racialized public discourse concerning illegal Latino immigration (e.g., Proposition 187) induced Latinos to feel under attack and as political outsiders as African Americans have felt for the bulk of American history. Finally, we think that their analysis does not measure their key conceptual variable very well. The acculturation variable, the centerpiece of their analysis, is only a weak approximation of subgroup attachment. Their measure categorized individuals by place of birth and language facility: U.S.-born Mexican Americans who were English speakers were regarded as the most acculturated while foreign-born Spanish speakers were classed as the least acculturated. Acculturation, however, is not the relevant variable. Although there is probably a relationship between the individual's level of acculturation and the strength of his or her preference for Mexicans over non-Mexican-Americans, there is no reason to assume that it is strong. It may, in fact, be extremely weak. Among European Americans (the Irish, Italians, Poles, etc.), identity with national origin is poorly related to rates of endogamy, the observance of ethnic customs, and facility with the immigrant language (Alba, 1990). *A priori*, there is no compelling reason to expect Mexican Americans to be different.

To be sure, the null results also appear with the one approximate measure of identity used in the analysis. Respondents classed as Latinos were those who, when asked their "racial" identity, chose the option "something else" rather than white. This group, slightly less than half of their sample, clearly thought of themselves in ethnic terms. In our experience, those who self-describe as Latinos are more ethnically identified than those who do not use this appellation—and this subgroup was not less patriotic or less individualistic in their study. However, an unwillingness of the respondent to choose the category "white" as their ethnic or racial group is a weak measure of identity, and the null results probably should not be surprising. Consider that it is fairly common for white Americans to respond with a national origin distinction when asked their nationality, but there is tremendous variability in the strength of attachment to the national origin of Americans who call themselves Italian, Polish, or Lithuanian when reporting their nationality. This variance almost certainly exists among Mexican Americans. It is at least reasonable to suspect that it does, and the weak relationship de la Garza and his colleagues report for the measure may only reflect the indeterminate property of the categorization.

The finding that Mexican Americans are more patriotic and individualistic than native-born whites is even less persuasive. As de la Garza and his colleagues note, the whites with whom they draw the contrast were available for the analysis only because they lived in areas with large Mexican-American populations. These whites are almost certainly not representative of the white population as a whole, given the patterns of residential segregation that exist in the United States. We would expect such whites to be poorer and less educated. Their social class is likely to orient them toward a preference for government action (the exact opposite of the "individualism" expected of the median American in the de la Garza et. al. formulation).[1] The social values that permit these whites to live comfortably in Mexican-American neighborhoods may also have negative implications for expressions of patriotism, depressing, or even reversing, therefore, the expected relationship between it and nativity and ethnicity.

Method and Design

We used five different data sets in these analyses and a total of 7,400 respondents.

Data set 1: UCLA Student Sample

This data set consisted of 725 randomly sampled UCLA undergraduates collected in the fall of 1993. The sampling frame stratified a list of all registered students into four "ethnic" strata (whites, blacks, Latinos, and Asians), and randomly sampled from each stratum. The subjects were enticed to participate by the offer of four $50 prizes. The ethnic breakdown of all of the samples is found in table 5.2. The students were given a questionnaire primarily assessing their attitudes toward patriotism and their affect toward various American ethnic groups. However, unlike the Sidanius et. al. (1997) study, in this chapter we will explore the responses of resident-aliens as well.

Patriotism Measures.   Kosterman and Feshbach (1989) and Sidanius et al. (1997) have shown that patriotism could be well measured by an eight-item scale consisting of items such as: "I am proud to be an American," and "Every time I hear the national anthem, I feel strongly moved." Not only did this scale have a high degree of face validity, but it also had a fairly high level of reliability (with a Cronbach α = .91). Because the patriotism measures were assessed using different scales across the different studies, in order to aid in cross-study comparisons, we transformed all of the patriotism measures to the same 0.00 to 1.00 scale, where 0 represents the lowest possible score a respondent can get and 1.00 represents the highest possible score a respondent can get.

Ethnocentrism.   While communal identity can be regarded as expressing the general salience of one's "racial," ethnic, or religious identity, we will use the term "ethnocentrism" to refer to *preference* for communal ingroups over communal outgroups. The ethnocentrism measures were operationalized by use of thermometer rating scales. The respondents were asked to indicate their degree of positive or negative feeling toward each of four ethnic groups using a seven-point rating scale (7–very positive, 4–neutral, 1–very negative). The groups were whites, African Americans, Latinos, and Asians.

Two different types of ethnocentrism scores were computed: (1) generalized ethnocentrism and (2) hierarchical ethnocentrism. Generalized ethnocentrism (GEI) was used to measure the respondents' degree of ethnocentrism against the "generalized other," regardless of whether this generalized other had relatively high or low ethnic status. GEI was computed simply by taking the thermometer rating given to one's ethnic ingroup minus the thermometer rating given to the average ethnic outgroup. *Hierarchical ethnocentrism* (HEI), on the other hand, was designed to be sensitive to the

TABLE 5.2 Data Sets and Ethnic Groups

	Samples					
Ethnic Group	Data Set 1 UCLA Students 1993	Data Set 2 LACSS 1997–98	Data Set 3 NES 1992	Data Set 4 NES 1996	Data Set 5 GSS 1996	Total
Whites	153	539	1,905	1,325	1,015	4,937
Blacks	113	139	312	191	170	925
Latinos	98	221	207	149	54	729
Asians	72	68	28	22	10	200
Jews	32	—	—	—	—	32
Immigrants	257	265	—	—	55	577
Total	725	1,232	2,452	1,687	1,304	7,400

hierarchical nature of the status differences among the ethnic groups. Thus, HEI was measured slightly differently, depending upon whether one was a member of a dominant or subordinate ethnic group. For whites, hierarchical ethnocentrism (HEI) was defined in precisely the same way as for generalized ethnocentrism (GEI). However, consistent with the notion of subordination to a dominant social group, HEI for the each of the three subordinates groups was defined as the positive rating given to one's ethnic ingroup minus the rating given to higher-status whites.

Data Set 2: Los Angeles County Social Survey (LACSS)

These data are drawn from two years (1997 and 1998) of the Los Angeles County Social Survey (LACSS). The LACSS is a countywide random-digit dial telephone survey of adults living in households conducted by the Computer Assisted Telephone Interviewing unit of UCLA's Survey Research Center. The LACSS employs a 12 call-back procedure, systematically varying the day of the week and the time of day, before dropping any numbers from the sample. A total of 1,232 respondents were interviewed (see table 5.2).

Patriotism Measures. Two items were used to operationalize patriotism: (1) "I find the sight of the American flag very moving," and (2) "I have great love for the United States." The questions were answered on a four-point scale from "4–strongly agree" to "1–strongly disagree." The reliability of the scale was considered adequate (Cronbach $\alpha = .68$).

Ethnocentrism. Generalized and hierarchical ethnocentrism were defined by use of affect differentials in the same manner as used in Data set 1, the UCLA student sample.

Ethnic Grievances. Another series of questions assessed respondents' "sense of ethnic grievance"—that is, the extent to which their ethnic or racial group has been disadvantaged by those in power. These questions assessed whether respondents: (1) believed that their group should have more influence in government; (2) believed that their group was often held back by other people; (3) believed that the government helps particular groups and does not pay enough attention to people in general; (4) believed that public officials from their own group would be more likely to do things respondents approved of; (5) would not vote for someone who was not likely to help their group; (6) oppose tax increases that help groups other than their own; and (7) would vote for a candidate from their own group, even if that candidate did not agree with them on every issue. All questions except the first two used an agree or disagree format (which also included options for don't know and refused, and neither agree or disagree if this was volunteered by the respondent). The response options for the first question were should have more influence, less influence, or just about right (as well as don't know and refused). The response options for the second question were often held back, sometimes held back, and treated as well as anybody else (as well as don't know and refused). For this question, both held back and sometimes held back were coded as "agreement" (i.e., agreeing that their group has been held back).

Data Set 3: National Election Study—1992 (NES)

The third data set was a national probability sample of Americans collected as part of the 1992 National Election Study (NES) conducted by the Center for Political Studies at the Institute for Social Research at the University of Michigan. Altogether, the 1992 study interviewed 2,452 respondents and the analysis is limited to the four major ethnic groups that are the focus of this study (i.e., whites, African Americans, Latinos, and Asians; see table 5.2 for details.

Patriotism. Patriotism was defined by two questions that had a content that was virtually identical to the patriotism questions used in data set 2: (1) "When you see the American flag flying does it make you feel extremely good, very good, somewhat good, or not very good?" (2) "How strong is your love for your country? Extremely strong, very strong, somewhat strong or not very strong?" (Cronbach $\alpha = .78$).

Ethnocentrism. Ethnocentrism was defined in precisely the same way in data sets 2 and 3.

Data Set 4: National Election Study—1996 (NES)

The fourth data set was the 1996 National Election Study (NES), also conducted by the Center for Political Studies at the Institute for Social Research at the University of Michigan (N = 1,687; see table 5.2). This data set did not contain measures of patriotism, but it did contain feeling thermometers that were used to compute ethnocentrism in the same way as in data sets 2 and 3. The 1996 NES permitted a replication of the communal identity patterns observed in the 1992 study, and a check against a one-time pattern.

Dataset 5: General Social Survey—1996 (GSS)

This data set (N = 1,304) was used to replicate earlier findings and examine dimensions of national identity beyond what was possible with the patriotism index used in the 1992 NES study (data set 3) and the LACSS samples (data set 2). While the dimension of patriotism, or love of the nation, is a central dimension of national attachment, it is clearly only one of several different possible ways in which citizens can be psychologically attached to the nation. Previous research (Kosterman & Feshbach, 1989; Sidanius et al., 1997; Hofstetter, Feierabend, & Klicperova-Baker, 1999) has shown that there are at least two important dimensions of national attachment: patriotism (love of country and its symbols) and nationalism (the desire that one's country dominate other countries). Previous research also suggests that while dominants are significantly more patriotic than subordinates, they are not more nationalistic than subordinates (see Sidanius et al., 1997).

The 1996 GSS permitted a further exploration (as well as replication) of the communal-national trade-off because it contained 34 questions concerning Americans' feelings of national attachment. While the 34 national attachment items formed a reasonable coherent and homogeneous scale (Cronbach α = .84), examination of the items revealed distinctly different types of national attachment within this scale. To further explore this issue and before any further analyses were attempted, we first factor-analyzed these items using an alpha factor extraction approach. While there were as many as 10 factors with eigen values greater than 1.00, the scree test suggested that only four of these factors were meaningful. Altogether these four factors accounted for approximately 37 percent of the total variance. The factors were interpreted as:

1. *Patriotism* or *pride in one's nation* (51 percent of the common variance) was primarily defined by nine items such as: "Proud of the way democracy works in America," "Proud of America's economic achievements," "Proud of America's political influence in the world," Proud of America's scientific and technical achievements."
2. *Nationalism* (20 percent of common variance) essentially embraced a chauvinistic and belligerent attitude toward other nations and peoples (see also Bar-tal & Staub, 1997). The items most strongly defining this dimension were: "TV should give preference to American films," "Foreigners should not be allowed to buy land,"

"America should follow its own interests," "People should support their country even when the country is wrong," and "People would be better off if they were more like Americans."

3. *Unwillingness to leave America* (16 percent of common variance) primarily expressed people's unwillingness to move away from America (e.g., "Willing to move outside of America," "Willing to move outside of North America").

4. *Importance of American identity* (13 percent of common variance), as distinct from patriotism or pride in one's nation, expressed people's sense of social identity as being American. The dimension was primarily defined by items such as: "It is important to have lived in America for life," "It is important to have been born in America," "It is important to have American citizenship."

Factor scores were computed for each respondent on each factor. Not surprisingly, these factor scores were positively correlated, with the strongest correlation found between "Patriotism" and "American identity" ($r = .42$), and the weakest between "nationalism" and "unwilling to leave America." ($r = .10$).

The 1996 GSS included one question that we used to assess the salience of ethnic identification. This question read "Compared to people who are not (your ethnicity), would you say that you feel much closer to people who are (your ethnicity), somewhat closer to them, or not closer at all?" The term "your ethnicity" did not actually appear—it was always replaced by the respondent's own ethnicity (e.g., if they said they were Asian, it read "Asian"; if they said they were "Latino" etc.).

Results

The alternative models of American society posit ethnic differences (or in the case of the melting-pot model, no ethnic differences) in: the salience of ethnic identity, group levels of patriotism, and the relationship between patriotism and ethnocentrism.

Issue 1: The Continued Salience of Ethnic Identity

Within the melting-pot model, ethnic identification should not be a salient social identity. We explored the validity of this assumption by examining: (1) the degree to which American citizens also think of themselves in "racial"/ethnic terms; (2) ethnocentric bias against other American ethnic groups, and (3) people's political grievances as a function of their own ethnic/racial ingroups. First Table 5.3 shows ethnicity to be a salient social identity for most Americans. For example, some 76 percent of European-Americans in the nation as a whole feel close (34 percent are very close) to

TABLE 5.3 Feelings of Closeness to One's Own Ethnic/Racial Group (Citizens Only)

	Whites		Blacks		Hispanics		Asians	
	USA	LA	USA	LA	USA	LA	USA	LA
Respondent feels:								
Very close	34%	27%	70%	58%	47%	43%	46%	37%
Some closeness	42	52	19	39	34	40	38	41
Not close	24	21	11	10	19	14	17	22
Total	100%	100%	100%	100%	100%	100%	100%	100%
Number of cases	975	559	166	140	343	432	14	95

Source: The U.S. national data are drawn from the 1996 General Social Survey. The Los Angeles data are from the 1997 Los Angeles County Social Survey.

other whites. Among, African, Latino and Asian Americans, this percentage is even greater at 89 percent, 81 percent, and 84 percent, respectively. The same general pattern was found for Americans in Los Angeles County. However, not surprisingly and in both cases, the salience of ethnicity varied significantly as a function of ethnic group membership. In both cases ethnicity was more salient for the ethnic minorities than for European Americans (national data set: $X^2_{(6)} = 81.71, p < .001$; LA dataset $X^2_{(6)} = 61.75, p < .001$).

Second, using the Los Angeles and national probability samples, we examined the generalized ethnocentrism scores of each ethnic group. If one's ethnic/racial particularism is no longer a salient feature of people's social identity, as a strict reading of the melting-pot model would expect, then Americans from one particular ethnic or "racial" group should not exhibit ethnocentric bias against other American "racial"/ethnic groups. However, as the data in table 5.4 show, all four major American ethnic/racial groups display an ethnocentric bias against other groups. While European Americans in Los Angeles appeared to be slightly less ethnocentric than members of the other major ethnic groups (the thermometer difference was approximately 3 degrees compared to differences of 8, 10 , and 8 degrees among blacks, Hispanics, and Asians, respectively), the level of general ethnocentric bias among European Americans in the nation as a whole appeared to be no more or less extreme than among other major ethnic groups in the nation as a whole (i.e., an 11 degree average difference compared to an average difference of 17 degrees for African Americans, 10 degrees for Latinos, and 8 degrees for Asians). This very broad and generalized level of ethnocentric bias is consistent with the thrust of social identity theory (Tajfel & Turner, 1986).

Finally, ethnic group membership also has political relevance and political overtones. Using the 1997 LACSS, we asked respondents from each of the major ethnic groups a series of questions concerning whether they felt

TABLE 5.4 Thermometer Differences Among Ethnic/Racial Groups (Citizens Only)

	Whites		Blacks		Hispanics		Asians	
	USA	LA	USA	LA	USA	LA	USA	LA
Rating of:								
Whites	71	81	73	79	71	75	67	74
Blacks	62	77	85	87	69	65	63	66
Hispanics	60	78	70	79	78	79	59	66
Asians	58	79	61	78	63	66	71	77
Own group	71	81	85	87	78	79	71	77
Average of								
other groups	60	78	68	79	68	69	63	69
Difference	+11	+3	+17	+8	+10	+10	+8	+8
Number of cases	3151	559	495	140	343	432	61	95

Source: The U.S. national data are drawn from the 1992 and 1996 National Election Study surveys of those years. The Los Angeles data are from the 1997 and 1998 Los Angeles County Social Survey.

that members of their own ethnic group were being fairly treated by the political system, whether public officials from their own ethnic group would treat them more fairly, and whether they would vote for a member of their own group, even if they disagreed with the respondent (see table 5.5). For example, while members of the ethnic minorities are significantly more likely than whites to feel that their own ethnic group needs more influence in the political system ($X^2_{(3)}$ = 15.82, p < .01), a majority of all groups feel that their ethnic ingroups need more political influence. Similarly, a majority of all ethnic groups believe that some groups get too much help and not enough attention is paid to what is good for all people. The only issue where one's ethnic identity does not seem to play a major role concerns respondents' willingness to vote for a member of one's own ethnic group, even when the respondent disagrees with the candidate. Table 5.5 shows that a distinct minority of respondents is willing to vote strictly on the basis of ethnicity, varying from 23 percent for blacks to 6 percent for Asians.

Altogether, ethnicity remains an important and salient social identity with clear political overtones. In general, the data give little support to the melting-pot image, at least to the extent that the melting pot assumes that Americans are blended and substantially unaware of their "racial" and ethnic differences. Table 5.5 also makes clear that the pluralist notion of contented collaboration among competing groups is at least contested. Ethnic minorities are particularly likely to believe that they suffer at the hands of others because of their communal identity and that members of their group are likely to be more sympathetic and protective.

TABLE 5.5 Sense of Grievance Among Those Identifying with an Ethnic/Racial Group (Citizens Only)

	White	Black	Hispanic	Asian
Percent agreeing:				
Believe that ones group needs more influence	58	86	71	67
Believe that he/she has been "held back" because of their ethnic/racial identity	27	77	88	67
Believe that some groups are helped too much and not enough attention is paid to what is good for all people	54	55	59	67
Believe that public officials from own group are more likely to do preferred things	30	41	59	56
Oppose programs that help some group but not mine	47	46	44	33
Would not vote for a candidate if he/she would not help people like respondent	55	73	61	28
Would vote for a candidate from my group even if I disagreed about some things	21	23	17	6
Number of cases	151	53	162	46

Source: The 1997 Los Angeles County Social Survey.

Issue 2: Ethnicity and Patriotism

Our second question concerns whether the degree of patriotic attachment to the nation is the same across all major ethnic groups. While both the melting-pot and pluralist models would expect no differences among the groups, the group dominance model of American society expects considerable differences. Dominant European Americans should have significantly higher levels of patriotism than Hispanics, Asians, and African Americans. In addition, since African Americans have long been, and remain, the group at the very bottom of America's ethnic hierarchy, the group dominance approach would expect the mean level of patriotism among African Americans to be relatively low and no greater than that found among resident-aliens, or people barred from participation in the political system. To explore these questions, we compared patriotism as a function of ethnicity across four of the five data sets (UCLA students, Los Angeles County residents, and two representative samples from the nation as a whole).

The results in table 5.6 are inconsistent with both the melting-pot and the pluralism models. Contradicting the melting-pot and the pluralist perspectives on America, patriotic attachment is not uniform across the ethnic status hierarchy. However, the differences are not substantially large. Moreover, the absolute scores indicate that all groups have relatively high patriotism scores. The bulk of the intergroup difference, reflected in the correlation ratios (varying between .14 and .35), is due to the relatively low

TABLE 5.6 Patriotic Attachment to America as a Function of Ethnicity Across Four Samples.

	Ethnic Group					Resident Alien in US	
	Whites	Asians	Latinos	Jews	Blacks	More than 5 yrs	Less than 5 yrs
Sample 1 (UCLA Students, 1993): $F_{(6,703)} = 16.64$, $p<.001$, $\eta = .35$							
Mean patriotism	.693	.628	.617	.555	.432	.585	.477
N	153	72	98	32	106	219	30
SD	.23	.20	.23	.23	.24	.20	.22
Sample 2 (L.A. County, 1997–98): $F_{(4,1203)} = 9.53$, $p<.001$, $\eta = .18$							
Mean patriotism	.849	.806	.818	—	.757	.763*	—
N	530	66	217	—	138	257	—
SD	.20	.19	.22	—	.25	.23	—
Sample 3 (NES-1992): $F_{(3,2206)} = 66.47$, $p<10^{-10}$, $\eta = .29$							
Mean patriotism	.794	.712	.789	—	.589	—	—
N	1,736	26	167	—	281	—	—
SD	.22	.22	.22	—	.29	—	—
Sample 5 (GSS-1996): $F_{(3,1204)} = 8.72$, $p<.01$, $\eta = .14$							
Mean patriotism	.531	—	.505	—	.488	.480*	—
N	973	—	48	—	38	49	—
SD	.11	—	.13	—	.13	.16	—

*Indicates that length of residency for this alien group is unknown.

patriotism scores of the African Americans. But even their scores are not particularly low, except in the UCLA student data set. In an absolute sense, then, no group is substantially alienated from the American polity, but there is a clear tendency for patriotism to be highest among European Americans and unequivocally lower among America's most subordinate group, African Americans.[2]

These differences survive our tests for the confounding effects of other social attitudes. The test used demographic information such as gender, age and socioeconomic status as proxies for confounding effects that might be correlated to a general sense of disaffection resulting from material disadvantages tied to social status. The analysis was done with multiple regression that controlled for gender, age, and SES while testing for the partial effect of a binary coded ethnic group membership variable. In all of the regression analyses, European-American ethnicity was treated as the contrast category. Use of this coding scheme had the distinct advantage of providing a direct test of the patriotism differences between the dominant ethnic group (i.e., whites) and each of the subordinate ethnic groups, net of the effects of all other factors.

The results of these analyses for the four different data sets are found in table 5.7. The table reports only the coefficients for the ethnic group contrasts (i.e., white vs. ethnic minority). The coefficients for gender, age, and various SES measures are not individually reported because they are only proxies for unexamined control variables that have no theoretical importance.[3] The tables show a moderate degree of consistency across data sets: after considering the effects of the major demographic factors, the patriotism differences among ethnic groups in table 5.6 persist in table 5.7. This was especially true among the college students. Without exception, the contrasts between socially dominant whites and all of the subordinates groups showed whites to have significantly higher patriotism scores, with, as before, the most powerful contrast being blacks versus whites ($t = -8.60$, $p < .001$, $b = -.39$). The contrasts between whites on the one hand, and Asian and Latino Americans on the other hand, tended not to be significant within the other general population samples.

African Americans, though exhibiting relatively high absolute levels of patriotic attachment and attaching relatively high importance to their American identity (see figure 5.1), express less patriotic sentiment than any of the other ethnic groups, and they are more likely to exhibit the exclusionary conflict between their communal identity and national sentiment. Indeed, African Americans tended to be no more patriotic than resident-aliens (see table 5.6). In the student data set, the patriotism scores among African Americans were significantly lower than those found among resident-aliens in the United States for more than five years (Scheffé post-hoc, $p < .001$). The effect is apparent even after controlling for demographic differences between groups: European Americans have a significantly greater level of patriotic attachment than resident-aliens (data set 1: $t = -4.79$, $p < .001$; $t = -4.54$, $p < .001$; dataset 2: $t = -2.02$, $p < .05$; dataset 5: $t = -1.83$, $p < .05$). African-

TABLE 5.7 Patriotism and Ethnocentrism Among Dominant and Subordinate-Groups

	European- vs. African-Americans		European- vs. Hispanic-Americans		European- vs. Asian-Americans	
	B	b	B	b	B	b
UCLA	−.25**	−.39**	−.06*	−.10*	−.08*	−.10*
LACSS 1997/1998	−.07**	−.11**	.01	.01	−.01	−.01
NES 1992	−.22**	−.30**	−.00	−.00	−.00	−.02
GSS 1996	−.04**	−.10**	.00	.00	NA	NA

Note: Numbers under the columns labeled "B" are standardized coefficients from a regression that controls for gender, age, and socio-economic status. Numbers in the "b" columns are the unstandardized coefficients.
**$p<.05$; *$p = .05$

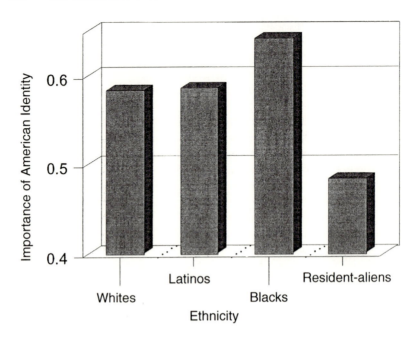

FIGURE 5.1 Importance of American Identity as a Function of Ethnicity

Americans, controlling for demographic differences, are never significantly more patriotic than resident-aliens. Among university students, African Americans had significantly lower patriotism scores than aliens residing in the United States five years or longer (data set 1: $-t = 5.20, p < .001$).

Issue 3: Patriotism and Communal Identity

Both the melting-pot and pluralist models of American society expect ethnocentrism and national attachment to be uncorrelated. This expectation is not met in these data. Feelings about the nation are related to communal identity. As one would infer from social dominance theory, this relationship is asymmetrical across the social status hierarchy. Ethnocentrism and national assessments are positively correlated for whites but negatively related for others, especially African Americans.

The following analysis regressed patriotism on the *hierarchical ethnocentrism* (HEI) index within each major ethnic group within the data sets where we had appropriate measures (data sets 1, 2, and 3). The results were reasonably consistent across all three data sets, but were, again, most consistent among the university students (see table 5.8). For example, the more white students were ethnocentric against African Americans, the more patriotic they were ($b = .37, p < .05$; see table 5.8). The same general tendency

TABLE 5.8 Patriotism Regressed upon Hierarchical Ethnocentrism Within Dominant and Subordinate Groups (Entries are unstandardized regression coefficients.)

Ethnocentrism Index among Dominant Group (i.e., Whites)			Ethnocentrism Index among Subordinate Groups			Interaction Statistics
Among Whites			Among Blacks	Among Latinos	Among Asians	
White-Black	White-Latino	White-Asian	Black-Whites	Latino-White	Asian-White	F-statistics for Slope Differences
UCLA Sample						
.37*			−.47***			19.63**
	.44**			−.49***		20.80**
		.41*			−.51*	17.78**
Los Angeles Sample 1997–98						
−.00$^{n.s.}$			−.09$^{n.s.}$			0.20$^{n.s.}$
	−.00$^{n.s.}$			−.19*		2.05$^{n.s.}$
		−.20**			−.10$^{n.s.}$	4.94*
NES 1992 Sample						
.15**			−.21**			30.09***
	.16**			−.12$^{n.s.}$		8.64**
		.16**			−.19$^{n.s.}$	0.73$^{n.s.}$

*$p<.05$, **$p<.01$ ***$p<.001$

held with respect to whites' HEI against both Latinos and Asians (i.e., $b = .44$, $p < .01$, and $b = .41$, $p < .05$, respectively). Among subordinates, on the other hand, the exact opposite trend was found. Without exception, ethnocentrism among subordinates was negatively related to patriotism. Thus, while the regression of patriotism upon ethnocentrism (HEI) among whites against Latinos was significantly positive (i.e., $b = .44$, $p <. 01$), the corresponding regression of patriotism on HEI against whites among Latinos was negative (i.e., $b = -.49$, $p <.01$). To test whether or not these asymmetries in the relationships between ethnocentrism and patriotism were statistically significant across the status continuum, we used simple slopes analyses to test for interaction between ethnic group and ethnocentrism (see Aiken & West, 1993). As can be seen for the student dataset in table 5.8, these slope differences were significant in all cases (i.e., $F = 19.63$, $p < .001$, $F = 20.80$, $p < .001$, $F = 17.78$, $p < .001$ for the white vs. black, white vs. Latino, and white vs. Asian contrasts, respectively).

The intergroup asymmetries were substantially weaker in the general population but generally consistent with expectations. Only two results are patently contrary to the exclusionary patriotism hypothesis: in the Los Angeles sample white ethnocentrism toward blacks and Hispanics is unrelated to patriotism. Every other coefficient is properly signed. The insignificant difference between whites and Asians in the 1992 NES is a product of a small number of cases; however, the numerical value of the differences is substantial. Altogether, six of the nine interactions showed that the slope of the relation between ethnocentrism and patriotism differed between dominants and subordinates. For whites, seven of nine correlations between ethnocentrism and patriotism were positive and significant. For the other ethnic groups, five of nine correlations between ethnocentrism and patriotism were negative and significant (see table 5.8).

Summary and Discussion

This paper offered three basic ways of thinking about the linkage between communal identity and national attachment in American society: (1) the traditional American melting-pot approach, (2) the pluralist model, and (3) the group dominance approach. In an effort to assess the relative validity of these different ways of thinking about the intersection of national and ethnic identity, we explored three issues (see table 5.1). These issues concerned: (1) the salience of ethnic identity and the presence of ethnocentrism against other groups of Americans, (2) the relationship between patriotic attachment to the nation and ethnic group membership, and (3) the nature of the interface between communal identity and patriotic attachment.

The results are mixed, but on balance more supportive of expectations proffered by social dominance theory. Ethnic subgroup identities remain a salient social identity for each of the major groups we examined and, consistent with the expectations of social identity theory (Tajfel & Turner, 1986), average Americans display clear ethnocentric bias against other ethnic groups of American citizens. Further, and inconsistent with both the melting-pot and pluralism perspectives, patriotic attachment to the nation was generally not uniform across ethnic groups. European Americans have stronger patriotic attachment than those from subordinate communal groups. This tendency was particularly strong and consistent with respect to the white/black contrast. There was not a single instance in which this white/black contrast failed to be statistically reliable.

Finally, the pluralism image of the society was contradicted by the correlation between ethnic and national attachment across ethnic groups. Within the pluralism model of American society, communal attachments should have no implication for national attachment. That is not the case, especially for black Americans. Here, the data were clearly more consistent with the group dominance thesis than with the pluralism perspective. The clear asymmetry in the relationship between communal identity and patriotism across the social status continuum can be regarded as a special case of *ideo-*

logical asymmetry discussed by social dominance theory and demonstrated in a number of studies (Fang, Sidanius, & Pratto, 1998; Levin & Sidanius, 1999; Levin, Sidanius, Rabinowitz, & Federico, 1998; Sidanius, Pratto, & Rabinowitz, 1994; Sidanius & Pratto, 1999).[4] The robustness of these basic asymmetrical findings is supported not only by their consistency with work generated by social dominance research but also by recent work outside of this tradition (Hofstetter et. al, 1999).

The distinctive relationships observed for black Americans raises the likelihood that the degree to which communal and national identity are connected depends upon contextual and situational factors that cannot be systematically considered in this chapter. For example, the degree to which the group dominance perspective accurately describes intergroup status relationships may well be the critical variable that links communal and extra-communal identities. African Americans, almost uniquely, have a history of subordination that makes it easy and reasonable to associate the institutions of the nation-state (and sentiments such as traditional patriotism) with abuse and oppression. In such an environment it is simple to understand why they, relative to Hispanics, Asians, or any other group of immigrants, are inclined to see a conflict between their communal identity and their sentiments about the nation. Many other groups, including European immigrants in their first decades in this country, also suffered (Freedman, 1996), but the severity of the oppression of American blacks is relatively unique.

The issue that policymakers and interpreters of the American social order need to address is whether the patterns characteristic of white/black communal and national sentiments can be approximated symbolically—in the absence of the distinctive history of blacks. We suspect that it can. Peter Skerry's (1993) analysis of Mexican Americans in San Antonio and Los Angeles offers affirmative evidence on this point. He persuasively argues that the ethnic politics practiced by Mexican Americans in San Antonio replicate the pluralist experiences of European immigrants, with the result that San Antonio Mexican Americans participate in and feel committed to the institutions of the society. In Los Angeles, by contrast, Skerry found an ethos that defined Mexican Americans as oppressed, a mind-set that created an insurgent political style, and a dramatically less supportive view of the society's institutions. In brief, in objectively similar conditions, an ideologically shaped political ethos in Los Angeles created among L.A. Mexican Americans a subordinate group perspective that established the conditions for exclusionary patriotism. We suspect, although the data to demonstrate it are lacking, that the strong asymmetry in the UCLA student data set is a reflection of the "oppressed minority" ethos of Hispanic and Asian politics in the region. This speculation suggests that future research in this area should explore the material and perceptual situational and contextual factors associated with the linkage of communal and national identity.

Notes

1. We have doubts about the appropriateness of measuring individualism with the questions used in their study. They are, more appropriately, viewed as measures of some attitude about the government's responsibility for the social welfare of the population. This is almost certainly related to an individualism-communitarian attitude, but it is a related orientation, not individualism itself. The failure of the three questions to form a reliable scale (de la Garza, 1996, p. 342) is a further indicator of the weakness of the questions as indicators of some underlying social orientation.

2. However, as mentioned before, unlike the other data sets examined, the 1996 GSS data set contained a much richer array of national attachment questions. These additional questions afforded us the opportunity to examine the connection between ethnic and national attachment across additional dimensions of national attachment. Thus, besides the dimension of patriotism, we were also able to identify three additional dimensions of national attachment: (1) *nationalism*—i.e., an aggressive and dominance-oriented stance toward other nations; (2) *unwillingness to leave America*, and (3) *importance of American identity*. Most interestingly, the ethnic differences with regard to these three additional dimensions of national attachment were very different from those found for patriotism. First, there were no significant ethnic groups differences with respect to *nationalism*. Second, while there was an overall difference with respect to *Unwillingness to leave America* (i.e., $F(3,1249) = 10.68$, $p < .001$, $\eta = .16$), inspection of Scheffé post-hoc comparisons showed that this difference was essentially due to the fact that resident-aliens were significantly less opposed to leaving the United States than all other American groups—not surprisingly.

The one national attachment dimension where the group differences were quite different from previous results was *importance of American identity*. Not only did the different ethnic groups show significant overall differences here ($F_{(3,1290)} = 13.68$, $p < .001$; $\eta = .18$), but the nature of these differences were qualitatively different from those found with respect to patriotism (see figure 5.1). As seen in figure 5.1, while one should expect resident-aliens to have the lowest level of American identity, given what we have already seen, it is not immediately obvious that African Americans should have the highest level of American identity. Furthermore, controlling for demographic differences did not substantially change this picture. The analyses showed that while the resident-aliens had significantly lower American identity scores than the dominant European Americans ($t = -3.74$, $p < .001$), African Americans had unambiguously *greater* American identity scores than the dominant European Americans ($t = 3.50$, $p < .001$). Rerunning these regression analyses and recoding ethnicity using blacks as the contrast group revealed that, everything else being equal, blacks also had significantly greater American identity than all groups except Latinos.

3. Gender had a significant relationship to patriotism in all the data sets; age was significant in every data set except the UCLA data (where age differences were attenuated). Patriotism was higher among males and older people. Income, education, and similar class measures were usually of trivial importance.

4. The ideological asymmetry hypothesis posits that while the correlations between ingroup bias and certain system-justifying ideologies will be positive among dominants, these correlations will be negative among subordinates.

References

Aiken, L. S., & West, S. G. (1993). *Multiple regression: Testing and interpreting interactions.* Newbury Park, CA: Sage Publications.

Alba, R. D. (1990). *Ethnic identity: The transformation of white America.* New Haven: Yale University Press.

Allen, J. P., & Turner, E. (1997). *The ethnic quilt. Population diversity in Southern California.* The Center for Geographical Studies, Department of Geography, California State University, Northridge.

Bar-tal, D., & Staub, E. (1997). *Patriotism in the lives of individuals and nations.* Chicago: Nelson-Hall.

Blumer, H. (1960). Race prejudice as a sense of group position. *Pacific Sociological Review,1,* 3-5.

Dahl, R. A. (1961). *Who governs?* New Haven: Yale University Press.

de la Garza, R. O., Falcon, A., & Garcia, F. C. (1996). Will the real Americans please stand up: Anglo and Mexican-American support of core American political values. *American Journal of Political Science, 40,* 335–351.

Fang, C. Y., Sidanius, J., & Pratto, F. (1998). Romance across the social status continuum: Interracial marriage and the ideological asymmetry effect. *Journal of Cross Cultural Psychology, 29,* 290–305.

Fredrickson, G. M. (1981). *White supremacy: A comparative study in American and South African history.* Oxford: Oxford University Press.

Freedman, S. G. (1996). *The inheritance: How three families and America moved from Roosevelt to Reagan and beyond.* New York: Simon and Schuster.

Gordon, M. (1964). *Assimilation in American life: The role of race, religion, and national origins.* New York: Oxford University Press.

Greeley, A. M. (1971). *Why can't they be like us.* New York: Dutton.

Greeley, A. M. (1976). *Ethnicity: A preliminary reconnaissance.* New York: Wiley.

Gurr, T. R., & Harff, B. (1994). *Ethnic conflict in world politics.* Boulder, CO: Westview.

Hofstetter, C. R., Feierabend, I. K., & Klicperova-Baker, M. (1999). Nationalism and ethnicity: A community study. Paper delivered at the Annual Meeting of the International Society for Political Psychology, Amsterdam, The Netherlands, July 17–21, 1999.

Horowitz, D. L. (1985). *Ethnic groups in conflict.* Berkeley: University of California Press.

Huckfeldt, R. & Kohfeld, C. W. (1989). *Race and the decline of class in American politics.* Urbana: University of Illinois Press.

Jackman, M. (1994). *The velvet glove: Paternalism and conflict in gender, class and race relations.* Berkeley: University of California Press.

Kelley, R. (1979). *The cultural pattern in American politics: The first century.* New York: Knopf.

Kleppner, P. J. (1970). *The cross of culture.* New York: Free Press.

Kosterman, R., & Feshbach, S. (1989). Toward a measure of patriotic and nationalistic attitudes. *Political Psychology, 10,* 257–274.

Levin, S., & Sidanius, J. (1999). Social dominance and social identity in the United States and Israel: Ingroup favoritism or outgroup derogation? *Political Psychology, 20,* 99–126.

Levin, S., Sidanius, J., Rabinowitz, J. L., & Federico, C. (1998). Ethnic identity, legitimizing ideologies and social status: A matter of ideological asymmetry. *Political Psychology, 19*, 373–404.

Lijphart, A. (1977). *Democracy in plural societies: A comparative exploration*. New Haven: Yale University Press.

Lijphart, A. (1979). Religious vs. linguistic vs. class voting: the "crucial experiment" In comparing Belgium, Canada, South Africa, and Switzerland. *American Political Science Review, 73* (June), 442–458.

Lipset, S. M., & Rokkan, S. (1967). Cleavage structures, party systems, and voter alignments: An introduction. In S. M. Lipset & S. Rokkan, (Eds.), *Party systems and voter alignments* (pp. 1–64) New York: Free Press.

Novak, M. (1971). *The rise of the unmeltable ethnics*. New York: Macmillan.

Parenti, M. (1967). Ethnic politics and the persistence of ethnic voting. *American Political Science Review, 61*, 717–725.

Petrocik, J. R. (1981). *Party coalitions: Realignments and the decline of the New Deal party system*. Chicago: University of Chicago Press.

Petrocik, J. R. (1998). Reformulating the party coalitions: The "Christian Democratic Republicans." Paper delivered at the 1998 annual meeting of the American Political Science Association. Sep 3-6. Boston Marriot Copley Place Hotel.

Polsby, N. W. (1963). *Community power and political theory*. New Haven, Yale University Press.

Powell, C. L. (1995). *My American journey*. New York: Random House.

Powell, G. B. Jr. (1982). *Contemporary democracies: Participation, stability, and violence*. Cambridge: Harvard University Press.

Pratto, F., Sidanius, J., Stallworth, L. M., and Malle, B. F. (1994). Social dominance orientation: A personality variable predicting social and political attitudes. *Journal of Personality and Social Psychology, 67*, 741–763.

Salins, P. D. (1997). *Assimilation, American style*. New York: Basic Books.

Schlesinger, A. M., Jr. (1992). *The disuniting of America*. New York: Norton.

Sidanius, J. (1993). The psychology of group conflict and the dynamics of oppression: A social dominance perspective. In S. Iyengar & W. McGuire (Eds.), *Explorations in political psychology* (pp. 183–219). Durham, NC: Duke University Press.

Sidanius, J., Feshbach, S., Levin, S., & Pratto, F. (1997). The interface between ethnic and national attachment: Ethnic pluralism or ethnic dominance? *Public Opinion Quarterly, 61*, 103–133.

Sidanius, J., & Pratto, F. (1993). The inevitability of oppression and the dynamics of social dominance. In P. Sniderman & P. Tetlock (Eds.), *Prejudice, Politics, and the American dilemma*. (pp. 173–211). Stanford University Press.

Sidanius, J., & Pratto, F. (1999). *Social dominance: An intergroup theory of social hierarchy and oppression*. New York: Cambridge University Press.

Sidanius, J., Pratto, F., & Rabinowitz, J. (1994). Gender, ethnic status, ingroup attachment and social dominance orientation. *Journal of Cross-Cultural Psychology, 25*, 194–216.

Skerry, P. (1993). *Mexican-Americans: The ambivalent minority*. New York: Free Press.

Smith, T. W. (1991). *What do Americans think about Jews? Working papers on contemporary anti-Semitism*. New York: The American Jewish Committee, Institute of Human Relations.

Tajfel, H., & Turner, J. C. (1986). The social identity theory of intergroup behavior.

In S. Worchel & W. G. Austin (Eds.), *Psychology of intergroup relations* (pp. 7–24). Chicago: Nelson-Hall.

Walch, T. (1994). *Immigrant America: European ethnicity in the United States.* New York: Garland Publishing.

Wolfinger, R. E. (1965). The development and persistence of ethnic voting. *American Political Science Review, 59:* 896–908.

PART III

THE CONTRIBUTION OF SOCIAL IDENTITY TO VIOLENT INTERGROUP CONFLICT

Social and Role Identities and Political Violence

Identity as a Window on Violence in Northern Ireland

Much of the violence in the contemporary world appears, on the surface, to involve two groups of people engaged in "them versus us" behavior. From this view, group members develop a social (group) identity in comparison with members of some other group. This comparative self-definition leads to heightened differences across some social category, for example, across tribes or ethnic groups, and, ultimately, violence. Examples of intergroup violence based on social identity might include Tutsi versus Hutu, Arab versus Israeli, and Serb versus Croat. I suspect, however, that much of this violence does not reduce to a straightforward "them versus us" situation.

It has been argued that violence in Northern Ireland, as an example, involves individuals with competing social identities based on religion—of Irish Protestants (the majority community) in conflict with Irish Catholics (the minority community); for example, Whyte, 1990, p. 97; Cairns, 1982. This view is subject to question. The Irish Republican Army (IRA) has been the most violent actor in Northern Ireland since 1969 (as measured by deaths caused). Typically, the IRA is viewed as a Catholic defense organization. Yet, the origins of the IRA lie in the Irish Protestant community, and there have been some Protestant members of the organization (see McKittrick, Kelters, Feeney, & Thornton, 1999, pp. 462–463; White, 1997a).

The complexity of the political violence in Northern Ireland may be demonstrated by a relatively straightforward examination of who has killed whom since 1969.[1] The examination shows that there are three broadly defined violent actors: Irish Republican paramilitaries, Protestant (or "Loyalist"—loyal to the British crown) paramilitaries, and the security forces.[2]

TABLE 6.1 Agency Causing Deaths and the Status of the Victims, Northern Ireland, 1969–1993

			Status of Agent			
				Security Forces		
Status of Victim	Irish Republican Paramilitaries	Protestant Paramilitaries	British Army	RUC-UDR/RIR[1]	Other	Total
British Army	494	1	3	2	3	503
RUC	280	6	2	1	3	292
UDR/RIR	196	3	2	0	1	202
Republican Paramilitaries	154	26	123	18	5	326
Protestant Paramilitaries	27	61	11	2	1	102
Catholic Civilians	181	612	134	30	30	987
Protestant Civilians	377	111	17	6	27	538
Political Activists	25	31	1	2	1	60
Prison Officers	23	2	0	0	0	25
Former Security Officers	62	0	0	0	0	62
Other	107	58	3	1	7	176
Totals	1926	911	296	62	78	3273

Source: Sutton, 1994.
1. The Royal Ulster Constabulary and the Ulster Defence Regiment/Royal Irish Regiment. The RUC is the local police force in Northern Ireland. The UDR, a locally recruited regiment of the British Army, was replaced by the Royal Irish Regiment.

Table 6.1 presents the number of persons killed by each actor for each "status" of victim in the Northern Ireland conflict (Sutton, 1994). This is one of the world's most studied conflicts, and these data are consistent with other attempts to enumerate the dead (see White, 1997a; McKittrick, et al., 1999, pp. 15–19, 1473–1493; Whyte 1990, p. viii).

The primary target of Protestant paramilitaries is Catholic civilians. Six hundred and twelve (67 percent) of their 911 victims were Catholic civilians. Only 26 (of 911—3 percent) of their victims were Irish Republicans. Irish Republicans killed the most people. And, Irish Republicans killed a large number of Protestant civilians (20 percent, or 377/1,926). However, the single largest group of Irish Republican victims was members of the British army. Adding in members of the Royal Ulster Constabulary (RUC), the police force in Northern Ireland, and the Ulster Defence Regiment (UDR; a locally recruited regiment of the British Army, later replaced by the Royal Irish Regiment; RIR) shows that about half (970 of 1926) of the victims of Republican paramilitaries were members of the security forces. Irish Republicans do not exclusively, or even primarily, target the Protestant community in Northern Ireland (see also White, 1997a, 1997b; Bruce, 1997; Drake, 1998).

State agents have killed a relatively large number of people in Northern Ireland. The British Army killed 296 people. The Royal Ulster Constabulary and the Ulster Defence Regiment/Royal Irish Regiment killed 62 people. The two communities have not suffered equally at the hands of the state. It is not surprising that state agents have killed a large number of Irish Republican paramilitaries, given that Republicans shoot and bomb them. However, state agents killed 164 Catholic civilians compared to 23 Protestant civilians (and 131 Republican paramilitaries). In Northern Ireland the state is not a neutral actor (see also White & White, 1995; White, 1999; Thatcher, 1993, pp. 384–385). Table 6.1 suggests that between 1969 and 1993, Irish Republicans and the security forces confronted each other with violence, while Protestant paramilitaries directed their violence against Catholic civilians (see also note 3).

My objective is to draw on the concepts of social and role identity to provide insight into the complexity of violence in places like Northern Ireland. This violence does not reduce to a "them versus us" model, but rather involves a complex mix of identities. I suspect that several conflicts in the world today, upon in-depth examination, will be shown to be as complex as the Northern Ireland conflict. With respect to Northern Ireland, I argue that the violence of Protestant paramilitaries may be understood in "them versus us," or in Irish Protestant versus Irish Catholic, terms. Protestant paramilitaries target their opponents because they are Catholic or Irish Catholic. Irish Republican paramilitary activity is best understood as a combination of behavior based on a social identity and behavior based on a role identity. However, for Republicans the social identity dimension of the conflict is not Irish Catholic versus Irish Protestant in Northern Ireland, but instead Irish Nationalist versus the British government and its agents, in Britain and Ireland. Also, an Irish Republican role identity (described below) complements the Irish social identity. Finally, the British view the conflict as an Irish problem—of Irish Protestants versus Irish Catholics (them vs. them). This has important implications for the behavior of British elites, British soldiers, and Protestant and Republican paramilitaries, as demonstrated below.

Like many other conflicts in the world, the violence in Northern Ireland is centuries in the making. Historical background is therefore presented first. An in-depth examination of the various identities at work in Northern Ireland follows.

The Historical Setting: Background to the Complexity

Norman/English soldiers invaded Ireland in the 12th century. From then until the mid-sixteenth century, political violence in Ireland was primarily motivated by what today is referred to as national identity. The English found a people different from themselves in language, customs, and outlook on life. For the next four hundred and so years there were numerous violent conflicts between native Irish and invading English (Cronin, 1980).

In the 16th century, with the Reformation, religion became important. The Irish and Old English in Ireland remained Catholic. Most people in Great Britain embraced Protestantism. In 1601, Irish Chiefs rebelled and lost. A few years later they fled to the European continent. Their lands—in Ulster in the North of Ireland—were confiscated and given to English and Scottish settlers. In the 1640s, the native Irish in Ulster rebelled. They were supported by the Old English in Ireland. Both groups were Catholic. From this point religion and national identity became intertwined in Anglo-Irish politics. When Oliver Cromwell invaded in 1649 he did so with particular, Protestant religious zeal. His zeal was also a function of the fact that it was *Irish* Catholics who were being pacified; Cromwell never treated Catholics in England as harshly as he did Catholics in Ireland (Fraser, 1973/1997; Cronin, 1980, pp. 488–489). There was a further confiscation of Irish land and property, which were placed in trustworthy, Protestant hands. In the late 1680s, William of Orange seized the throne in England. James II, a Catholic, fled to Ireland. He was supported by his fellow Catholics in Ireland, who sought relief from Protestant domination. William's army defeated James's army at the Battle of the Boyne, and for the third time in a century the Irish suffered the results of a lost war (e.g., O'Leary & McGarry, 1993).

These 17th century wars established a Protestant ascendancy in Ireland. By the end of the century roughly 10 percent of Irish land was in Catholic hands, though perhaps 90 percent of the population was Catholic (i.e., "native Irish"; O'Leary & McGarry, 1993, pp. 66–69). The wars were about religion and political and social control of Ireland. The native Irish were virtually excluded from Irish social and political affairs. In the process, a siege mentality was generated among the Protestant elite. Placed in control of a conquered people were a Protestant Ascendancy that was vastly outnumbered and constantly fearful.

In the late 18th century the political philosophy of Republicanism was introduced into the mix. The United Irishmen, the first Irish Republicans, were founded by Presbyterian merchants and manufacturers in Belfast and Dublin. They were influenced by the French and American Revolutions, and by a desire for economic and political freedom. They found allies in Irish Catholics, who sought political and social relief. Republican ideology is a political philosophy, not a religious or ethnic one. In the 1790s, it was a radical philosophy. The United Irishmen sought such reforms as universal (male) suffrage and no property qualification (see Cronin, 1980). The United Irishmen rebelled in 1798. Unlike the republicans in the United States and France, they failed.

In response to the violence in Ireland, the Act of Union (effective January 1, 1801) disbanded an independent Irish parliament and created the United Kingdom of Great Britain and Ireland. This did not end political violence in Ireland. Irish Nationalists rejected the Union and aspired for an independent Irish nation. Irish Republicans sought to achieve this nation through force of arms. There were Republican rebellions in 1803, 1848, and 1867. The rebellions failed, but there remained in Ireland persons committed to an independent Irish Republic. Throughout the 1870s and 1880s there was Republican-inspired violence. Throughout the 19th century, the general Protestant community in Ireland—"Unionists"—supported the Union. This was especially so in northeast Ireland, where the descendants of the 17th-century settlers feared that "Home Rule" would lead to "Rome Rule." In Belfast in the 1880s, for example, there was widespread rioting in opposition to a Home Rule Bill for Ireland (see Cronin, 1980; Lyons, 1973).

Northern Ireland dates from events in 1916–1922. In 1916, there was a rebellion the day after Easter. The rebels lost, but they reorganized as the Irish Republican Army (IRA) and the political party Sinn Féin (founded 1905). The two organizations worked to break the connection with the United Kingdom. They established a revolutionary Irish government in Dublin and carried out military activities against the British presence in Ireland. The IRA and Sinn Féin were successful throughout most of Ireland. In the northeast, the IRA and Sinn Féin were opposed by both the state's security agents—for example, the Royal Irish Constabulary—and by a Protestant paramilitary organization, the Ulster Volunteer Force. In response to the political unrest, the British passed the Government of Ireland Act (1920), which partitioned Ireland. The Act created Northern Ireland, which comprised six of the nine counties of the province of Ulster, and the Irish Free State. The parliamentary headquarters for Northern Ireland was established in Belfast. Dublin became the seat of power for the Free State. At its creation, Northern Ireland was approximately two-thirds Protestant and one-third Catholic. The Irish Free State (declared a republic in 1949), was (and is) approximately 95 percent Catholic.

In 1921, negotiations between Republicans and British representatives led to a treaty. The IRA and Sinn Féin split over the Anglo-Irish Treaty (1921), and a civil war ensued. Those Republicans opposed to the treaty maintained the IRA and Sinn Féin, and fought against former comrades who accepted the treaty and the new Irish Free State. Pro-treaty forces won the war, and, among other things, this cemented partition. Those who remained in Sinn Féin and the IRA refused to recognize partition and the governments in Dublin and Belfast. They also maintained their organizations. From 1939 to 1945 and from 1956 to 1962, the IRA engaged in unsuccessful paramilitary campaigns in England and Northern Ireland, in an attempt to create a united Ireland (see Bell, 1979).

In Northern Ireland, the Protestant community embraced the new province. The Catholic community, both in Northern Ireland and in the Irish Free State, largely rejected it. Thus, partition created a double minority situation. In Northern Ireland Protestants dominated a minority Catholic community who believed they had been gerrymandered into a Protestant state. Within Ireland as a whole the Protestant community was in the minority. The government of the Free State/Republic rejected Northern Ireland and claimed the entire island for itself.

In the 1960s, there was a civil rights campaign in Northern Ireland. The campaign sought to redress grievances that Nationalists/Catholics had faced since the founding of the province. Civil rights protests led to counterdemonstrations by Protestant extremists, which led to widespread rioting in Northern Ireland in August 1969. The British government sent in troops to restore order. It is out of events in the mid-to late 1960s that the three actors of table 6.1 are derived: Irish Republican paramilitaries, Protestant paramilitaries, and the security forces (Bell, 1979, 1993).

Organizationally, Irish Republicans can legitimately trace themselves to the rebellion in 1848. Veterans of 1848 were involved in rebellious activity in the 1860s, and some of those involved in the 1860s (and 1870s and 1880s) took part in the 1916 Easter Rising (see Bell, 1979, 1987, p. 136). In 1969 and early 1970, the IRA and its political wing, Sinn Féin, split again and the Provisional IRA (hereafter, IRA) and Provisional Sinn Féin (hereafter, Sinn Féin) were created. The founders of the Provisionals were Republican veterans, some with activist histories that dated to 1916. Contemporary Protestant paramilitary organizations date from the mid-1960s and the creation of the Ulster Volunteer Force (named for the UVF of the 1910s). In 1971 the Ulster Defence Association (UDA) was started as a coordinating body for vigilante groups. The Ulster Freedom Fighters (UFF) became the paramilitary wing of the UDA (see Flackes & Elliott, 1989, pp. 272–277, 278).

Political violence in Northern Ireland is hundreds of years in the making. It is not simply about religion, but instead involves a complex mix of national identity, religion, and political aspirations. Social identities and role identities, as described below, provide an insight into this complexity.

Identities: Social (Group) and Role

According to Tajfel (1981, p. 255), social identity is that "part of an individual's self-concept that derives from his knowledge of his membership of a social group." Tajfel typically refers to groups based on race, ethnicity, or religious identification. For Tajfel, the need to view oneself positively may heighten differences between groups and lead to conflict. While Tajfel focuses on intergroup relations, Turner, Hogg, Oakes, Reicher, & Blackwell (1987) extend the social identity perspective to emphasize intragroup behavior. They define social identity as self-categorizations that "define the individual in terms of his or her shared similarities with members of certain social categories in contrast to other social categories" (Turner, Oakes, Haslam, & McGarty, 1994, p. 454). Thoits and Virshup (1997) summarize these two perspectives by noting that they focus on "we's," in the sense that social identities are "collective identities." The focus is on how the individual and the group mesh together. While the social groups around which a collective "weness" develops are often described in terms of race, gender, and ethnicity, a social identity may also develop around a political grouping—for example, the Ulster Volunteer Force or the Irish Republican Army. My use of the term "social identity" is consistent with Thoits and Virshup's (1997) usage, in which they refer to a collective "weness" that exists in comparison to a collective "other."

Role identities focus on "me's" (Thoits & Virshup, 1997). Role identities act as "internalized positional designations" (Stryker, 1980, pp. 60–61; see also McCall and Simmons, 1978) that locate and define individuals within a group. Role identities refer to individual-level self-conceptions of the requirements attached to social positions. Individuals internalize these requirements, which become identified as a part of the self. Role identities have "salience" for individuals (Stryker, 1980, 1968). In certain situations one role identity may be more salient for an individual than another role identity. In addition, there is the potential for significant role conflict and role strain—when the expectations associated with roles conflict or compete (Stryker, 1980). My use of the term "role identity" follows the definition of Stryker and refers to self-conceptions of the requirements attached to a social position that develop from social interaction—for example, by learning to be a Volunteer in the Irish Republican Army from other IRA Volunteers.

The social or group (collective) identity is conceived of as a group-level phenomenon, where the individual conceives of the self as one of "us"— often in contrast to "them." The focus is on cognitive processes, comparing one's group to some other group. As Thoits and Virshup (1997, p. 115) state, "Group- or category-based identities are collective-level self-conceptions; they are identifications of the self *with* a collectivity." In contrast, role identities focus on who the individual is. Instead of comparing "us" vs. "them," the individual considers "Who am I?" by drawing on social interaction and incorporating the expectations of other people into their self-conceptualization. Both kinds of identity are social, but in different ways (see also Stryker, 2000; Klandermans and de Weerd, 2000). For those who employ the concept of social identity, the self is a product of comparison and categorization processes in which "the perceiver appraises the self *in relation to others*." For those who employ the concept of role identity, the self is a product of incorporating others' expectations and appraisals, of appraising the self from the perspective of others—for example, in role-taking exercises (see Thoits & Virshup, 1997, pp. 120–122). In terms of violent political activists in Northern Ireland, persons may kill on behalf of their group, and/or they may kill because they have internalized such behavior as part of the role of being a particular political activist. Indeed, activists may kill because they are motivated simultaneously by both a social identity and a role identity.

In the following, I argue that the violence of Protestant paramilitaries is best understood from a social identity perspective. Protestant paramilitaries act in defense of their social group by killing members of the other (Catholic) social group. In contrast, I argue that Irish Republican paramilitaries are motivated by both social and role identities. Irish Republicans target the security forces in Ireland because these forces represent an oppressor of their "Irishness" (the British government) and because they have internalized the role requirements of being an Irish Republican. Finally, I argue that the British perspective may be understood in social identity terms. However, instead of taking a "them versus us" perspective—for example, British forces versus Irish Republican forces—the British take a "them versus them" perspective and view the violence as an Irish problem, involving Irish Protestants versus Irish Catholics.[3]

Data Sources: Accounts from Activists

The accounts below are from very different sources. None of the data were collected with this particular research topic in mind. The accounts from Irish Republicans are from my ongoing research on the causes and consequences of small-group political violence. These accounts are taken from interviews that centered on why the respondents became involved in the Irish Republican movement. The Republican accounts represent my interpretation of how Irish Republicans may be understood in terms of social and role identities. This interpretation is based on interaction with Irish Republicans over a 17-year period. I have formally interviewed perhaps 100 Irish Republicans, and have informally met with an unknown number of others. Many of the respondents were low-level Sinn Féin workers, such as advice center staffers. Included among the respondents are several prominent Republicans and several veterans of the IRA. Many of the respondents were born and raised in families where a parent or other significant adult was active in Republican politics or had strong Republican sympathies (see White, 1993; White & Fraser, 2000).

The accounts from Protestant paramilitaries, British elites, and British soldiers are taken from secondary sources. These sources include interviews with journalists, memoirs, and published accounts of speeches. I did not collect these data. My interpretation of the accounts of Protestant paramilitaries, British elites, and British soldiers, therefore, is qualified. With respect to Protestant paramilitaries, I present the accounts to illustrate the conventional wisdom with respect to these people—that is, that the motive of these paramilitaries is sectarian and is based on a strong identification with being Protestant. This conventional wisdom is based on solid social science research (e.g., Bruce, 1992). The statements from British elites and British soldiers are consistent with survey data, noted below, which shows that Northern Ireland is not a high-priority item for the British public. This is one indicator that British people may interpret the conflict as one of "them versus them."

Northern Ireland: The Actors and Their Identities

In Northern Ireland, political actors represent two communities that reside there and one external interest group: the Protestant community, the Irish Nationalist community, and British representatives. Within the Protestant community, there are Unionists and Loyalists. Unionists want Northern Ireland to remain part of the United Kingdom. Loyalists are Unionists who take an extreme position on the Union and are willing to defend it with paramilitary activity. Irish Nationalists, who are predominantly Catholic, seek an end to the Union and a united Ireland. Among Irish Nationalists are Irish Republicans, who are willing to use paramilitary activity to bring about a united Ireland. British interests are represented by political appointees, for example, the secretary of state for Northern Ireland, and persons involved with the security apparatus, such as the British army.

The Protestant Community: Unionists.

In many ways, the Unionist mentality is a siege mentality. In spite of their political power in Ireland, Unionists have always been in the minority, and they have, therefore, always perceived their position to be threatened. When it was created, Northern Ireland offered Unionists a gerrymandered majority situation, but this was not guaranteed to last forever. Historically, the Protestant ascendancy in Ireland maintained their position only with the help of the English and British state. The British parliament created Northern Ireland as a haven for pro-British Protestants; the Protestant community in Northern Ireland did not do this on its own.

Today, most Protestants in Northern Ireland are Unionists (there are some Catholic Unionists). In addition, many Protestants in Northern Ireland identify not with Ireland but with Britain. When asked in 1968, on the eve of the current violence, which term best describes themselves (Irish, British, Ulster, Sometimes British-Sometimes Irish, Anglo-Irish), only 39 percent of Protestants chose "British." An additional 32 percent chose "Ulster." Perhaps surprising, the first choice of 20 percent of Protestants to this question was "Irish" (see Rose, 1971, p. 485). In 1978, in the midst of a violent conflict, the question was repeated on a survey by Edward Moxon-

Browne. Moxon-Browne found that the number of Protestants whose first identity was "British" increased significantly, to 67 percent. The number who chose "Ulster" fell to 20 percent, and only 8 percent chose "Irish" (Moxon-Browne 1983, pp. 5–7).

The Protestant Community: Loyalists

Loyalists (loyal to the British crown) tend to be working-class Unionists who view violent opposition to Irish nationalism as both justified and necessary; they support, or are, Protestant paramilitaries (see Bruce, 1992, pp. 14–15; Nelson, 1984). There is general agreement that Protestant paramilitaries are motivated by sectarianism, by deep-seated mistrust, and by hatred of Catholics. Steve Bruce, an authority on Protestant paramilitaries, stated in 1994:

> Although leaders of the UDA [Ulster Defence Association] and UVF [Ulster Volunteer Force] have periodically tried to confine the violence of their members to some notion of "legitimate targets" (that is, republicans) or have claimed to be trying so to restrict the deaths, very many of their victims were chosen simply because they were Catholics. Even in these more publicity-conscious days there are loyalist paramilitary leaders who say that they like to kill republicans but an ordinary Catholic will do. (1994, p. 125)

The data in table 6.1 support this interpretation. The majority of victims of Protestant paramilitaries are Catholic civilians. Because Catholics tend to be Irish Nationalists, they are by (Protestant paramilitary) definition traitors and subject to violence. Protestant paramilitaries punish the general Catholic community when they are threatened or want to hit back. Because Irish Republicans are hard to target, the objective is to create enough fear in the Catholic community that they, in turn, will force the Republican paramilitaries to quit. At its most basic level, Loyalists view themselves as fighting for tribal survival (Bruce, 1992, p. 55).

In identity terms, Protestant paramilitaries view the world from a Protestant social identity, in opposition to Catholics. Consider the following from a former Protestant paramilitary, John White. White was a leading member of the Ulster Freedom Fighters (UFF). He describes his upbringing:

> I remember my mother, an uneducated working-class woman, saying to me, Son, we don't go into a united Ireland, and me saying, why not, Mammy, and I remember her saying, because you'll not get a job, and you'll probably not get a house, and they'll murder us, you know. And my Da, he just had a confirmed hatred for Roman Catholicism. I remember one time my brother brought a Roman Catholic to the house, a girlfriend, and my Da told her to get out of the house and not come back again. So, you know, I thought there must be some genuine fears there, when even my Da was saying, no bringing Taigs home to this house. (Stevenson, 1996, p. 62)[4]

In 1976, White confessed to the 1973 murders of Paddy Wilson and Irene Andrews. Wilson was a member of the Social, Democratic, and Labour Party (SDLP), a moderate, middle-class political party associated with the Catholic community in Northern Ireland. The SDLP then, and now, advocated a united Ireland, but through peaceful means. Now out of prison, John White commented on why Wilson, who was publicly known to be unarmed, was a target:

> My analysis then was that he [Wilson] supported the concept of a united Ireland; the IRA were trying to pursue a united Ireland; therefore, by his rhetoric, he was supporting the IRA. It may have been warped at that time, but that was the way I viewed it when I was twenty two years of age. (Stevenson, 1996, pp. 59–61)

John White's account is not unique among former Protestant paramilitaries. The following is from Alex Calderwood, a veteran of the Ulster Defence Association (UDA). He states, "I grew up hating Catholics."

> I admit that I was a sectarian bigot. . . . It was my background and the society that programmed me in a sense, but I was responsible for what I done. I was a bigot and I hated Catholics. (Stevenson, 1996, p. 65)

A central theme in the accounts of Protestant paramilitaries is a sense of "us versus them," Protestant versus Catholic. The account of another former Protestant paramilitary, William Smith, is consistent with this:

> In the seventies these communities were close-knit communities. . . . You still had the extended family situation, and word-of-mouth and rumor was far more valid than printed matter or television. But there's no one thing, it was the whole situation at the that time. You had segregated schools, you had segregated areas, you had a whole history dealt down to you by word-of-mouth about troubles, the IRA, and all that—that was all part of your dogma the whole way through your life. So whenever the bogeyman appeared in 1970, this was the bogeyman we were told about. The bogeyman appeared and the rest became part of life—there was thousands and thousands, I mean, the vast majority of people were involved in it. So when your community felt threatened, you felt threatened. (Stevenson, 1996, p. 67)

Based on these accounts, it appears that persons who became Protestant paramilitaries were motivated by an "us versus them" perspective. These accounts suggest that the paramilitaries learned this perspective because they were encouraged, by family, friends, and the Protestant community around them, to view things comparatively—Protestant versus Catholic. Thus, Catholics are people to be hated because "they'll murder us."

Beginning in the early 1970s, large numbers of people were recruited into Protestant paramilitary organizations like the Ulster Volunteer Force, the Ulster Defence Association, and the Ulster Freedom Fighters. It can be expected that members of these groups developed social identities that were particular to these groups—that is in addition to their Protestant social identity they probably also developed social/collective identities based on their membership in a particular paramilitary group. As members of these groups they may also have developed role identities (see below). However, the key to understanding these groups and their members remains their Protestant social identity. This social identity is common to most if not all Protestant paramilitaries, and is probably the most important motivator of their behavior.

The Irish Community: Nationalists

An Irish Nationalist is a person who wants all of Ireland to be ruled by Irish people (Irish people being defined as people living in Ireland, even if they identify themselves as British). Irish Nationalism predates the Reformation and the Act of Union (effective January 1, 1801; Cronin, 1980). Today, most Irish Nationalists are Catholic. With respect to Northern Irish politics, the terms "Catholic" and "Nationalist" are often used interchangeably, but they are not synonymous. Catholics in Northern Ireland do not exclusively identify themselves as Irish. When Richard Rose (1971) surveyed the Northern Irish public in 1968, he found that when asked which term "best describes the way you think of yourself" (British, Irish, Ulster, sometimes British-sometimes Irish, Anglo-Irish), 76 percent of Northern Irish Catholics chose the "Irish" option. Only 15 percent of Catholics identified themselves as "British," and even fewer (5 percent) identified themselves as "Ulster." Ten years later, in the midst of violence, when Edward Moxon-Browne included the question on his survey, the percentage had fallen; 69 percent of Catholics chose "Irish" as their first option. Again, only 15 percent of Catholics identified themselves as "British," and few (6 percent in 1978) identified themselves as "Ulster." Also in 1978, when asked "which of these would you least like to call yourself? British, Irish, Ulster, sometimes British-sometimes Irish, Anglo-Irish, Other?", less than 2 percent (1.7 percent) of Catholics chose "Irish"—that is, very few Catholics rejected the Irish national identity (see Moxon-Browne, 1983, pp. 6–9). In contrast to the Protestant community, the national identity of Catholics/Nationalists in Northern Ireland appears to be more stable (see also Moxon-Browne, 1983).

The Irish Community: Irish Republicans

At its most basic level, an Irish Republican is someone who "seeks to separate Ireland from England by force" (Cronin, 1980, p. 23). At their core, all Republicans agree on two things: (1) the British government is the cause of political strife in Ireland, and (2) a British withdrawal from Ireland can be gained only through force of arms (see White & Fraser, 2000). These beliefs are evident in accounts from Republicans and may be interpreted in both social and role identity terms.

Consider the following from Respondent 1. He describes events that led him into the Irish Republican Army. Recognizing that he is Irish and that the British were killing "our people" was essential for his recruitment into the IRA. In the early 1970s he went to school in England:

RESPONDENT 1 [Hereafter, R]: I went to England and as I say everything then was at a distance, it wasn't as immediate. . . . But then Bloody Sunday [in which British troops shot dead 14 Nationalist civilian protesters, in 1972] happened and again this incredible sense of outrage. And then, just through-out the year, watching the British, some of the British people—their attitudes to us, the Irish. And it was just—fuck sake. The attitudes were just that— you're "Paddy." They automatically call you Paddy when you go over there. I'd say, "My name's Ruairí." "Sure, you're Paddy. You're all called Paddy and Mick." I said, "No, my name's Ruairí." I took it from my friends there because it was usually a joke, there was no malevolence in it. But, there were people who used it as a derogatory term. And just throughout the year, watching things going at home. And following along Bloody Sunday I decided that what I was doing, which I wasn't happy with anyway, that I was wanting to go home more and more. And then when I left England to travel for a couple of months, hitched around, and I came home. And as soon as I came home I got into Sinn Féin and it was a natural progression from there. Because my beliefs were fairly well formulated at the time. *The British were killing our people*, they were locking them up and they were nothing more than Stormont [the Northern Ireland parliament]. (emphasis added)

Similar comments were offered by a Protestant Republican (see also Hynd-man, 1996). He was born and raised in East Belfast. By his background he was an unlikely candidate for involvement with Irish Republicans. When he moved to England, he discovered that he was Irish.

INTERVIEWER [Hereafter, I]: You mentioned our people, you said they were killing our people or shooting our people. Do you consider yourself Irish?

R: Oh yes, I am Irish you see.

I: But I mean, the typical—

R: (Laughs) I know it's uh—I understand what you mean. Given my back-ground, right? For a long time I thought I was British. I didn't really know what I was, actually. When I was younger I went to England to work due to the high unemployment at home. *And, then I was made very aware of my iden-tity, and it was Irish.* I was left in no doubt that I was a Paddy. And uh, you know the old stories about people going to try to find flats, you know, some-where to live in London, where the signs are in the window, "No Irish," "No Coloureds." It was a good thing to experience because it did give me a per-ception, it did give me an education which I might not necessarily have gotten if I had stayed in the North [of Ireland]. But certainly that made me very aware of my identity. Then moving from my Loyalist area, through other lo-cations, finally to end up in a Republican area was a great experience. Living there which had always—had been a place which I had visited quite a lot, but living in it is a lot different from visiting. To experience the continual daily harassment, the constant harassment. It's a great education as well. To see the poverty as well. [RESPONDENT 2, emphasis added]

These two respondents acquired an Irish social identity by personally experiencing discrimination and devaluation of their Irishness. The development of this social identity helped to make them potential recruits to Irish Republicanism. Their recruitment was also influenced by their acquiring a Republican role identity.[5]

Respondents 1 and 2 became Republicans when they were adults. Many Republicans, however, are born and raised in Republican families and they are influenced by Republicanism at an early age. One result of this influence is an Irish social identity. Respondent 3 was raised in a Republican family:

R: the only solution to our problems, and it has been my opinion all down through the years, is a united Ireland. It's the only way forward for us. There is no other way. The other way is a creeping, cringing, crawling spirit of the Irish nation. We desire freedom, we seek freedom, and it's not too much to demand. All we're seeking is our own country. . . . I think it only makes good common sense that if you are the owner of a house, I always make this analogy, that if you've got a four-roomed house, and there's one person occupying the house. And there's quite a large family of you. And you make a democratic decision time after time for the person that's occupying your house, undemocratically, for to remove . . . to get out of the house. That democratic decision is taken. But the man won't move. What's your alternative? Get him by the scruff of the neck and throw him out. It's the only way. *Our people has taken the democratic decision in this country here several times to ask Britain to leave this country.* So as we can apply our own national government. But she hasn't adhered to that democratic decision, and that's why this struggle is still going on. (Respondent 3, emphasis added)

Respondent 4 was also raised in a Republican family. He stated the following:

R: [When I joined, my goal for the Movement] was to see the complete freedom of this country. In other words, what the Republican goal always was, *to break the connection with England and to establish an Irish Republic.* An Irish Socialist Republic. And that was my reason for joining the Movement and that is why I got involved. (Respondent 4, emphasis added)

Like Protestant paramilitaries, Republicans—both from Republican families and not—develop a social identity that places them in an "us versus them" situation. The "them," however, is the British government, not the Protestant community in Northern Ireland.

There is evidence that Irish Republicans develop a role identity that complements their Irish social identity, and that this role identity develops through social interaction with family members and/or peers who are Republicans. Consider the following from the three respondents raised in Republican families:

I: Why in general did you get involved in the Movement?

R: Well, Bob, I was involved with the Republican Movement at a very early age because of my father being a member of the Republican Movement as well. From 1916 'til the Civil War my home was a place for anybody who came on the run, or to seek help. It was always given to them. So I was sort of brought up, you know what I mean, within Republican circles, my father being a Republican. And uh, I suppose it rubbed off on me. I always had Republican ideals, you know? (Respondent 3)

R: Well, the reason why I decided to get involved in the Republican Movement was that I was born into the Republican tradition. Both on my father's and my mother's side. And that is one of the reasons. And reading Irish history I realized and came to the conclusion that the Republican Movement were the true inheritance of the Republican faith. That is the reason why I became [involved].
. . .

R: [Reading the question] Did any particular person have a strong influence—eh, to get involved? Well, I wouldn't just say to get involved, but, there was one woman, she was my grandmother. Incidentally my four grandparents were teachers. But this particular—my mother's mother, she was an outstanding republican sort of thing, you know? When she died in 1969—She never wavered. . . . She was strong in her Republican [beliefs] to the day she died. And when she—her house, as a matter of fact, was the headquarters of the Irish Republican Army [in her area]. . . . she was a very highly respected woman sort of thing there. . . . And she had a big influence on my life there because as you may know you're—well, in this country anyway your grandchildren go on holidays with their grandparents. . . . She never wavered, as I said. And she had a big influence. And even up to this day, if any questions come up [I would refer to her Republicanism]. (Respondent 4)

R: Republicanism in our house was a—sort of what would be termed now as pure Republicanism, in that my father wouldn't of been very sympathetic toward a socialist line of thinking. It would of been more of a Republican principled directly. And, uh, seen the great danger in socialist tendencies within it. And, to some extent that would of influenced my direction for a number of years. And even yet to some extent that you would fear a socialist—too big a socialist involvement within it. And uh, he was very much just a straight line Republican.

I: Is that why you would have gone with Provisional rather than Official [when the Republican Movement split in 1969/70]?

R: That's right. That would of been a big influence actually. And uh, not only from hearing it in the past but actually hearing him talking about it at that particular time, eh, that the split come. My direction like would of been influenced a big part by his sort of talking to me. (Respondent 5)

It appears that these children of Republicans were raised such that they acquired Republican principles and learned the role of being a Republican—for example, to help other Republicans "on the run" and to never "waver" in your commitment. This acquisition and learning occurred through interaction with other Republicans. Accounts from Republicans not born and raised in Republican families suggest that they also acquire a role identity through interaction with both their family members (even though they are not Republican) and their peers who are Republicans. The following is from Respondent 1. He is not from a Republican family. He joined the IRA in the early 1970s. He was strongly influenced by his personal experiences with peers who were involved in the Irish Republican Movement. His involvement stems from a family background that stressed being a responsible person, and his social interaction with people who he believed were being responsible—that is, persons who were willing to risk their lives in a just struggle against a much stronger opponent (and his development of an Irish social identity, as noted earlier).[6]

> R: The main reason that I got involved with the Republican Movement is that I was brought up to believe that you should treat people as equals and that nobody had the right to walk over you, nor did you, more importantly, did you have the right to walk over anybody else. And the Republican Movement, it may have historical background, yes, but essentially it got off the ground because it came out of the community and it was a community that accepted it because it was its own people. And therefore I suppose you could say it was my contemporaries that, if anybody influenced, would have influenced me to join. But it was just a natural thing because it was the time of ferment, of political ferment that was in it. I felt that I couldn't close my eyes to it and that I had a responsibility to do something. I'm not sure, mind you, that would be everybody's reply—it sounds terribly altruistic [laughs]. But the point is that that's just the way I felt about it. I just felt that I had had a pretty good life compared to most of the lads that would have been in the movement in Derry. I come from a middle class background and I never really had to worry about anything and I just felt there was a responsibility for me to do something. But it wasn't as clear cut as that.
>
> . . .
>
> R: I didn't join because my friends were in the movement. That's not the reason I joined. I was motivated to join the Republican Movement because I knew that the people who were in it were sincere. I mean, a 19-year-old kid or an 18-year-old kid who makes a conscious decision to go out and fight a vastly superior army on the streets, to take on a government and all its forms, and to change society—He may not think in terms of vast political thought about how society's going to be changed by him. But if he makes that conscious decision instead of happily waiting until he get his welfare check, and then goes off and plays pool or drinks beer and goes to dances—I mean they're denounced as being mindless thugs but that is just not true. It could never for me be a description of them. (Respondent 1)

As it was for Protestant paramilitary organizations, in the early 1970s Irish Republican organizations received large numbers of recruits. As with Protestant paramilitaries, the new Republican paramilitary recruits were influenced by a social identity. Unlike Protestant paramilitaries, the Republican recruits did not interpret their activity as Catholic versus Protestant, but rather as Irish versus British. In addition, and also unlike Protestant paramilitaries, the Republican paramilitary recruits joined a movement with a lengthy history. Along with this history came established roles for members of the Republican Movement—"she never wavered." Out of interaction with persons who were already Republican (be they family members or peers) the Republicans acquired a role identity that complemented their social identity.

The British Perspective: "Them vs. Them"

The British interpretation of the violence is that it is an Irish problem in which members of two Irish communities, Protestant and Catholic, cannot get along. This is implied in the accounts of Respondent 1 and Respondent 2, one Catholic and the other Protestant, but both "Paddy" in Britain. In effect, the British deny the social identity of Protestant paramilitaries, who view themselves as British, and they deny the political aspirations of Irish Republican paramilitaries, who do not want to be citizens of the United Kingdom.

This is not a new phenomenon. In 1921, on a visit to Belfast, King George V said:

> I speak from a full heart when I pray that my coming to Ireland today may prove to be the first step towards an end of strife amongst her peoples, whatever their race or creed. In that hope I appeal to all Irishmen to pause, to stretch out the hand of forgiveness and conciliation, to forgive and forget and to join in making for the land which they love a new era of peace, contentment and goodwill. (see Lyons 1973, p. 426)

Fifty years later, Reginald Maudling was the British Home Secretary responsible for Northern Ireland affairs at Westminster (from 1970-1972). In his memoirs, he described how the "Irish" problem perplexed him, an Englishman.

> It is very hard for an Englishman to understand the feelings of those who live in Northern Ireland. The history of their struggles is a long one, and they tend to cherish every moment of hatred in it. The deep divide between Catholic and Protestant, which, incidentally, is more racial than religious, had been handed down faithfully from generation to generation. (Maudling 1978, p. 180)

Traditionally, Ireland is not that important for British elites. This makes the violence that much more an "Irish problem." After helping execute Charles I, Oliver Cromwell spent nine and one-half months in Ireland, pacified the country, and then returned to the real business at hand—running England (Fraser, 1973/1997). In the early part of this century, there were a series of debates and proposals associated with the Home Rule [for Ireland] Bill in 1914. William Manchester, in his biography of Winston

Churchill, describes the Irish situation as being, "foremost in everybody's mind, so certain to burst into flames at any moment" (1983, p. 463). But, as a meeting concluded Sir Edward Grey read out a document from the Foreign Office. It was an ultimatum from Austria to Serbia, part of the beginning of what became World War I. The war developed, and the Irish issue was "deferred." Churchill later recalled,

> The parishes of Fermanagh and Tyrone faded back into the mists and squalls of Ireland, and a strange light began immediately, but by perceptible gradations, to fall and grow upon the map of Europe. (Manchester, 1983, p. 463)

The "Irish question" also has not had an impact on the voting British public. Northern Ireland constitutes less than 3 percent of the population of the United Kingdom. Since 1983, the province has sent only 17 (of 635) MPs to Westminster. In response to Gallup polls on important issues in the United Kingdom, Northern Ireland traditionally has "fluctuated between nil mention and coming at the bottom of a list of ten or a dozen issues" (see O'Malley, 1990, p. 226).

Because Northern Ireland has not been a high priority for the British public, British soldiers, recruited from that public, appear to be relatively unaware of the politics of the situation (at least in the early years of the recent conflict). Consider the following from two soldiers sent to Northern Ireland in 1969.

> BRITISH SOLDIER 1: The boys knew where they were supposed to go in terms of sealing off streets, so it was then a question of getting men down to the corners and road junctions and giving them cover in case there was shooting. *We hadn't a clue what was going on really*, but the feeling I got within half an hour was one of relief, on both sides. *The Irish are terribly curious* and they came out of all sorts of corners, and I think both Protestants and Catholics were relieved that there might be some stability. . . . (emphasis added; Arthur, 1987, p. 7)

> BRITISH SOLDIER 2: For the first week I slept underneath an awning by a baker's shop. I'd chosen the baker's shop because I knew we'd get fresh bread and buns each day. This was the period of complete daze, immediately after the initial rioting. *No one knew what was going on, so we had to start talking to the people to find out what might happen.* We felt we were terribly welcome, particularly by the Protestants, but they kept on saying: 'Why have you got your rifles pointing at us, and your backs to the Catholics, when they're the ones who started it?' So immediately we came up against the sectarian problem: *which way do you face? Who do you defend? Which side do you protect?* (emphasis added; Arthur, 1987, pp. 9–10)

The perspective on Ireland of British elites, citizens, and soldiers may best be described as viewing the conflict as "them versus them." The degree to which Britishers identify with Britain and adopt potential role identities—"As a British soldier my job here is to keep the peace"—may be less important than the fact that they view what happens in Northern Ireland as external to themselves, or at least not of their own making, that it is a conflict caused by "others" and it is not a reflection of British policies or actions.

By denying the identity of those Protestants in Ulster who identify themselves as British, British elites contribute to the fears of these people. By refusing to recognize the political claims of the Republicans, and by actively denying these claims, British elites leave Republicans with violence as a means of expressing their political desires. Perhaps most important, viewing the conflict as external, or involving "them versus them," contributes to policy mistakes on the part of the British government, as described below.

Implications

In Ireland there are three violent political actors: Protestant paramilitaries, Irish Republican paramilitaries, and state agents. Each perceives the violence in Northern Ireland from a different perspective. These perceptions have real consequences. This is demonstrated in the British policies of criminalization and Ulsterization, which were implemented in the mid-1970s. Their impact is still felt today.

In 1972, IRA prisoners led by Billy McKee, an IRA veteran of the 1930s and 1940s, went on a hunger strike in order to gain political status. In the midst of negotiations that led to a truce between the British government and the IRA in late June, political status was granted to both Republican and Protestant paramilitary prisoners. Criminalization revoked this status. After March 1, 1976, persons convicted of paramilitary crimes were treated as ordinary criminals. The British government denied the political nature of the IRA's activity and equated IRA violence with the sectarian violence of Protestant paramilitaries. Ulsterization dates from 1977 and is designed to make the Royal Ulster Constabulary the primary policing agent in Northern Ireland (e.g., Flackes & Elliott, 1989, p. 392 ; see also Bell, 1993, p. 517). As a result, the violence became that much more an Irish problem (of "them vs. them").

The implications of criminalization and Ulsterization were profound. Irish Republican prisoners rejected criminalization. They refused to wear prison clothes and wrapped themselves only in blankets. The protest escalated, ultimately resulting in the hunger-strike of 1981. In an attempt to regain political status, 10 Irish Republican prisoners fasted to death (see Bell, 1993). The behavior of the Republican prisoners on the strike may be understood in terms of a role identity and role behavior. Hunger-striking has a lengthy history among Republicans; the hunger-strike weapon is part of the Republican repertoire. The first Republican to die on a hunger strike in this century was Thomas Ashe, in 1917. There were deaths by Republicans on hunger strike in the 1910s, 1920s, 1940s, and the 1970s. People like Ashe, it can be argued, were role models. One dimension of the role identity of being an Irish Republican is to confront the state while in prison with the weapon of the hunger strike. Billy McKee, the senior Republican hunger striker in Belfast in 1972, was active in the IRA in the 1940s when then senior Republicans were on hunger strike. Some of those on the hunger strike in 1981 were under the command of people like McKee (if not McKee himself) when they were new recruits to the Republican Movement in the early 1970s.

The hunger strike in 1981 led to a mass mobilization of the general Nationalist community in Ireland. One of the strikers, Bobby Sands, was elected as an abstentionist MP to Westminster. The chief beneficiary of the hunger strike was the Republican movement. Both Sinn Féin and the IRA attracted large numbers of new recruits (see Bell, 1993; White, 1993). For the British government, who held firm against the hunger strike, it was a disaster. Ulsterization probably saved the lives of British soldiers, but it, like criminalization, did not stop Irish Republicans, who claim that they 'target the uniform' rather than the religion of members of the security forces (see Flackes & Elliott, 1989, p. 414, table 4). While killing a British soldier may have more of an impact, Republicans were quite willing to kill members of the RUC (see White, 1997a, 1997b; Bruce, 1997)).

Criminalization and Ulsterization had very different results for Protestant paramilitaries. Criminalization did not lead to deaths from hunger strikes by Protestant paramilitary prisoners. Although there have been Protestant paramilitary prisoners on hunger strike, none have maintained a fast to the death. There are a number of reasons for this and two are important here. First, it must be acknowledged that the conditions for Protestant paramilitary prisoners have never been as severe as they have been for Irish Republican paramilitaries. Pro-British Protestant paramilitary prisoners are less of a threat to the state than are anti-state Republican prisoners (see White, 1999). Second, and very important for present purposes, there is no history of hunger striking to the death by Protestant paramilitaries. The historic and contemporary "role models" (martyrs) that Irish Republicans have—Thomas Ashe in 1917, Sean McCaughey in 1946, Michael Gaughan in 1974, and Bobby Sands in 1981, for example—are not available to Protestant paramilitaries. The role identity of a Protestant paramilitary prisoner confronting the British government by dying on hunger strike does not exist.

Indeed, at the beginning of the violence a Protestant paramilitary role identity could not exist because such people, and such organizations, had not yet formed. When the Ulster Volunteer Force and the Ulster Freedom Fighters were created in the mid-1960s and early 1970s, a previous generation of Protestant paramilitaries was not there to serve as paramilitary leaders (role models). The original UVF was largely recruited into the security forces of Northern Ireland in the 1920s. That organization ceased to exist, and its former members became police agents of Northern Ireland (see Farrell, 1980, pp. 35, 44–45). While some of the parents of the Protestant paramilitary recruits of the 1960s and 1970s were members of the RUC and the Ulster Defence Regiment (UDR; e.g., Taylor, 1999, p. 82), this is qualitatively different from being raised in a family with a tradition of involvement in illegal paramilitary activity. A leader of a vigilante group described their activity at the beginning of the current violence:

> *We never planned to go on the kill.* There was no time that we sat down and said 'That's it. Stiff a Taig.' Mind, we planned doing something to the Ardoyne after the three Scots boys [three British soldiers] were killed [in 1971] but for some reason it never came off. No, it was ground up. One or two volunteers just started doing it. (taken from Bruce, 1992, p. 54; emphasis added)

Contrast this with the description of Billy McKee's activities in the early 1970s. The interviewer, the journalist Peter Taylor, asked a Republican who was recruited back into the IRA by McKee to comment on his activities in the early 1970s:

> What did he [McKee] tell you about the policy towards British soldiers?
> He didn't indicate that there was going to be an immediate offensive against the British army. He said, "These things take time. *People have to be trained. People have to be motivated. People have to be equipped.* All this won't happen overnight." But the intention was there and it sounded good to me. (Taylor, 1998, p. 74; emphasis added)

For Protestant paramilitaries, criminalization reinforced their interpretation that Republicans are out to destroy their community. While Republicans state that they only target uniforms, not the ethnic/religious belief of the occupant, Protestants (paramilitaries and in general) view attacks on the RUC as sectarian because the force is 90 to 95 percent Protestant. In response to the killing of members of the RUC, Protestant paramilitaries killed Catholic civilians (see White, 1997a, 1997b; Bruce, 1997).

The accounts from Protestant paramilitaries suggested that they do not interpret their behavior in terms of a role identity. However, these accounts are from secondary sources and social and role identities were not the focus of those who collected the accounts. Also, the accounts are from activists who were not born and raised in Protestant paramilitary families. The violence in Northern Ireland has spanned a generation. Many of the Protestant (and Republican) paramilitaries of the 1970s and early 1980s now have adult children. It is very possible that with the continuity of the Protestant struggle there has developed among Protestant paramilitaries a role identity that has been passed to another generation in the same manner as Irish Republicans pass on their role identity. Today, the leader of the Ulster Democratic Party, the political wing of the Ulster Defence Association, is Gary McMichael. Gary McMichael is the son of John McMichael, a leading Protestant paramilitary who was killed by the IRA in 1987 (Cusack & McDonald 1997, p. 267; Bruce, 1992, pp. 232–233). If a Protestant paramilitary role identity has developed, this identity should be consistent with the

Protestant social identity, and the basic social identity differences among Protestant paramilitaries, Irish Republican paramilitaries, and the British should remain.

Conclusion

Much of the violence in the world today appears to be caused by heightened social identities, by groups that define themselves as "us versus them." On the surface, violence in Northern Ireland fits this pattern. The above case study reveals, however, that there are three significant violent actors in Northern Ireland, not two. These actors are Protestant paramilitaries, Irish Republican paramilitaries, and the state's security forces. Each of the actors interprets the violence in different social identity terms. Protestant paramilitaries see themselves as British and they define themselves as Protestants in contrast to Irish Catholics. Further, they perceive that Irish Republicans act in a manner consistent with an *Irish Catholic* identity. Irish Republicans, in contrast, act in a manner consistent with an Irish social identity. Their conflict is not with Irish Protestants but with British parliaments that lay claim to Irish territory. They view themselves as being in a war of national liberation against the British government. Protestant paramilitaries interpret Republican activity differently. For Protestant paramilitaries, targeting the British in Northern Ireland means targeting Protestants in Northern Ireland—they view themselves as the British in Northern Ireland. In the midst of these different interpretations, British people have traditionally viewed the violence in Ireland from an outsider's perspective. The violence is between Protestant Irish and Catholic Irish, and the British, as the lawful government, are caught in the middle. This adds to the complexity of the situation, especially because British government actions are subject to different interpretations by Protestant paramilitaries and Irish Republican paramilitaries.

In addition to their Irish social identity, the data suggest that there is an Irish Republican role identity and that this influences Republicans' behavior. This role identity develops through social interaction with other Republicans. Although the data did not necessarily indicate the development of a Protestant paramilitary role identity, there is no reason to believe that such an identity has not developed over time. Similarly, British elites and British soldiers probably have role identities. As with Republicans, these role identities probably develop through social interaction.

At the moment, there is a peace process underway in Northern Ireland. It has been a long time coming, with origins that date from events in the mid- to late-1980s. As of yet, peace has not been fully confirmed. Involved in this peace process are the three general actors that are the subject of this paper—Protestant paramilitaries, Irish Republican paramilitaries, and the British government (also involved are several other actors, including nonviolent political activists and the Irish Government in Dublin). The different perceptions that the actors have of themselves and their counterparts contribute to the difficulty of achieving a lasting peace in Ireland.

The Northern Ireland conflict is hundreds of years in the making. The conflict is not unique. Many of the conflicts that attract our attention today are decades, if not centuries, old. Serb versus Croat and Hutu versus Tutsi are centuries old conflicts. There are more than two violent actors in Northern Ireland. Other violent settings also involve more than two actors, if not currently then historically. The British were key actors in the carving up of Palestine. Today, the United States plays a key role in that conflict, as Arab states and Palestinian paramilitaries are aware. Similarly, for the victims of the bombing of Kosovo (whether or not it was justified), the United States and its allies were significant actors. An in-depth investigation of many conflicts that appear to involve two actors engaged in "them versus us" behavior may show them to be as complex as the Northern Ireland conflict.

Acknowledgment

This research was supported by grants from the Harry Frank Guggenheim Foundation, the National Science Foundation (grant SES-8318161), and the IUPUI Office of Faculty Development. I thank Stephen Heathorn, Shel Stryker, Peggy Thoits, Eric Wright, the participants in the Symposium, and the reviewers for their comments.

Notes

1. My use of the term "political violence" follows Tilly's conception of the term "any observable interaction in the course of which persons or objects are seized or physically damaged in spite of resistance" (Tilly, 1978, p. 176). Political violence in Ireland is not confined to Northern Ireland. The Irish Republican Army recruits and carries out operations on an all-Ireland basis. Protestant paramilitaries have killed people in the Irish Republic, and the IRA has been active throughout Ireland, England, and on the European continent. Included in the Sutton (1994) data in table 6.1 are persons who were killed outside of Northern Ireland, in events related to the conflict there. By far the vast majority of persons killed because of the Northern Ireland conflict were killed in Northern Ireland (see White, 1997a).

2. These actors are "broadly" defined because there are in fact several different Republican, Protestant, and security force organizations active in Northern Ireland. These include the Irish Republican Army, the Irish National Liberation Army, the Ulster Volunteer Force, the Ulster Freedom Fighters, the British army, and the Royal Ulster Constabulary.

3. This is too simple a description of a complex situation. While Irish people are in general "thems" to Britishers (as described below), there are probably degrees of "themness." In particular, one group of "them"—Ulster Protestants—identifies with Britain, is devoted to the British crown, proudly flies the Union Jack, etc., while an-

other group of "them"—Irish Nationalists—identifies with Ireland, rejects the British crown, flies the Irish flag, etc. While Irish people may be "them," some of "them" are likely to be more tolerable than others. This helps to explain differences in state repression, whereby Republican paramilitaries experience more repression at the hands of the British than do Protestant paramilitaries (e.g., White, 1999). It also helps explain the much larger number of Catholic civilians versus the relatively small number of Protestant civilians killed by the security forces. Catholic civilians come from the dis-loyal "them" community. They are subject to much more state repression (see White & White, 1995).

4. "Taig" is a slang term for a Catholic person. It is typically used by Protestants in a derogatory fashion. It is a corruption of the Irish first-name, "Tadhg."

5. In order to demonstrate the development of an Irish identity I present information from two respondents who lived in England prior to their joining the IRA. The life stories of these two respondents are such that their understanding of their Irishness was practically forced on them, which makes for a good presentation. The other Republican respondents (Respondents 3, 4, and 5), developed an Irish social identity without first living in Britain.

6. Determining when a person acquires a role identity is difficult. Some people may acquire role identities only after joining an organization and formally moving into the role. Others may acquire role identities from interaction with persons in roles prior to their actually joining a given organization. In a sense, they may find themselves in the role, and then join the organization. Imagine the potential recruit who goes out on an operation or two with his friends and quickly finds herself a regular member of an IRA unit. Similarly, consider the child of a Republican who, at the age of 18, is interned under the assumption that he is a member of the IRA, but is not. Interred without trial with other Republican prisoners, having been brought up in Republican surroundings, this individual probably knows the role—or learns it very quickly—of being an IRA prisoner, adapts quickly to prison, and joins the IRA.

References

Arthur, M. (1987). *Northern Ireland: Soldiers talking*. London: Sidgwick & Jackson.

Bell, J. B. (1979). *The secret army: The IRA 1916–*. Dublin: Irish Academy Press.

Bell, J. B. (1987). *The gun in politics: An analysis of Irish political conflict, 1916–86*. New Brunswick, NJ: Transaction.

Bell, J. B. (1993). *The Irish troubles: A generation of violence*. New York: St. Martin's.

Bruce, S. (1992). *The red hand: Protestant paramilitaries in Northern Ireland*. Oxford: Oxford University Press.

Bruce, S. (1994). *The edge of the Union: The Ulster Loyalist political vision*. Oxford: Oxford University Press.

Bruce, S. (1997). Victim selection in ethnic conflict: Motives and attitudes in Irish Republicanism. *Terrorism and Political Violence, 9*, 56–71.

Cairnes, E. (1982). Intergroup conflict in Northern Ireland. In H. Tajfel (Ed.), *Social identity and intergroup relations* (pp. 277–297) Cambridge: Cambridge University Press.

Cronin, S. (1980). *Irish nationalism: Its roots and ideology*. Dublin: Irish Academy Press.

Cusack, J. & McDonald, H. (1997). *UVF*. Dublin: Poolbeg Press.

Drake, C. J. M. (1998). The role of ideology in terrorists' target selection. *Terrorism and Political Violence, 10* (Summer), 53–85.

Farrell, M. (1980). *Northern Ireland: The orange state.* London: Pluto Press.

Flackes, W. D., & Elliott, S. (1989). *Northern Ireland: A political directory.* Belfast: Blackstaff Press.

Fraser, A. (1973/1997). *Cromwell: Our chief of men.* London: Weidenfeld and Nicolson.

Hyndman, M. (1996). *Further afield: Journeys from a Protestant past.* Belfast: Beyond the Pale Publications.

Klandermans, B., & de Weerd, M. (2000). Group identification and political protest. In S. Stryker, T. J. Owens, & R. W. White, *Self, identity, and social movements.* (pp. 68–90) Minneapolis: University of Minnesota Press.

Lyons, F. S. L. (1973). *Ireland since the famine.* London: Fontana.

Manchester, W. (1983). *The last lion: Winston Churchill, 1874–1932, Visions of glory.* New York: Little, Brown and Co.

Maudling, R. (1978). *Memoirs.* London: Sidgwick & Jackson.

McCall, G., & J. L. Simmons. (1978). *Identities and interactions.* New York: Free Press.

McGarry, J., & O'Leary, B. (1995). *Explaining Northern Ireland.* Oxford: Blackwell Publishers.

McKittrick, D., Kelters, S. Feeney, B., & C. Thorton. (1999). *Lost lives: The stories of the men, women, and children who died as a result of the Northern Ireland troubles.* Edinburgh: Mainstream Publishing.

Moxon-Browne, E. (1983). *Nation, class and creed in Northern Ireland.* Aldershot: Gower Publishing.

Nelson, S. (1984). *Ulster's uncertain defenders: Protestant political, paramilitary, and community groups and the Northern Ireland conflict.* Belfast: Appletree Press; Syracuse, NY: Syracuse University Press.

O'Leary, B., & McGarry, J. (1993). *The politics of antagonism: Understanding Northern Ireland.* London: Athlone Press.

O'Malley, P. (1990). *The uncivil wars: Ireland today.* Boston: Beacon.

Rose, R. (1971). *Governing without consensus: An Irish perspective.* Boston: Beacon Press.

Stevenson, J. (1996). *"We wrecked the place": Contemplating an end to the Northern Irish troubles.* London: The Free Press.

Stryker, S. (1968). Identity salience and role performance: The relevance of symbolic interaction theory for family research. *Journal of Marriage and the Family, 30,* 558–564.

Stryker, S. (1980). *Symbolic interactionism: A social structural version.* Menlo Park, CA: Benjamin/Cummings.

Stryker, S. (2000). Identity competition: Key to differential social movement participation? In S. Stryker, T. J. Owens, & R. W. White, *Self, identity, and social movements* (pp. 21–40). Minneapolis: University of Minnesota Press.

Sutton, M. (1994). *An index of deaths from the conflict in Northern Ireland, 1969–1993.* Belfast: Beyond the Pale Publications.

Tajfel, H. (1981). *Human groups and social categories: Studies in social psychology.* Cambridge: Cambridge University Press.

Taylor, P. (1999). *Loyalists.* London: Bloomsbury.

Thatcher, M. (1993). *The Downing Street years, 1979–1990.* New York: Harper-Collins

Thoits, P. A., and Virshup, L. K. (1997). Me's and we's: Forms and functions of social identities. In R. Ashmore & L. Jussim (Eds.), *Self and identity: Fundamental issues*. New York: Oxford University Press.

Tilly, C. (1978). *From mobilization to revolution*. Reading, MA: Addison-Wesley.

Turner, J. C., Oaks, P. J. Haslam, S. A. & McGarty. C. (1994). Self and collective: Cognition and social context. *Personality and Social Psychology, Bulletin 20*, 454–463.

Turner, J. C., with Hogg, M. A., Oakes, P. J., Reicher, S. D., & Blackwell, M. S. (1987*). Rediscovering the social group: A self-categorization theory*. Oxford: Basil Blackwell.

White, R. W. (1993). *Provisional Irish Republicans: An oral and interpretive history*. Westport, CT: Greenwood Press

White, R. W. (1997a). The Irish Republican Army: An assessment of sectarianism. *Terrorism and Political Violence, 9* (Spring), 20–55.

White. R. W. (1997b). The Irish Republican Army and sectarianism: Moving beyond the anecdote. *Terrorism and Political Violence, 9*, 120–131.

White, R. W. (1999). Comparing state repression of pro-state vigilantes and anti-state insurgents: Northern Ireland, 1972-75. *Mobilization, 4*, 189–202.

White, R. W., & Fraser, M. R. (2000). Identities and long term movement activism: Republican Sinn Féin. In S. Stryker, T. J. Owens, & R. W. White (Ed.), *Self, identity, and social movements*. (pp. 324–346). Minneapolis: University of Minnesota Press.

White, R. W. & White, T. F. (1995). Repression and the liberal state: Northern Ireland, 1969-72. *Journal of Conflict Resolution, 39*, 330–352.

Whyte, J. (1990). *Interpreting Northern Ireland*. Oxford: Clarendon Press.

Individual and Group Identities in Genocide and Mass Killing

Mass killing and genocide, in which a group turns against another with systematic and widespread violence, has been a tragic aspect of life in the 20th century. How does such violence, especially its most extreme form, genocide, come about? What is the motivation for such violence and how does it evolve? What are the social conditions, characteristics of cultures, and psychological processes of individuals that make it more likely? Most important for the present volume, what role do individual and group identities play in genocide and mass killing?

The U.N. Genocide Convention has defined genocide as "acts committed with intent to destroy, in whole or in part, a national, ethnic, racial or religious group." I see the words "in part" in the definition above as problematic. When some people in a group are killed, for example, to intimidate the whole group, or when members of the population are killed in the belief that this will eliminate support for guerrillas, as in Guatemala, this may best be considered mass killing, not genocide. However, genocide and mass killing have similar origins and prevention requires similar actions. Because some nations objected to the inclusion of political groups, they have not been included in the Genocide Convention. Some authors have called violence that aims to eliminate a political group, "politicide" (Harff & Gurr, 1990) while others, including myself, prefer the term "genocide". Influences leading to genocide against political and other kinds of groups and the preventive efforts required seem to be the same (Staub, 1989b).

I define "mass killing" as killing many members of a group without the intention to eliminate the group (Staub, 1989b). Such killings can be part of an evolution toward genocide. It is important for both understanding and prediction, and therefore prevention, that similar influences lead to mass killing and genocide. While the likelihood of group or collective violence is predictable, its exact nature, whether it will be mass killing or genocide, may not be.

In this chapter I first outline a conception of the origins of genocide and other collective violence that I have developed over the last 20 years and have applied to the analysis of a number of specific instances of genocides and mass killing (see Staub, 1989b, 1996a, 1999b). I next examine elements of this conception in detail as I extend it by exploring the role of identity in the generation of such violence. I will look at different types of and aspects of identities: individual identity and varied forms of it; social identity, the extent to which a person's identity is based on membership in the group; group self-concept, or how the members see and define their group. I will also discuss the psychological and social processes through which people strengthen their identities in difficult times, often in destructive ways.

One of the important reasons for understanding the origins of genocide and mass killing is to find ways to prevent them. Thus, in the last section of the chapter I will consider prevention and the role of identities in prevention.

The Origins of Genocide and Mass Killing

Over the years I have developed a model of the origins of genocide and mass killing (Staub 1989b, 1996b, 2000). This is depicted schematically in figure 7.1. Genocide or mass killing usually begins with some form of "instigation." Instigation may have little to do with the group that ends up as the victim. Difficult life conditions in a society are such instigators: severe economic problems, such as inflation, depression, and unemployment; political disorganization or political chaos; and rapid social changes.

Difficult life conditions usually frustrate fundamental human needs— what I have called "basic needs." All of the following psychological needs may be frustrated by difficult life conditions: the need for security, for a positive identity, for effectiveness and control, for connection to other people, and for a meaningful comprehension of reality and of one's own place in the scheme of things. These needs are viewed here as universal, even though culture may shape their strength, manifestation, and available avenues for fulfillment. Especially when these needs are reasonably fulfilled, another important need also enters—the higher need for spirituality or transcendence, the need to go beyond a focus on one's own self, needs, and concerns (Staub, 1989b, 1996a, 1998a, 1999a, 1999b, 1999c).

Conflict between groups is another instigator. One type of conflict has to do with vital needs, such as territory needed for living space. Conflicts can be intractable, often for psychological reasons, such as a group's identity be-

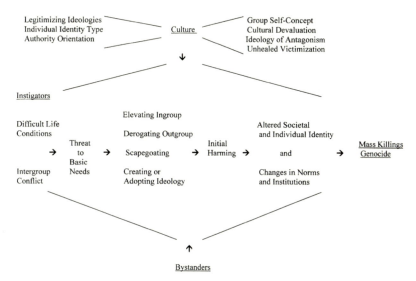

FIGURE 7.1 Influences and Processes Contributing to Genocide and Mass Killing

ing tied to living in a certain territory. Another type of conflict occurs when a powerful group limits the opportunities and resources of a subordinate, powerless group.

Group conflict also frustrates basic needs. What needs it affects will depend on specific conditions, but it is likely to affect security and identity. Conflict between superordinate and subordinate groups, as well as the uneven effects of difficult life conditions on different groups, may give rise to a sense of injustice. While justice may not be a fundamental need in the same way as the needs described to this point, it is nonetheless a powerful human motive.

The instigation and the resulting frustration of basic needs leads to psychological and social processes that turn a group against others. These include individuals turning to some group for identity; people elevating the group by devaluing other groups and taking action against their members; the ingroup scapegoating outgroups; and ideologies or visions of social arrangements that promise a better life but also identify enemies.

One example is Rwanda. All the instigators were present there. There were increasing economic problems, starting in the late 1980s. The invasion of a Tutsi-led group of rebels in 1990, consisting of refugees from violence against Tutsis in previous decades or the children of refugees, began a civil war. Political demands by varied groups added to political chaos and disorganization. The Tutsis were scapegoated for all the problems. An intense ideology of "Hutu power" was developed and propagated, with the

Tutsis defined as enemies to be destroyed (des Forges, 1999; Prunier, 1995; Staub, 1999b).

These psychological and social processes often lead to action against the devalued, scapegoated group, or a group that is seen as an ideological enemy, and thus is the starting point for an evolution toward possible mass killing or genocide. Individuals and groups change as they harm others. They justify their actions by devaluing their victims more and more. They become desensitized to the suffering of their victims. The standards of acceptable social behavior change, allowing and even encouraging violence. Institutions change or new ones are established that serve discrimination and violence. In the end, there may be a reversal of morality: killing the scapegoat or ideological enemy may become a "higher good" (Staub, 1989b).

Unless halted by bystanders, the violence evolves in intensity. Unfortunately, both internal bystanders (members of the involved groups) and external bystanders (other nations and the international community) tend to remain passive. This affirms and encourages the perpetrators. At times outsiders—groups and nations—support the perpetrators because of past ties or a desire to promote what they define as their own national interests. When the kind of psychological and social processes here described do not lead to genocide, usually bystanders are involved in a positive way—they intervene in some way to alter the processes leading to collective violence (Staub, 1989b, 1999b, 2000).

Certain characteristics of cultures make the genocide or mass killing process more likely. A history of devaluation of a group of people is a primary characteristic. Very strong respect for authority and a monolithic society with a limited range of values, in contrast to a pluralistic society, are also important. Unhealed wounds in a group owing to past victimization, which lead members of the group to feel easily threatened and respond with what they see as defensive aggression, make it more likely that such a genocidal process unfolds in response to instigation. The nature of individual identities that the society has fostered and the nature of group self-concept are also important.

The influences here described do not act separately and independently. They interrelate and join in meaningful ways. I will examine here some aspects of this interrelation; others can be seen and deduced from the subsequent discussion (see figure 7.1 and Staub, 1989b). It is the frustration of basic needs by instigating conditions that leads group members, whose individual identity is shaken, to turn to the group for identity, to focus more on their social identity, or to "give themselves over" to an identity group. This frustration also leads to scapegoating and the creation of destructive ideologies (which identify enemies), that turns the group against another group. The kind of ideology that is adopted, and the scapegoat and ideological enemy that is selected, very much depend on characteristics of the culture.

Whether the group turns against another depends in part on whether the devaluation of some group is part of the culture, the nature of that de-valuation, and how intense it is (Staub, 1989b, 1999b). It depends on past victimization of the group and unhealed wounds, which make it more vul-nerable to threat. It depends on the strength of "authority orientation," how deeply and unconditionally people are accustomed to be led, to respect and obey authorities and the extent they are accustomed to gain support from their group. The stronger this orientation, the more they will be af-fected by difficult life conditions and other instigators, and the more diffi-cult it will be to stand on their own. Their need to turn to new authorities who might be able to guide and support them will be greater.

A history of devaluation of a group, which all members of a society tend to absorb to some extent, a strong authority orientation, and a monolithic rather than pluralistic-democratic culture, as well as other cultural charac-teristics (Staub, 1989b), all make it less likely that people will oppose initial actions against a victim group, or initial "steps along the continuum of de-struction." The passivity of bystanders has the effect of allowing and even encouraging the evolution of violence.

The psychological processes that initiate and maintain the increasing violence are fostered both by intense instigators and the presence of cul-tural characteristics. The social conditions that constitute the instigators af-fect both perpetrators and internal bystanders. As the violence evolves, it constitutes culture change; further evolution happens in a changing and changed cultural context.

Identity and the Origins of Mass Killing and Genocide

I now describe how individual and group identities are involved in the paths to genocide or mass killing depicted in figure 7.1. To begin, severe eco-nomic problems deeply impact people. Unemployment, or the inability to provide for oneself and one's family owing to severe inflation, makes people feel insecure and ineffective. Such conditions call into question people's personal identity and self-worth: Who am I if I have no work and cannot take care of the basic material needs of myself and my family? At the same time that identity is questioned, ties to one's group can also weaken because the problems originate in society and social conditions.

Intense political conflict and disorganization also affect people's experi-ence of their group and perception of the world. Rapid social change, which often occurs at times of economic and political crises, adds to social chaos and disorganization. Since substantial social change requires adjustment, even positive change places demands on people.

The different elements of difficult life conditions, which may occur sepa-rately but frequently are present in some combination, frustrate many of the basic needs. In difficult times, focusing on their own needs, people be-come disconnected from each other. At times when they need it most, people lack connection and support. The social upheaval makes their old worldview inadequate in providing a comprehension of reality: an understanding of how people, society, and the world operate, and of their own role or place in the scheme of things.

As a result, when a society experiences persistent, intense life problems, its members desperately need a renewed basis for identity, security, a sense of effectiveness, connection to other people, and comprehension of reality. They turn for identity and the fulfillment of other basic needs to a new group, or to leaders who strengthen the group through scapegoating outsiders or offer it new identity, meaning, and hope through ideologies that promise a better life and offer the fulfillment of basic needs.

Identity, Scapegoating, and Ideology

Three types of "identities" are discussed in this chapter: first, *personal identities*, or the ways in which individuals answer the question, who am I?; second, *social identities*, or the extent to which individual identity is rooted in, or connected to, the group; third, *group self-concepts*, or the socially shared way members perceive and experience their group. Relevant to all of them is a group's culture and the social and political institutions that both express and shape that culture. The nature of individual identity is shaped by culture; in turn, the identities that characterize individuals maintain the culture. Social identity theory has focused on how people categorize themselves (and others) as members of groups, how they identify themselves with certain groups, and the tendency they have to enhance themselves by comparing their group favorably with other groups (Tajfel, 1982; Turner, 1987; Myers, 1999). It emphasizes the psychological experience of rootedness in and connection to the group.

But social identities also have content, as defined by the culture. "We" are intelligent and hardworking, or easygoing and ready to enjoy life, or brave and ready to fight for our rights or for maintaining important values. The content of social identity is what I refer to as group self-concept. While social identity theory stresses the tendency to favorably evaluate one's group, group self-concept can be positive or negative (superior or weak and vulnerable). As in the case of individual identity, consciously held views and evaluations of the group can exist side by side with feelings about and valuations of the group that may not be consciously held, such as a sense of vulnerability or weakness.

Individual identity is, in part, a social identity rooted in groups to which one belongs ranging from family to nation (Tajfel, 1978, 1982; Turner, 1987; Bar-Tal & Staub, 1997). It is not surprising, therefore, that in difficult times people try to strengthen their identity through personal identification with some group. A good social identity—an identity based in a group that is seen in a positive light, for example, as effective and powerful—can also be a good source of security, feelings of effectiveness and control, and connection. The values and worldview of the group also provide a comprehension of reality.

Scapegoating some other group can strengthen both individual and group identity and also help fulfill other needs. If another group is viewed as responsible for life problems, then neither I nor my group are to blame. Scapegoating at such times is usually a social process in that it is done together with like-minded others. This not only builds identity but strengthens security and connection.

Ideologies are almost always a part of the genocidal process. I see ideologies as visions of social arrangements that tell people how to live life. They are blueprints for the organization of societies and relations among individuals. The ideologies created or adopted in difficult times offer the satisfaction of basic needs. They promise people a better life. Sometimes their stated purpose is to improve life for all human beings—what I have called "better world ideologies." Communism has been such an ideology. Nationalistic ideologies promise better life to people in a particular group by enhancing the group's wealth, power, or purity (Staub, 1989b).

Often, ideologies have both better life and nationalistic components. This was true of the Nazi ideology. The Khmer Rouge ideology was ostensibly a better world ideology, focusing on total social equality. But it was group based, looking to the group's history as a simple agricultural society for ways to create this social equality. Without explicit elaboration it also included a strongly nationalistic agenda. This expressed itself in the especially intense violence against the Vietnamese in Cambodia, in hostility to Vietnam, an ancient enemy, and in genocidal violence against other minorities in Cambodia.

Legitimizing ideologies (Levin, Sidanius, Rabinotitz, & Frederico, 1998; Staub, 1989b, 1999b) offer justifications for the power and privilege of dominant groups. Violent reactions by powerful groups to demands by subordinate groups for rights and privilege have been one of the most frequent sources of mass killing since World War II (Fein, 1993). In my view, this response of dominant groups is not simply to a threat to their power and privilege. They also respond to a threat to their identity and worldview (Staub, 1989b). They have come to see themselves as rightfully occupying positions of power and influence, owing to their background, history, diligence, intelligence, bravery, or other aspects of their presumed nature. The world is arranged the "right way" with them in power (see Sidanius & Petrocik, this volume).

People usually hold or turn to and adopt ideologies as part of a group or a movement. At times some people create or put together ideas that form the ideology, as did Hitler (1925) or the leaders of the Khmer Rouge in Cambodia (Staub, 1989b). However, it is when shared among a group of people that an ideology comes to life. The ideology defines the group and gives the group and its individual members a positive social identity. It also provides a basis for connection. Participating in the movement can make people feel effective and in control. The goals of the movement become the motivating force for members. The ideology and the movement that arise from it often become central sources of people's identity and comprehension of reality.

While human beings need positive visions in difficult times, the ideologies that emerge usually identify another group as an enemy. This group is seen either as the cause of problems, or as standing in the way of the ideology's fulfillment, or both. They, therefore, become the objects of hostility. Harmful actions begin to be directed at them.

The Role of Individual Identities in Genocide

Certain individual identities that a culture promotes make the genocidal process more likely. Research and theory have identified differences in the type of self-concept or individual identity that is shaped by individualist and collectivist cultures (Triandis, 1994). Differences in women's and men's identities in Western societies, including the United States, have also been noted (Sampson, 1988). It has been proposed, for example, that male identity is more autonomous, more like the identity shaped by individualistic cultures, while female identity is more relational, like identities shaped by collectivist cultures.

Considering conditions that give rise to genocide, both relational/collectivist and autonomous/individualist identities may have vulnerabilities. Difficult life conditions may especially frustrate autonomous persons. They have learned to stand on their own, but now they are unable to effectively fend for themselves or their families. American soldiers who became prisoners of war in the Korean War had more difficulty in resisting brainwashing than, for example, Turkish soldiers, seemingly because the former were trying to face it alone while the latter supported each other (Kincaid, 1959).

Relational identities may also create difficulties. People with such identities may feel interconnected with other people in a way that makes it especially difficult to speak out against and oppose the direction the group is beginning to take. As their group or society begins to scapegoat, identify an enemy, discriminate, or take other harmful actions against another group, they are more likely to remain silent and go along. This makes more probable the evolution of increasing discrimination and violence.

I have suggested that relational/collectivist identities may be differentiated into *embedded* and *connected* (Staub, 1993a). The embedded identity, which I just described, is characterized by a strong connection to other people that also embodies dependence on the group and an inability to separate from it. In contrast, people who have developed connection to others as inherent to their identities, but who also have learned to stand on their own, to be separate, have connected selves or identities.

The nature of personal identity has implications for peoples' relationship to their group. People with connected selves may be less likely to give themselves up to the group in difficult times. They may be less likely to relinquish their own identity and give themselves over to a social or group identity than people with embedded selves. Seemingly paradoxically, because they can use others for support more effectively, those with connected self-concepts may be even less likely to do this than people with autonomous/individualist identities. As a result, people with connected selves may be less likely than those with either embedded or autonomous identities to remain passive as the evolution of harm-doing begins. They may be more likely to speak out and oppose actions contrary to their own values, or to the values they believe the group ascribes to. This is extremely difficult to do but is essential in halting the evolution of increasing violence.

I am suggesting that identity-related differences in individuals' relationship to the group have implications for group violence. Related to this, I have proposed that some individuals are "constructively" patriotic while others are "blindly" patriotic (Staub, 1997). In research exploring this we find that constructive patriots express love for their group, but also a willingness to question and criticize the policies and practices of the group that are contrary to caring values and concern for human welfare, or contrary to what they see as important group values (Schatz & Staub, 1997; Schatz, Staub, & Lavine, 1999). Although this has not been assessed in the research, I expect that constructive patriots would have connected identities. In contrast, blind patriots, who I expect to have either individualist or embedded self-concepts, love their group but are unwilling to criticize it or to question its policies or practices. Different identity types and associated relationships to the group have clear implications for supporting or opposing destructive views and group practices.

Other classifications of individual identities that are relevant to genocide are possible. Some people may have secure identities (Staub, 1993a). Presumably their basic need for security has been fulfilled in the course of their lives, especially early lives. Perhaps they also have had experiences with taking effective action to protect themselves. As a result they feel reasonably secure in the world. They would be less affected by instigating conditions, such as difficult life conditions, and less moved to the psychological and social processes that were described as a consequence of such conditions. Others, perhaps due to the frustration of the need for security early in life, including victimization or other traumas, may develop insecure identities, making it more likely that these psychological processes leading to genocide unfold in response to instigating conditions.

Authority Orientation and Identity

Observation and research indicate that in many cases of genocide or mass killing the society has been characterized by strong respect for authority (Gourevich, 1998; Kressel, 1996; Smith, 1998; Staub, 1989b,1999b). "Authority orientation" in the culture is a term I prefer to "authoritarian personality" because it focuses purely on respect for authority and hierarchy, without implications of repression of sexual feelings and other characteristics that have been described as aspects of the authoritarian personality.

Authority orientation affects the nature of identity in a number of ways. Individuals who have embedded selves are connected to others through networks of dependent relationships. People in an authority-oriented culture also seem deeply embedded in the group, but this is based on their orientation to authority. The experiences they have as this orientation is developed in them, normally from early childhood on, diminishes the evolution of a strong independent self.

In the face of difficult life conditions or group conflict, people who have relied on leaders for guidance and protection will find it more difficult to bear the threat, anxiety, and frustration of basic needs. When policies and practices are instituted in a group that harm others, they will be less willing to speak out and to oppose the authorities and the rest of the group. Strong respect for authority also makes obedience to immoral orders by authorities more likely.

The Nature of Group Self-concept

Weakness, Superiority, and a Positive Self-Concept.   The nature of group self-concept (by which I mean the way members consensually see and experience their group) is also important. How do members of a group, people who identify with a group, see their group? What is their conception and experience of the group? And, how do differences in group self-concept predispose toward mass killing or genocide? I have hypothesized (Staub, 1989b) that *both* a sense of weakness and vulnerability, *and* feelings and beliefs of superiority, may make it more likely that groups will turn to and engage in systematic violence against others. When a group feels weak and vulnerable, life problems in the society or conflict with other groups will intensify vulnerability and the need to defend oneself. Elevating the group, scapegoating another group, creating "positive visions" that identify enemies, and self-defense through aggression become more likely.

A sense of superiority, when frustrated, may also become a powerful source of psychological processes and actions that contribute to genocide. Feeling superior makes individuals and groups vulnerable to disconfirmation of their superiority and, as a result, likely to experience narcissistic wounds (Baumeister, 1997). However, a self-concept of superiority is different from a high self-esteem. Feelings of superiority may be the result of a history of success by a society in many realms combined with the usual ethnocentrism of groups that leads to interpretation of this success as evidence of the group's superiority. But more often, a belief in one's superiority is exaggerated and may represent a compensatory identity. In the lives of most individuals and groups there are enough small and large experiences of ineffectiveness, failure, and loss that, under normal conditions, a more moderate sense of self would develop.

A positive identity in individuals is likely to arise from experiences of nurturance and affirmation and from success in overcoming obstacles. Comparable experiences on the group level can give rise to positive group self-concepts. The absence of these may lead to low self-concept. Their absence, or negative experiences, overlaid with experiences of success but without incorporating the difficult, painful experiences into one's identity, can lead to a feeling of superiority, which is what I regard as a compensatory identity. In children a defensive self-esteem or defensive egotism, which was found to be different from high self-esteem, was associated with more bullying of others. Defensive self-esteem was ascribed to children who described themselves and were described by others as having positive self-esteem, but were also described by others as "always wants to be the center of attention; thinks too much of himself or herself; can't take criticism" (Salmivalli, Kaukiasnen, Kaistaniemi, & Lagerspetz, 1999, p. 1271).

Germany may be a good example of having a superior group self-concept. The group self-concept of Germans early in this century was extremely positive, of a kind that may be described as a superior compensatory identity. This was due to recent military successes, economic strength, a history of cultural achievement, effective civic institutions, and an internal climate that propagated self-satisfaction with German culture and society beyond what is "normal" ethnocentrism (Staub, 1989b).

These positive experiences might account for what seems was an early 20th-century German sense of superiority. But Germans also had a history of problems and suffering. Many Germans died in wars in previous centuries. During the Thirty Years' War (1618–1648), a third of Germany's population died (Craig, 1982). After struggles among many smaller units, Germany became a single country only late in the 19th century. History leaves its mark, and perhaps underlying the outward sense of group superiority there was also a deep-seated national vulnerability. Germany was then frustrated by a series of events beginning with the loss of World War I. These included a revolution that overthrew the monarchy, hyperinflation, economic depression, political chaos, and actions by other countries that Germans felt were humiliating to them (e. g., the French occupying the Ruhr district to ensure the receipt of compensation Germany was forced to pay after World War I). Whether it was defensive egoism, or normal ethnocentrism, or even a "genuine" sense of superiority, the nature of their group identity was likely important in Germans' reactions to the intense life problems following World War I.

A decade ago I wrote: "in groups and in individuals very high self-evaluation often masks self-doubt. Persistent life difficulties may contradict high self-evaluation and bring self-doubt to the surface. Even when there is no underlying self-doubt, a very high self-evaluation may be associated with limited concern for others. Among individuals, a *moderately* positive self concept is most strongly associated with sensitivity and responsiveness to other people" (from Staub, 1989, p. 55; see also Jarymowitz, 1977; Reese, 1961). This still seems a reasonable conclusion. Both individuals and groups have to value themselves in order to value other people, but not value themselves so strongly that others do not matter, or so highly and unrealistically that setbacks are experienced as devastating blows to collective and personal self-worth.

Cultural Devaluation and Ideologies of Antagonism

A form of group identity that I have called "ideology of antagonism" is especially important in genocide and collective violence. Inherent in group identity is a differentiation between "us" and "them." In my view a devaluation of "them" is not inherent in, but easily arises out of, this differentiation (see Brewer, this volume). There are many factors that develop a persistent devaluation of one group by another, which then becomes part of the group's culture. They include justification of past mistreatment of the other group, fear of the other's difference, and the need to create identity when one group has split off the other. (The latter may be an important origin of Christian anti-semitism [Staub, 1989b]). Devaluation embedded in a culture is a crucial cultural source of a group turning against another.

At times, two groups have had a long history of conflict with mutual violence. The evolution of increasing violence has already occurred, and as a result new violence easily flares up. In the course of this past history, not only the view of the other but the identity of each group as well has come to be defined around this enmity: the other is my enemy, and I am the enemy of the other. In short, group self-concept comes to center on violent conflict with the other group (see Kelman, this volume).

The Hutus and Tutsis in Rwanda seem to be an example of ideologies of antagonism. Up to the 20th century, the Tutsis were dominant, but group membership was defined by a complex combination of ethnic origin and class, with rich Hutus sometimes acquiring a classification as Tutsis. Under colonial rule by the Belgians, Tutsi dominance was intentionally enhanced, with Hutus receiving increasingly bad treatment. They became an underclass with limited rights and privilege. In 1959, in a violent revolt, they killed about 50,000 Tutsis. The Hutus ruled the country after it gained independence in 1962. There were significant massacres of Tutsis in the 1960s and 1970s, with continued discrimination and more limited, sporadic violence against them after that.

In the 1990s, a Tutsi-led group, consisting mainly of descendants of refugees over the past few decades, invaded Rwanda. In the course of the following few years, a complex political and military situation developed in the country. Dominant Hutus increasingly advocated "Hutu power," with media propaganda explicitly or implicitly promoting the destruction of Tutsis. The genocide of 1994 followed. It was stopped by the victory of the

Tutsi-led army over the government (see des Forges, 1999; Prunier, 1995; Staub, 1999b).

Cultural devaluation is extremely persistent, and ideology of antagonism is even more so. Neither tend to go away on their own, unattended, simply with the passage of time. They remain part of the culture, expressed in literature, in everyday relations, and in the life of institutions. They remain part of the identity of individuals and groups. Active social processes are required to change them.

Victimization, Healing, and Identity

When a group has been victimized in the past, without significant healing, it has an increased likelihood of becoming a perpetrator of mass violence (see Eriksen, this volume). People who experience trauma are deeply affected (Herman, 1992; Janoff-Bulman, 1992; McCann & Pearlman, 1990). Group victimization diminishes the different selves—the individual self, social identity, and group self-concept. Who am I and who are we, if we are so treated? Since individual identity is partly based on group identity, even those members of the group who are not present and have not been individually in danger are deeply affected.

Victimized groups are more likely to respond to threat with violence. In case of conflict, their understandable self-focus makes it difficult for them to consider the needs of others. Feeling insecure, their self vulnerable, and perceiving the world as a dangerous place, they experience threat as more intense than it is. They are more likely to engage, therefore, in aggression which they see as defensive (Staub, 1998b).

Healing following victimization makes it less likely that a group turns against another and perpetrates violence. Acknowledgment of the group's suffering by others and the expression of caring and empathy contribute to healing. The group itself can also promote healing by directly engaging with its past experience, including certain kinds of memorials and rituals of mourning and remembrance (Staub, 1998b). Healing from both individual trauma and group victimization involve repair of identity, as well as connections to other people (Pennebaker & Keough, 1999). The two are inherently related. The reestablishment of trust in people and the capacity to experience connection to them help repair identity.

Perpetrators also need to heal. At times, their woundedness has contributed to their actions. Their own violence further wounds them. It seems impossible to inflict tremendous harm on others, to kill many people and not become wounded or damaged. When perpetrators and victims continue to live together, as in Bosnia and Rwanda, for reconciliation to take place, some healing by both groups has to precede it. Reconciliation is required, in turn, to stop a continuing cycle of violence.

In the case of the Armenians who survived the genocide by the Turks in 1915–1916, healing was interfered with by the denial of Turkey that a genocide had taken place and by the complicity in this denial of many other countries. The relationships of the recently created Armenia to other nations, especially Turkey and Azerbaijan populated by ethnic Turks, have been affected by this history and the identity it has helped create. That identity has components of vulnerability, including a view of the world as dangerous and, perhaps, an ideology of antagonism in relation to Turks.

It is difficult to identify victim and perpetrator groups that have healed and thus see the consequences of such healing. While there has been awareness of the need for individuals to heal following the mass killing in Bosnia and the genocide in Rwanda, there has been little prior consciousness of the need for whole groups to heal. There have certainly been natural processes that have moved groups toward healing, but there have probably been no intentional efforts specifically aimed at this by victimized groups themselves or by the community of nations or by other bystanders.

A consciousness about the need for healing seemed to have emerged, at least in contemporary times, with respect to individual survivors of the Holocaust, and later Vietnam veterans, as well as victims of individual violence such as sexual or physical abuse (Herman, 1992; McCann & Pearlman, 1990). The aim of such healing has been to improve individual lives, not reducing the likelihood of later group violence.

Germany might serve as an example of healing, even if far from complete. Germany was wounded by the sequence of events that contributed to the Holocaust and by its own horrific actions during World War II and the Holocaust. Afterwards, the Germans were led to hesitantly engage with their past through the Nuremberg trials, other trials, and through the rest of the world reminding Germans of their conduct. At the same time, instead of acting in a generally punitive and harsh way, the world offered support, help, and connection to Germany. This ranged from the Marshall plan, to the willingness by French leaders to make connections with Germany, to Germany's becoming a member of the European Community, and to other demonstrations of the world accepting Germany into the international community. In different ways and for different reasons, this was true of both West and East Germany. Reconnecting with others is an avenue to healing for both victims and perpetrators.

Changes in Identities as Harm Doing Evolves

As noted above and depicted in figure 7.1, genocide and mass killing are usually the outcome of an evolution of increasing harm doing by perpetrators. There may be one victim group, although in the course of this evolution the boundaries expand and violence toward other groups also becomes probable. How do individual and group identities change along the way?

The perpetrators come to devalue members of the victim group more and more. They justify their actions, in part, by the nature of the victim, who is not only increasingly devalued but also increasingly excluded from the moral realm, the realm of people to whom moral values and moral considerations apply (Opotow, 1990; Staub, 1989b). Perpetrators also justify their actions by the "higher" values of their ideology. Along the way the perpetrators may come to see themselves as people who are willing to make the sacrifices required, including the killing of the victims, to fulfill important goals. Thus, they may see themselves, as Himmler encouraged the SS to see themselves, as bearing noble sacrifice for their higher cause (Hilberg, 1961).

In addition to their identity changing in relation to the victims, perpetrators are likely to become desensitized to human suffering in general. Devaluation tends to extend from the original victims to new groups, which prepares the way for the extension of violence (Staub, 1989a, 1989b). In Germany, for example, after the euthanasia program, the killing of physically handicapped, mentally ill, and other "inferior" Germans, after the genocide of the Jews and gypsies, and after violence against people in occupied countries, the authorities began to consider the killing of physically ugly German prison inmates (Lifton, 1986).

As boundaries weaken and new groups are devalued and become potential or actual victims, the perpetrators' identity as people who value human beings and human welfare is likely to change. As this process unfolds perpetrators are likely to distance themselves from all human beings not a part of their group, however that is defined. At the extreme, might it be the case that even the welfare of one's ingroup and of friends and family become of less concern?

The identity of bystanders also changes. Internal bystanders—members of the perpetrator group who are not themselves perpetrators—usually remain passive. They are also affected by instigating conditions. They have grown up in a culture that imbues members with respect for authority and devalues the victim group. Thus, they share a "cultural tilt" with perpetrators. This cultural background, often in combination with fear of a repressive system, reduces the motivation to oppose the group as it moves along a continuum of increasing violence.

Passivity changes bystanders. It is difficult to see others suffer and do nothing. To justify their passivity, reduce their guilt, and reduce empathy with victims that would make them suffer, passive bystanders tend to distance themselves from victims, in part by increasingly devaluing them. This makes it even more likely that they will remain passive. It also leads some bystanders to join perpetrators.

For example, a group of psychoanalysts in Berlin remained passive as their fellow Jewish analysts were the object of harassment and persecution. They began to use racially appropriate Nazi terms to refer to Jewish colleagues, like "not pure Germans." These served both as euphemisms and as means to distance and objectify their fellow analysts. They accepted a relative of Herman Goring, untrained in psychoanalysis, as the head of their Institute. They began to rewrite psychoanalytic theory to fit Nazi ideology and doctrine. Some of them became participants in the euthanasia program, and in the end some got involved in the extermination of Jews (Staub, 1989a).

The process in this specific instance may be an example of how by-standers distance themselves, even from familiar others and from close asso-ciates. Adopting at first an "objective," disinterested stance, and introducing ideological thinking change both the view of and emotional relationship to the other. Through this process bystanders, as well as perpetrators, change the nature of their own self. Those changes in identity are intertwined with changes in society and culture. As violence evolves, the norms and standards of society change, allowing and often promoting actions that were previ-ously inconceivable. For instance, in Rwanda, neighbors killed neighbors and people gave up members of their families to the killers (des Forges, 1999; Gourevich, 1998; Staub & Pearlman, in press).

I have suggested that these changes in perpetrators and bystanders repre-sent changes in identity. Although identity is a broad concept, we may see it as including a person's self-concept and orientation to and evaluation of the self, as well as values relating to and orientation toward and evaluation of other people. Thus, I am proposing here that a person's view of the world is also part of personal identity (Epstein, 1980). Some or all of these elements of identity will change in the course of a societal evolution toward genocide. The changes in a person's self-concept and in the group's collective sense of self mutually reinforce each other.

However, the negative changes in the view of the other, and the changes in the self, as individuals and a society move along a "continuum of destruc-tion" (Staub, 1989a, 1989b), are not the whole story. Even in very simple societies there is variation in personality and, presumably, self-concept. Only a small percentage of people have the "modal identity type" that may be seen as characteristic of the society (Konner, 1978). In genocidal soci-eties, in addition to perpetrators and passive bystanders, there are usually some people who attempt to help victims. The rescuers of Jews in Nazi Eu-rope have been the primary group of such helpers who have been exten-sively studied (Fogelman, 1994; Oliner & Oliner, 1988; Tec, 1986). But in other societies as well, there have been heroes who have endangered them-selves to save lives.

I have heard several such stories in Rwanda, both in conversation and in formal interviews I conducted with people whose lives were saved. In one case, for example, a Hutu man who had worked for a woman sent another man to help her after her husband was killed. The man who came, a stranger carrying a Bible, repeatedly endangered himself as he faced off people who came to the house wanting to take her away. The woman telling this story was unclear about his motivation to help: she suggested his reli-gion, his being a good man. Having some difficulty accepting such self-sacrificial behavior, she wondered about possible selfish motives but could not identify any.

Once people begin to help in some limited way, they are further shaped by their own actions. Like violence, so helping evolves. People who have agreed to help for a short time, or to a limited extent, change as a result of their actions. They become more committed to the welfare of those they have helped and often to the welfare of human beings in general. They come to see themselves as people who are willing to endanger themselves to help others. Their values and identity change (Staub, 1989b, 1993b).

The Role of Identity in the Prevention of Genocide and Mass Killing

The Role of Leaders

How can genocide and mass killing be prevented and what is the role of different kinds of identities in prevention? How can people gain positive identities in difficult times without turning to destructive groups or making their groups destructive? One way is for leaders to offer positive visions that are constructive, visions that offer hope but are realistically aimed at solving life problems without identifying enemies, visions that connect rather than separate people. The New Deal under Roosevelt was one example of this. This can be difficult and at times even dangerous for leaders when there is already strong enmity against a potential victim group.

Healing by Victimized Groups

An important contributor to prevention is healing by victimized groups. Healing can help repair damaged identities and worldviews (as well as fulfill other frustrated needs). It can recreate some sense of security and trust in the world. As a result, it makes it less likely that a victim group becomes a perpetrator. Acknowledgement of the group's suffering, expressions of empathy and sorrow, and other forms of affirmation by the rest of the world can contribute to healing. Punishment of perpetrators can also help victims. It can communicate to victims that what was done to them is not regarded as normal and acceptable by the world. That message, in turn, makes it seem less likely that it will happen again (Staub, 1998b, 1999c).

Engaging with their painful experiences can also help survivors of group violence heal. Trauma victims frequently avoid such engagement even though they are often affected by what has happened to them in many ways: through intrusive imagery, hyper arousal, negative feelings about the self, mistrust and difficulty in relating to people (Herman, 1992; McCann & Pearlman, 1990). Engagement can lead to integration of the self and reconnection with people (Pennebaker & Keough, 1999). It can lead to finding meaning, perhaps in helping other people, working for the prevention of similar violence against people, or living life in a different way.

Healing makes reconciliation possible. In places like Rwanda and Bosnia, where victims and perpetrators live together, or where mutual violence has occurred, reconciliation is essential to prevent continued cycles of violence. The self is to a significant extent defined by relationships to others. Ideologies of antagonism, intense devaluation and hostility toward another, or strong fear of a neighbor are central aspects of identity. Reconciliation, which when genuine requires forgiveness and overcoming devaluation and antagonism, changes identity in central ways. As a result of healing and reconciliation, feelings of diminished self-worth and vulnerability can lessen. Mistrust in people and in the world can also be reduced. Both the desire for revenge as a form of justice and the readiness to use force to defend oneself and one's group can decrease. Trust in people, trust in the world as a livable place, and hope for the future can reemerge.

How can healing, reconciliation, and positive connection to others in general be promoted in previously victimized groups? We have so far only a limited repertoire of skills and techniques for this. To begin with, victimized groups have to start with at least some desire for change, which, in case of intense antagonism, may be lacking. When there is some openness, contexts for healing can be created by bringing members of different groups together. People can write about and talk to each other about what has happened to them (Pennebaker & Keough, 1999). They can talk about their pain, sorrow, loss, and anger. As they listen to each other and respond with empathy, pain, which has been a source of disconnection, can become a source of connection (Staub & Pearlman, 1996).

This is one aspect of a project that we have been conducting in Rwanda on "healing, forgiveness, and reconciliation." In addition to such experiential aspects of promoting healing and reconciliation, the training we have used also had psycho-educational aspects. Participants learned about and discussed the impact of trauma on people in the hope that this would help them understand their own experience better. They learned about avenues to healing. They heard about the fulfillment and frustration of basic needs and they received information and engaged in discussion about the origins of genocide (Staub, 2000; Staub & Pearlman, in press).

This last element of the training has had seemingly dramatic effects. Learning about a number of other genocides and about how genocide comes about seemed to reaffirm for participants their own humanity. If these terrible things have been done to others as well, and if there are understandable human processes that give rise to them, then the victims in Rwanda remain part of the human realm in spite of what happened to them. In addition, understanding the forces that led to genocide seemed to humanize the perpetrators, both in the survivors' eyes and, perhaps, in their own, thereby contributing to reconciliation. The type of training described, which we conducted in Rwanda, can help not only victims but also members of the perpetrator group. Genocide and mass killing, inflicting violence on others, deeply wounds the perpetrators. It also wounds members of the perpetrator group who have remained passive bystanders. They also are in need of healing. Healing, in turn, can open the way to reconciliation. As reconciliation enhances a feeling of security, it furthers the possibility of healing.

Some of the participants in our project used the approach provided in the training, integrated with their own traditional approach, with groups in the community. Formal, experimental assessment showed that trauma symptoms decreased among community members who participated in meetings led by people we trained, both over time, and in comparison to groups led by different trainers who used their organizations' traditional approach, as well as in comparison to no treatment control groups. Orientation to members of the other ethnic group became more positive among community members who participated in the meetings that used this integrated approach, both over time and in comparison to people in the other groups (Staub, Pearlman, Gubin and Hagengimana, unpublished research).

Healing by leaders is also important. Like the other members of a victimized group, so the people who emerge as leaders have been affected by past victimization. In Bosnia, a number of the Serb leaders have had members of their families killed by the Croat regime that killed many Serbs and Jews during World War II. Outsiders who engage with such leaders need to be aware of and attempt to address their wounds to individual and group identity, if they are to effectively influence policies and practices (Staub, 1999c).

Hostile groups can also benefit from joint efforts in behalf of shared goals. Depending on the nature of hostility and past injuries, this may require prior dialogue, problem solving in small groups (see Kelman, in this book), or healing. But significant engagement by members of groups with each other in the course of working together for shared goals can bring benefits in overcoming devaluation and antagonism (Allport, 1954; Pettigrew, 1997; Staub, 1989b, 1999c).

Culture Change

Another group-level issue is culture change. Cultural devaluation and authority orientation shape identities. Monolithic cultures, with a limited set of values and limited access of at least some groups of people to the public domain, also make genocide more likely, while pluralistic cultures make genocide less likely. When respect for authorities is moderate and there are varied values and points of view that can be expressed in the public domain, people are more able to tolerate uncertainty and therefore social upheaval (Soeters, 1996).

Democracies, which are pluralistic, are unlikely to engage in genocide (Rummel, 1994). This, however, seems especially true of "mature" democracies. (Staub, 1996b) These are democracies in which laws are enforced, in which all groups can participate in public life, and which have a "civil society " (i. e., well-established civic institutions). Germany was not this kind of democracy at the time of the Weimar Republic, nor was Argentina at the time of "the disappearances" (Staub, 1989b), when elected governments were regularly replaced by military rule. Working to create democracy and a civil society is one way to bring about culture change that makes genocide less likely. Such a culture is likely to form individuals whose relationship to the group is more akin to constructive, rather than blind, patriotism and who are less likely to be embedded in their group.

Multiple group identities seem important in preventing genocide. When people can gain identity and fulfill other basic needs through connection to a variety of groups, they are less likely to give themselves over to and lose themselves in a group that turns against others. Their ability to oppose destructive ideologies and practices will increase.

However, these groups need to be reasonably independent of each other. In many cases of genocide, subgroups of society, which could have been the source of at least somewhat independent identities, have subordinated themselves to or have become embedded in the state or in an ideological movement. This was recently the case with the churches in Rwanda. Many church leaders, both in the dominant Catholic Church and in the minority Protestant churches, were long connected to the ruling elements of the country. They became accomplices during the genocide, facilitating the killing of Tutsis (des Forges, 1999; Gourevich, 1998).

Inclusive Caring, Moral Courage, and the Behavior of Bystanders

What type of socialization will lead children to speak out against harmful practices within their groups? What is required for people to exert influence within their group so that it does not remain a passive bystander in the face of violence against people outside the group? Warmth, affection, effective but not punitive guidance, allowing children reasonable autonomy, helping them develop a sense of significance and a "voice," and guiding children to help and not harm others make it likely that they will develop inclusive caring, connected identities and constructive patriotism, as well as moral courage (Staub, 1996a). Such characteristics would make genocide less likely.

Constructive patriotism has a value basis in caring about human welfare. Holding such a value motivates criticism and opposition to harmful policies and practices of the group. Caring about human welfare is a value that has to develop in children through experiential learning. Without love and affection and positive guidance in their own lives, without feeling valued, children are unlikely to learn to value others.

To publicly oppose harmful practices and advocate benevolent ones often requires moral courage. This is not necessarily physical courage, but the ability and willingness to tolerate conflict. The kind of individual identities people develop and the nature of social identities, what the group requires of its members, are central to this. Even when there is no physical danger, people often won't speak out against harmful and potentially violent practices out of concern for ostracism or exclusion from the group. Is it possible to create cultures in which opposition for the sake of human welfare is valued?

It is relevant in this context that, according to one researcher, about one-third of rescuers of Jews in Nazi Europe were marginal to their group (Tec, 1986). They had a different religion, or one foreign parent, or moved to their community from some other place, or may have been simply personally different and therefore less taken in by or less invested in their community. This marginality may have made them less identified with their group, perhaps fearing less the possibility of ostracism and enabling them to have a separate, independent perspective.

Inclusive caring means the development of caring for people beyond the group. It has to do with the relationship of "us" and "them," with the development of an identity that makes individuals and groups not draw a line at the boundary of their group that diminishes concern for the welfare of those beyond the group. (Staub, 1996a). Many of the rescuers grew up in families where this line between their group and minorities was not as sharply drawn as in the rest of the group. The parents and the family engaged with people outside the "ingroup," often including Jews (Oliner & Oliner, 1988).

Individual identities based on inclusive caring would lead people to want their countries to be active bystanders, who would respond when there is violence against people outside their borders. Self-concepts that embody inclusive caring would be likely to move individuals to exert influence on their governments not to remain passive. This is essential for the prevention of mass killing and genocide. While this has rarely happened, the limited examples that exist strongly suggest that if the community of nations responds early, as harm doing just begins, the evolution of increasing violence can usually be stopped.

Even groups of individuals can exert significant influence. After the revolution in Iran the Bahai, for a long time a devalued and persecuted group, were immediately intensely persecuted. Over 200 Bahai were executed. The international Bahai community immediately made representations to the various governments where Bahai lived and to the international community. The United Nations, as well as individual nations, passed resolutions condemning the killing and persecution. While the persecution did not stop, the killings did (Bigelow, 1993), with some limited resumption, unfortunately, in the 1990s.

In places where violence could have been much greater, as in Northern Ireland, or between Israelis and Palestinians, usually external bystanders had some role in limiting violence. Internal bystanders, members of different groups reaching out to each other, perhaps enabled by the behavior of external bystanders, also seems to have had a role (Staub, 1999b). In Northern Ireland, the British military and political presence provided support to political and social leaders who have worked for opportunities in jobs and more social equality for Catholics, as well as to community organizations that brought members of the two groups together for dialogue and other forms of engagement with each other (Cairns & Darby, 1998; Staub, 1999b; see, however, White, this volume).

With early, committed, and resolute actions by the community of nations, the evolution of violence can probably be inhibited much of the time without the use of military force (Staub, 1999b). But for this to happen requires important changes in identities: in individuals' views of themselves and their nations and in nations' views of themselves and of the international community. It requires committed bystanders and the creation of an international system that leads to action when action is required.

Summary and Conclusions

Identities of individuals, the nature of the relationship to the group in which they invest their identity, and group-self concept are all important in the generation of genocide, mass killing, and other harmful behavior by groups toward other groups. They are also important in prevention. However, identities must be considered in the context of other aspects of individual and group psychology. Identity is a concept that refers to certain structures in individual personality with related processes. In reality, of course, human beings (and cultures and societies), are unitary wholes with interrelated structures and processes.

Important concepts related to identity that have relevance to genocide and mass killing include values, the way the self and others are divided ("us" and "them"), orientation to authority, the individual's relationship to the group, and basic human needs (figure 7.1). One may conceptualize all these as part of identity, or separate them and see them as concepts with their own structures and processes. I find it useful to separate these and then consider the relationships among them. As I suggested in this chapter, the nature of a person's identity and group self-concept will certainly affect orientation to authority, divisions between "us" and "them," and so on.

I have proposed a series of steps that can take members of a group from instigating factors (left side of figure 7.1) to full-fledged genocide or mass murder (right side of figure 7.1). Instigating factors include intergroup conflict and difficult life circumstances (e.g., poverty) that threaten basic needs (e.g., need for security, sense of self-worth, connections to others). Behaviors that elevate the ingroup and derogate outgroups (e.g., scapegoating) provide means of coping with these threats to the self. Derogation of the outgroup can encourage initial acts of violence against the outgroup. Initial violence, in turn, sets in motion a cycle of further violence and polarization

that becomes tied to self and group identity. This cycle may eventually escalate to mass killing and genocide. The development of this chain of events is
moderated by both cultural variables (top of figure 7.1) and the behavior of
bystanders (bottom of figure 7.1). For example, ideologies that legitimize
violence and a group's history of being a victim of violence are two cultural
factors that can increase the likelihood that initial instigators will lead to
mass killing or genocide. On the other hand, involvement of bystanders
(whether ingroup members or outsiders, such as the international community) can mitigate the march from instigators to eventual genocide.

One of the important relationships suggested by this chapter is that between identity and basic needs (figure 7.1). Security, connection, and effectiveness are important from birth on, and their fulfillment and frustration
begin at birth. When we consider motivation for action that may have to do
with identity, under many conditions a complex of motives and needs will
be involved. When people engage in destructive ways of fulfilling their need
for identity (for example, by joining an ideological movement that aims to
destroy "enemies"), they are also usually seeking to satisfy other basic needs
that I have proposed: security, connection, a sense of effectiveness and control, and the need for comprehension of reality. The same is true when people act in positive ways. Reconciliation with others may arise from and has
effects on identity, but also fulfills varied basic needs and expresses and affirms certain values.

Individual identity is a storehouse of and is shaped by all the experiences
a person has, at least all significant experiences. For example, it is shaped by
a history of fulfillment and frustration of basic needs. Some may regard it,
therefore, as superordinate to other aspects of personality and their related
processes. In my view, however, the most useful theory will maintain and
develop conceptual distinctions. The important task for basic theory building is to identify the interrelations of concepts and related processes.

How are these concepts, underlying structures, and processes interrelated in the tragic domain of human life this chapter addresses? Is identity a
more basic need than others? When a basic need such as security or connection is fulfilled, does that automatically strengthen identity? How can
basic needs be fulfilled constructively for whole groups of people? Will
answers to these and other questions help in halting and preventing group
violence? How can we apply gains we make in theoretical understanding to
help us in the practical realm, in preventing violence?

These questions point to an obligation of psychologists. The obligation
is even deeper than applying knowledge to the great practical issues of human life. It is to be purposeful in our efforts to gain knowledge, whether in
the laboratory or through experience in real-life settings. The obligation is
to be guided by a vision of reducing human suffering and enhancing human
welfare, especially when the knowledge we seek relates to such important
matters as the origins and prevention of genocide and mass killing.

References

Allport, G. W. (1954). *The nature of predjudice*. Reading, MA: Addison-Wesley.

Bar-Tal, D., & Staub, E. (1997). Introduction: The nature and forms of patriotism. In D. Bar-Tal & E. Staub (Eds.), *Patriotism in the lives of individuals and groups*. Chicago: Nelson-Hall.

Baumeister, R. F. (1997). *Evil: Inside human violence and cruelty*. New York: W.H. Freeman.

Bigelow, K. R. (1993). A campaign to deter genocide: The Baha'i experience. In H. Fein, (Ed.), *Genocide watch*. New Haven: Yale University Press.

Cairns, E., & Darby, J. (1998). The conflict in Northern Ireland. *American Psychologist, 53*, 754–760.

Craig, G. A. (1982). *The Germans*. New York: New American Library.

des Forges, A. (1999). *Leave none to tell the story: Genocide in Rwanda*. New York: Human Rights Watch.

Epstein, S. (1980). The self-concept: A review and the proposal of an integrated theory of personality. In E. Staub (Ed.), *Personality: Basic aspects and current research*. Englewood Cliffs, NJ: Prentice-Hall.

Fein, H. (1993). Accounting for Genocide after 1945: Theories and some findings. *International Journal of Group Rights, 1*, 79–106.

Fogelman, E. (1994). *Conscience and courage: Rescuers of Jews during the Holocaust*. New York: Anchor Books.

Harff, B., & Gurr, T. R. (1990). Victims of the state genocides, politicides and group repression since 1945. *International Review of Victimology, 1*, 1–19.

Gourevich, P. (1998). *We wish to inform you that tomorrow we will be killed with our families*. New York: Farrar, Straus and Giroux.

Herman, J. (1992). *Trauma and recovery*. New York: Basic Books.

Hilberg, R. (1961). *The Destruction of the European Jews*. New York: Harper & Row.

Hitler, A. (1925). *Mein Kampf*. Translated by Ralph Manheim. Boston, MA: Houghton Mifflin Company.

Janoff-Bulman, R. (1992). *Shattered assumptions*. New York: The Tree Press.

Jarymowitz, M. (1977). Modification of self-worth and increment of prosocial sensitivity. *Polish Psychological Bulletin, 8*, 45–53.

Kincaid, E. (1959). *In every war but one*. New York: Norton.

Konner, M. (1978). Social and personality development: An anthropological perspective. In M. Lamb (Ed.), *Social and personality development*. New York: Holt.

Kressel, N. J. (1996). *Mass hate: The global rise of genocide and terror*. New York: Plenum Press.

Levin, S., Sidanius, J., Rebinowitz, J. L., & Frederico, C. (1998). Ethnic identity, legitimizing ideologies and social status: A matter of ideological asymmetry. *Political Psychology, 19*, 373–404.

Lifton, R. J. (1986). *The Nazi doctors: Medical killing and the psychology of genocide*. New York: Basic Books.

McCann, L. I., & Pearlman, L. A. (1990). *Psychological trauma and the adult survivor: Theory, therapy, and transformation*. New York: Bruner/Mazel.

Miller, A. (1982). *For your own good: Hidden cruelty in child-rearing and the roots of violence*. New York: Farrar, Straus and Giroux.

Myers, D. (1999). *Social psychology*. New York: McGraw-Hill.

Oliner, S. B., & Oliner, D. (1988). *The altruistic personality: Rescuers of Jews in Nazi Europe.* New York: Free Press.

Opotow, S. (Ed.). (1990). Moral exclusion and injustice. *Journal of Social Issues, 46* (1).

Pennebaker, J. W., & Keough, K. A. (1999). Revealing, organizing and reorganizing the self in response to stress and emotion. In R. J. Contrada, & R. D. Ashmore (Eds.), *Self, social identity, and physical health.* (pp. 101-121) London: Oxford.

Pettigrew, T. F. (1997). Generalized intergroup contact effects on prejudice. *Personality and Social Psychology Bulletin, 23,* (2), 173–185.

Prunier, G. (1995). *The Rwanda crisis: History of a genocide.* New York: Columbia University Press.

Reese, H. (1961). Relationships between self-acceptance and sociometric choices. *Journal of Abnormal and Social Psychology, 62.*

Rummel, R. J (1994). *Death by government.* New Brunswick, NJ: Transaction Publishers.

Salmivalli, C., Kaukiainen, A., Kaistaniemi, L., & Lagerspetz, K. M. J. (1999). Self-evaluated self-esteem, peer-evaluated self-esteem, and defensive egotism as predictors of adolescents' participation in bullying situations. *Personality and Social Psychology Bulletin, 25,* 1268–1278.

Sampson, E. E. (1988). The debate on individualism. *American Psychologist, 47,* 15–22.

Schatz, R., & Staub, E. (1997). Manifestations of blind and constructive patriotism. In D. Bar-Tal & E. Staub (Eds.), *Patriotism in the lives of individuals and groups.* Chicago: Nelson-Hall.

Schatz, R., Staub, E. & Lavine, H. (1999). On the varieties of national attachment: Blind versus constructive patriotism. *Political Psychology, 20.* 151–175.

Simpson, C. (1993). *The splendid blond beast.* New York: Grove Press.

Smith, N. S. (1998). The psychocultural roots of genocide. *American Psychologist, 53,* 743–753.

Soetters, J. L. (1996). Culture and conflict: An application of Hofstede's theory to the conflict in the former Yugoslavia. *Peace and Conflict: Journal of Peace Psychology, 2* (3), 233–244.

Staub, E. (1989a). Steps along the continuum of destruction: The evolution of bystanders, German psychoanalysts and lessons for today. *Political Psychology, 10,* 39–53.

Staub, E. (1989b). *The roots of evil: The origins of genocide and other group violence.* New York: Cambridge University Press.

Staub, E. (1993a). Individual and group selves, motivation and morality. In T. Wren, and G. Noam, (Eds.), *Morality and the self.* (pp. 337–359) Cambridge: MIT Press.

Staub, E. (1993b). The psychology of bystanders, perpetrators and heroic helpers. *International Journal of Intercultural Relations, 17,* 315–341.

Staub, E. (1996a). Altruism and aggression in children and youth: Origins and cures. In R. Feldman, (Ed.), *The psychology of adversity.* Amherst: University Massachusetts Press.

Staub, E. (1996b). Cultural-societal roots of violence: The examples of genocidal violence and of contemporary youth violence in the United States. *American Psychologist, 51,* 117–132.

Staub, E. (1997). Blind versus constructive patriotism: Moving from embeddedness in the group to critical loyalty and action. In E. Staub & D. Bar-Tal (Eds.), *Patriotism.* Chicago: Nelson-Hall.

Staub, E. (1998a). Basic human needs and their role in altruism and aggression. Unpublished manuscript. Department of Psychology. University of Massachusetts at Amherst.

Staub, E. (1998b). Breaking the cycle of genocidal violence: Healing and reconciliation. In J. Harvey (Ed.), *Perspectives on loss: A sourcebook*. Philadelphia: Taylor and Francis.

Staub, E. (1999a). A brighter future: The evolution of caring and nonviolent children. Book in preparation.

Staub, E. (1999b). The origins and prevention of genocide, mass killing, and other collective violence. *Peace and Conflict: Journal of Peace Psychology, 5* (4), 303–336.

Staub, E. (1999c). The roots of evil: Social conditions, culture, personality and basic human needs. *Personality and Social Psychology Review, 3*, 179–192.

Staub, E. (2000a). Genocide and mass killing: Origins, prevention, healing and reconcilation. *Political Psychology, 21*, 367–382.

Staub, E. (2000b). Mass murder: Origins, prevention and U.S. involvement. *Encyclopedia of violence in the United States*. New York: Charles Scribner's Sons, Reference Books.

Staub, E., & Pearlman, L. (1996). Trauma and the fulfillment of the human potential. Workshop presented of the meetings of the International Society for Traumatic Stress Studies. November, San Francisco.

Staub, E., & Pearlman, L. A. (in press). Healing, reconciliation and forgiving after genocide and other collective violence. In *Forgiveness and Reconciliation*, Radnor, PA. Templeton Foundation Press.

Staub, E., Pearlman, L. A., Gubin, A., and Hagengimana, A. Healing, forgiveness and reconciliation in Rwanda: Intervention and experimental evaluation. Manuscript in preperation. Department of Psychology, University of Massachusetts at Amherst.

Tajfel, H. (1978). Social categorization, social identity and social comparison. In H. Tajfel (Ed.), *Differentiation between social groups* (pp. 61–76). London: Academic Press.

Tajfel, H. (1982). Social psychology of intergroup relations. *Annual Review of Psychology, 33*, 1–39.

Tec, N. (1986). *When light pierced the darkness: Christian rescue of Jews in Nazi-occupied Poland*. New York: Oxford University Press.

Triandis, H. C. (1994). *Culture and social behavior*. New York: McGraw-Hill.

Turner, J. C. (1987). *Rediscovering the social group: A self-categorization theory*. New York: Basic Blackwell.

PART IV

THE ROLE OF SOCIAL IDENTITY IN REDUCING INTERGROUP CONFLICT

The Role of National Identity in Conflict Resolution

Experiences from Israeli-Palestinian Problem-Solving Workshops

My colleagues' and my work as scholar-practitioners has focused on analysis and resolution of protracted, seemingly intractable conflicts between national, ethnic, or other kinds of identity groups, best exemplified by intercommunal conflicts, such as those in Cyprus, Northern Ireland, Sri Lanka, Bosnia, and apartheid South Africa. My own most intensive and extensive experience, over the past quarter-century, has been with the Israeli-Palestinian conflict, and my analysis draws primarily on that experience.[1]

Using the Israeli-Palestinian conflict as a case in point, this chapter examines the way in which issues of national identity can exacerbate an international or intercommunal conflict and the way in which such issues can be addressed in conflict-resolution efforts. The chapter starts out with a brief history of the Israeli-Palestinian conflict, setting the stage for the identity issues at the heart of the conflict. It then proceeds to describe the struggle over national identity between the two peoples, which has led them to perceive their conflict in zero-sum terms, with respect to not only territory and resources but also national identity and national existence. Next, it argues that long-term resolution of this and similar deep-rooted conflicts requires changes in the groups' national identities, such that affirmation of one group's identity is no longer predicated on negation of the other's identity. Such identity changes are possible as long as they leave the core of each group's national identity intact. Furthermore, the chapter proceeds to argue, such changes *need* to be and *can* be "negotiated" between the two groups. One venue for negotiating identity, described in the next section, is provided by the problem-solving workshops between Israeli and Palestinian elites that my colleagues and I have convened for many years. Finally, the paper concludes with an illustration of the possibilities and limits of the ne-gotiation of identity, based on a joint Israeli-Palestinian exploration of the problem of Palestinian refugees.

The Israeli-Palestinian Conflict

The Israeli-Palestinian conflict is now more than a century old (see Tessler, 1994, for a comprehensive account of the history of the conflict, or Mendelsohn, 1989, and Gerner, 1991, for shorter accounts). Its origins go back to the birth of political Zionism at the end of the 19th century (see Halpern, 1969, and Hertzberg, 1973). The early decades of the 20th cen-tury brought to Palestine waves of Jewish immigrants who purchased land, built settlements and social institutions, and clearly signaled their intention to establish a Jewish homeland and ultimately a Jewish state in Palestine. The growing Jewish presence was soon perceived as a threat by the Arab population of the land, which was itself influenced by the development of Arab nationalism and the construction of a specifically Palestinian identity (see Muslih, 1988, and Khalidi, 1997). Violence first erupted in the 1920s and has continued to mark the relationship between the two peoples ever since.

During the period of the British mandate, which was established after World War I, various formulas for the political future of Palestine were ex-plored, including partition and establishment of a federal state, but none was found to be acceptable to both the Arab and the Jewish populations (or indeed to either one of them). In November 1947—in the wake of World War II and the decimation of European Jewry—the United Nations Gen-eral Assembly voted to end the British mandate over Palestine (on May 15, 1948) and to partition the land into a Jewish and an Arab state. The Zionist leadership accepted the partition plan, with reservations. The Arab leader-ship, both within Palestine and in the neighboring states, rejected it. Fight-ing between the two sides broke out immediately after adoption of the UN resolution and turned into all-out war after May 15, 1948, when the British forces withdrew, the Jewish leadership in Palestine declared the indepen-dent state of Israel, and regular armies from the neighboring Arab states joined the fray. Fighting continued until early 1949.

In July of 1949, Israel and the Arab states signed armistice agreements (though the state of war continued). The armistice lines became the official borders of the State of Israel. These borders included a larger portion of Palestine than the UN partition plan had allotted to the Jewish state. The Arab state envisioned by the partition plan did not come into being. Two parts of mandatory Palestine remained under Arab control: the West Bank, which was eventually annexed by Jordan, and the Gaza Strip, which came under Egyptian administration. The establishment of Israel and the war of 1948–49 also created a massive refugee problem, with the flight or expulsion of hundreds of thousands of Palestinian Arabs from their homes in the part of Palestine that became the State of Israel. I shall return to the refugee problem later in this chapter.

The map changed radically as a result of the Arab-Israeli war of June 1967—and, along with it, the political atmosphere in the Middle East. By the end of the Six-Day War, as Israelis called it, Israel occupied the West Bank and the Gaza Strip, thus extending its control over the entire territory of mandatory Palestine. It also occupied the Sinai Peninsula and the Golan Heights—Egyptian and Syrian territories, respectively. The new geopolitical and strategic situation created by the 1967 War led to the Palestinianization of the Arab-Israeli conflict, bringing it back to its origin as a conflict between two peoples over—and increasingly within—the land they both claimed (Kelman, 1988).

The Palestinianization (or re-Palestinianization) of the conflict has manifested itself in the actions of the Arab states, of the Palestinian community itself, and of Israel. Israel's neighboring Arab states gradually withdrew from the military struggle against Israel—though not before another major war in 1973—leaving it, essentially, to the Palestinians themselves. The disengagement of the Arab states became dramatically clear with the 1977 visit to Jerusalem of President Anwar Sadat of Egypt, the largest and most powerful Arab state, an initiative that led to the Camp David accord of 1978 and the Egyptian-Israeli peace treaty of 1979. The Palestinians took repossession of their struggle, which in the years between 1949 and 1967 had been mostly in the hands of the Arab states. Fatah, under the leadership of Yasser Arafat, and other Palestinian guerrilla organizations grew in strength and eventually took over the Palestine Liberation Organization (PLO), which was originally a creature of the Arab League. Between the 1960s and the 1980s, the Palestinian movement gradually shifted its emphasis from the liberation of all of Palestine through armed struggle against Israel to the establishment of an independent Palestinian state in the West Bank and Gaza through largely political means. The end of the occupation became the immediate goal of the movement and, with the onset of the *intifada*—the uprising in the West Bank and Gaza—in December 1987, the occupied territories became the focal point of its struggle.

On the Israeli side, the *intifada* further underlined the Palestinianization of the conflict in the wake of the 1967 War. What had been largely an interstate conflict between 1948 and 1967 had now been internalized by Israel—that is, transformed into a continuous confrontation with a resentful Palestinian population, living under occupation within Israel's post-1967 borders. Many Israelis were persuaded by the *intifada* that continuing occupation was not tenable and that the Palestinians were indeed a people, whose national movement had to find some political expression if there was to be a peaceful accommodation between the two sides (Kelman, 1997c).

By the end of the 1980s, there was a strong interest on all sides in finding a peaceful accommodation and an increasing recognition that some version of a two-state solution would provide the best formula for a broadly accept-able historic compromise. The political obstacles to such a solution, how-ever, remained severe. A number of strategic and micropolitical considera-tions—traceable, in particular, to the end of the Cold War and the aftermath of the Gulf War—eventually brought the leaderships on both sides to the negotiating table at the Madrid Conference in 1991 and the subsequent talks in Washington. These talks, however, never developed momentum. It was only after Prime Minister Yitzhak Rabin came into power in Israel in 1992, at the head of a government led by the Labor Party, and gradually (and reluctantly) concluded that Israel would have to deal di-rectly with the PLO leadership in order to make progress in the negotia-tions, that a breakthrough was finally achieved. This breakthrough oc-curred in the secret Oslo talks, which culminated in the exchange of letters of mutual recognition between the PLO and the State of Israel (which, in my view, was the most significant achievement of the Oslo process) and the Declaration of Principles signed in Washington in September 1993 (see Kelman, 1997c, for further details).

The Oslo breakthrough occurred because a number of long-term and short-term interests of the parties—to which I alluded briefly—persuaded them of the necessity of reaching an agreement. "But a significant factor contributing to the breakthrough was the conclusion, on both sides, that negotiations were not only necessary but also possible—that they could yield an acceptable agreement without jeopardizing their national existence. This sense of possibility evolved out of interactions between the two sides that produced the individuals, the ideas, and the political atmosphere re-quired for negotiations" (Kelman, 1997d, p. 213). A variety of unofficial contacts between the two sides, including the workshops to be described in this chapter, contributed to creating this sense of possibility and the climate conducive to negotiations (see Kelman, 1995).

Though the Oslo agreement was a genuine breakthrough in the effort to resolve the Israeli-Palestinian conflict, the process of negotiating an interim agreement and initiating final-status negotiations has faced numerous ob-stacles and experienced dangerous setbacks, all reminding us of the in-tractability of conflicts between identity groups, such as the Israeli-Palestin-ian conflict. Significant changes in the conflict have taken place with the establishment of a Palestinian Authority (PA) in the West Bank and Gaza Strip, which constitutes the scaffolding for a Palestinian state. But the path to a negotiated agreement has been obstructed by such events as the He-bron massacre of Palestinians at prayer, the assassination of Yitzhak Rabin, the suicide bombings against Israeli civilians, the continuation of the Israeli settlement process in the West Bank, the deteriorating economy and quality of life in the West Bank and Gaza, the corrupt and autocratic leadership of the PA, and the three-year rule of Prime Minister Netanyahu in Israel.

The election of a new Israeli government in May of 1999 brought new hope that serious negotiations of the final-status issues will be pursued. But the negotiations failed and, in late September 2000, a new *intifada* broke out, producing a violent Israeli response and a serious deterioration of the peace process. Nevertheless I feel fairly confident that the negotiations will eventually succeed in establishing a Palestinian state. I am less confident that this new state will be truly independent, secure, and viable, and that its establishment will form the basis of a long-term peace and a cooperative, mutually enhancing relationship with Israel, conducive to ultimate reconciliation between the two peoples. How the identity issues that divide the two peoples are addressed in the negotiations and the public debates that surround them will play a major role in determining the quality and durability of the solution achieved at the negotiating table.

The Struggle over National Identity

Although national identity is carried by the individual members of a national group and can thus be studied as a property of individuals, the present chapter refers to it as a collective phenomenon—as a property of the group. "Insofar as a group of people have come to see themselves as constituting a unique, identifiable entity, with a claim to continuity over time, to unity across geographical distance, and to the right to various forms of self-expression, we can say that they have acquired a sense of national identity. National identity is the group's definition of itself as a group—its conception of its enduring characteristics and basic values; its strengths and weaknesses; its hopes and fears; its reputation and conditions of existence; its institutions and traditions; and its past history, current purposes, and future prospects" (Kelman, 1997a, p. 171; see also Kelman, 1998b).

In the Israeli-Palestinian and other such conflicts, the threat to collective identity is a core issue in the conflict, which is integrally related to the struggle over territory and resources. Both peoples and their national movements claim the same territory, and each seeks ownership of that territory and control over its resources as the basis of an independent state that gives political expression to its national identity. The integrity of this collective identity is critical to each group for several reasons. First, the integrity of the national identity is an end in itself, in that the identity serves as a source of distinctiveness, unity, and continuity for the group and of a sense of belongingness for its members. Second, the national identity constitutes the ultimate justification of the group's claim to ownership of the land and control of its resources. And third, the national identity provides a focus for developing and maintaining the group's distinctive culture, religion, and way of life. The collective identity of each group is bolstered by a national narrative—an account of the group's origins, its history, and its relationship to the land—that explains and supports its sense of distinctiveness, its positive self-image, and the justice of its claims and grievances.

In conflicts such as that between Israelis and Palestinians, in which the two sides live in the same space and claim ownership of the same territory, it is not only the actions of the other but also the identity and the very existence of the other that are a threat to the group's own identity. The other's identity and its associated narrative challenge the group's claims to ownership—at least to exclusive ownership—of the land and its resources. The other's presence in the same space, particularly if it is accompanied by demands for a share of the power and for recognition of the other culture, religion, and/or language, is perceived as a threat to the integrity and cohesiveness of the group's society and its way of life.

These dynamics lead to a view of the conflict as a zero-sum struggle, not only around territory but also around identity (Kelman, 1987). Acknowledging the other's identity becomes tantamount to jeopardizing the identity—and indeed the national existence—of one's own group. Each side "holds the view that only one can be a nation: Either we are or they are. *They* can acquire national identity and rights only at the expense of *our* identity and rights" (Kelman, 1987, p. 354). Thus, over the course of the Israeli-Palestinian conflict, there has been a systematic tendency on each side to deny the other's identity as a people, the authenticity of the other's links to the land, the legitimacy of the other's claims to national rights, and the very existence of the other as a national group (Kelman, 1978, 1982). Negation of the other's identity and of the narrative in which it is embedded becomes so important to the conflict that it is incorporated in the identity that each group constructs for itself and in the narrative that it presents to the world (Kelman, 1999).

The contrasting Israeli and Palestinian narratives about the creation of the State of Israel in 1948 both rely on the negation of the other to bolster the justice of their own cause. For Israelis, the creation of Israel represented a rightful return of the Jewish people to its ancestral homeland. Establishment of a Jewish state in Palestine did not, in their eyes, constitute an injustice to the Arabs who resided there, because Palestinian Arabs were not a people, distinct from the Arab inhabitants of surrounding countries, and never exercised sovereignty in Palestine. Moreover, in the Israeli narrative, the responsibility for the Palestinian refugee problem and the suffering of the Palestinian Arab population rests with their own aggressive and incompetent leadership, which rejected all compromise and initiated violent attacks in the effort to block the establishment of Israel. For Palestinians, by contrast, the creation of Israel represented an act of usurpation by European settlers, who forcefully displaced the indigenous population and destroyed their society, their property, and their way of life. In the Palestinian narrative, Jews are a religious group, not a nation entitled to its own state, and Zionism is a form of settler colonialism that imposed itself on a region in which it has no roots. Each identity gains some of its strength and legitimacy from negating and delegitimizing the other.

Identities that rest in part on negation of the other inevitably take on an exclusivist and monolithic character (Kelman, 1997b). In the Israeli-

Palestinian conflict, such exclusivist and monolithic definitions of identity have begun to give way in recent years. For significant segments of the two population, however—and in some respects even for large majorities—such definitions still prevail.

In the Israeli-Palestinian case, a defining element of each group's identity is its relationship to the land and its history. Insofar as this relationship is *exclusive*—that is, insofar as the group's identity rests on the view that the land and its history belong to it alone and that the other's claims on them as part of its own identity are illegitimate and inauthentic—there is little room for conflict resolution. Conflict resolution becomes an option when the parties accept the possibility that certain elements of identity may be *shared* with the other, acknowledging that the other also has a profound attachment to the land, anchored in authentic historical ties to it. Israelis and Palestinians have been gradually moving toward acceptance of shared elements of identity as they have been searching for a political formula for sharing the land. It has proved more difficult for the two sides, so far, to accept Jerusalem as a shared element of the two identities and to develop a political formula to reflect that view.

Identities that rest on negation of the other also take on a *monolithic* character; that is, all dimensions of the group's identity—such as ethnicity, religion, and language—tend to be viewed as highly correlated. The ideology calls for complete correspondence between ethnic boundaries, political boundaries, boundaries of emotional attachment, and boundaries of intensive interaction. Self and other are, in principle, completely separated along all of these lines. The Israeli-Palestinian conflict, as well as other protracted conflicts, particularly between identity groups living in close proximity within a small space (such as Northern Ireland or Cyprus), might be more amenable to resolution if there were some degree of disaggregation of the monolithic identity, based on distinctions between different types of boundaries. Such distinctions would allow for the development of a *transcendent* identity—not in place of the particular ethnonational identities, but alongside of them. In the Israeli-Palestinian case, a transcendent identity could be fostered by separating the concept of the state, as a sovereign political entity, from that of the country, as a geographical entity. This distinction would allow the two communities to treat the entire country (Eretz Yisrael or Palestine) as an object of common sentimental attachment and as the framework for common instrumental pursuits (in such areas as development and use of water resources, environmental protection, public health, and tourism), while living in and identifying with separate political states within that country.

The zero-sum view of identity and the mutual denial of the other's identity that I have described create serious obstacles to conflict resolution. All issues tend to become existential—matters of life and death for each side. Compromise solutions that involve sharing of the land or agreeing on different boundaries for different purposes are likely to threaten exclusivist and monolithic identities. The demonized other is not trusted to negotiate in good faith and respect agreements. In short, when acceptance of the other's national rights and recognition of the other's national identity are seen as relinquishing the group's own rights and jeopardizing its own identity, distributive solutions based on compromise are hard to achieve. Even if the parties agree to make certain compromises in response to reality demands and external pressures, these compromises are unlikely to lead to durable changes in the relationship between the conflicting groups, conducive to stable peace, mutually enhancing interaction, and ultimate reconciliation. Lasting change requires mutual adjustments in collective identity.

Identity Changes

The stubborn resistance to change in collective identities is widely recognized and taken for granted. Yet identities have to change, at least tacitly, if protracted identity conflicts are to be settled and, certainly, if they are to be resolved in a way that transforms the relationship and opens the way to reconciliation. South Africa provides perhaps the best illustration of an arena of intense, protracted conflict in which fundamental identity changes paved the way to resolution and reconciliation, although it also illustrates the difficulties in changing the worldviews and the structural realities that became entrenched in the apartheid era.

Despite their undeniable rigidities, identities are potentially changeable (and indeed negotiable) for two reasons: First, unlike territory and resources, they are not inherently zero-sum; though they are perceived and debated as such in intense conflicts, it is in fact not the case that A's identity can be recognized and expressed only if B's identity is denied and suppressed.

If the two identities are to become compatible, however, they have to be redefined. And this points to the second reason for the potential changeability of group identities: they can be redefined because they are to a large extent constructed. To view national identity as a social construction does not imply that it is manufactured out of nothing. There may be cases in which one can properly speak of an imagined past, invented to buttress a newly formed identity (cf. Anderson, 1983). Generally, however, the social construction of an identity draws on a variety of authentic elements held in common within a group: a common history, language, or religion; common customs, cultural expressions, experiences, values, grievances, aspirations (Kelman 1997b). Typically, the social construction of an identity involves a dual process of *discovery* (or rediscovery) and *creation* of such common elements (Kelman, 1997a). The social construction of the identity implies a degree of arbitrariness and flexibility in the way the identity is composed (which elements are admitted into it and which omitted from it), and in what its boundaries are (who is included and who is excluded). These choices depend on the opportunities and necessities perceived by the elites that are engaged in mobilizing ethnonational consciousness for their political, economic, or religious purposes (Kelman, 1997b). Serbs and Croats, for example, share a common language and culture, but differ in religion and historical experiences. Political leaders have at times focused on the similarities in the effort to shape them into a single nation; at other times they have magnified the differences to define them as separate—and mutually antagonistic—nations.

Thus, although national identities are generally constructed out of real experiences, these experiences can be ordered in different ways, resulting in different boundaries and priorities. As a consequence, they can be—and typically are—deconstructed and reconstructed. "In fact, the reconstruction of identity is a regular, ongoing process in the life of any national group. Identities are commonly reconstructed, sometimes gradually and sometimes radically, as historical circumstances change, crises emerge, opportunities present themselves, or new elites come to the fore" (Kelman, 1997b, p. 338). Clearly, therefore, there is room for maneuver in a group's self-definition, particularly with respect to the definition of group boundaries and the priorities among different elements of the group's identity.

Changes in identity over the course of a protracted conflict come about through a combination of changed perceptions of the *necessity* and the *possibility* of resolving a conflict that has become increasingly costly to the parties. The mounting costs and dwindling prospects of governing Algeria for the French, of maintaining apartheid for white South Africans, of the occupation of Palestinian territories for Israelis, and of the armed struggle for the Palestinians created the *necessity* for changes in identity: Algeria as an integral part of France, South Africa under exclusive white control, Israel within the borders of Greater Israel, and Palestinian repossession of the entire homeland were assigned lower priority in the national identities of these groups as it became clear to a majority that these aspirations could not be realized at an acceptable cost.

What made it *possible* to change these priorities was often the discovery that accommodation of the other's identity need not destroy the core of the group's own identity, and that a compromise solution to the conflict was therefore negotiable. This kind of learning can take place in the course of official or unofficial interactions between the groups or their members, including the problem-solving workshops that my colleagues and I have conducted: In the course of Israeli-Palestinian workshops, for example, participants have learned to differentiate their image of the enemy by discovering that there are potential negotiating partners on the other side, that there is a distinction between the other's ideological dreams and operational programs, and that the other has positive goals beyond destruction of their group (Kelman, 1987). They were enabled to enter into the enemy's perspective, thus discovering the historical sources of the other's claims and grievances, the depth of the other's fears, and the authenticity of the other's sense of peoplehood. They began to visualize a different future, discovering possibilities for mutually beneficial coexistence and cooperation. As such experiences multiply, and as the learnings produced by them are infused into the two political cultures, each group may gradually change its identity by eliminating the negation of the other's identity as an element of its own identity and perhaps even admitting the possibility of a partnership as a new element of its own identity.

Negotiating Identity

The changes I have described are often the result of an explicit or implicit process of negotiating identity. At its core, national identity is clearly non-negotiable; indeed, the very idea of negotiating identity sounds like an oxymoron. National identity is a collective psychological conception, which cannot be dictated or prescribed by outsiders. A group of people who define themselves as a nation cannot be told that they have no right to do so because their self-definition does not conform to some set of theoretical, juridical, or historical criteria for doing so, or because their nationhood is inconvenient to others. Nor does it make sense to tell them how to draw the boundaries of the group: whom to include and whom to exclude. People are a nation if they perceive themselves as such and are prepared to invest energy and make sacrifices in terms of that perception (Kelman, 1978). Neither Palestinians nor Israelis will give up the core of their identity: their sense of peoplehood, their attachment to the land, their conviction about the historical authenticity of their links to that land, their commitment to their national culture, language, and way of life. Nor will they give up the national narrative that substantiates the justice of their cause.

But there are many elements that can be added to or subtracted from an identity without jeopardizing its core. In fact, changes in less central elements of the identity are often advocated precisely in order to protect the core of the identity. It was on that basis that the majority of Israelis and Palestinians came to accept territorial compromise—that is, a shrinking of the territorial dimension of their identity—as the best available option for maintaining their national identity. The Peace Now movement in Israel, for example, advocated withdrawal from the occupied territories largely on the grounds that this was the only way in which Israel could maintain its character as both a Jewish state and a democratic state. Yehoshafat Harkabi (1986), a former chief of Israeli military intelligence and a prophetic voice in the debate about Israeli-Palestinian peace, explicitly advocated a "smaller Israel"—a "Zionism of quality" rather than a "Zionism of acreage." He argued that Israel had to choose between withdrawing from the West Bank and making way for a Palestinian state there, or annexing the West Bank with the consequence that Israel would eventually *become* a Palestinian state. On the Palestinian side, the territorial dimension of the Palestinian identity has gradually changed as the movement reflected on its realistic options. The thinking of the PLO evolved from advocacy of a Palestinian Arab state in the whole of Palestine, to a secular democratic state, and eventually to a Palestinian state alongside of Israel comprising the West Bank and Gaza (cf. Muslih, 1990). Significant segments of both societies still reject territorial compromise on religious or ideological grounds and link their national identity to possession of the land in its entirety. But the Palestinian and Israeli mainstreams have by now come to terms with a national identity that finds its political expression in only part of the land, as evidenced by the opinion polls that are now conducted on a regular basis in both societies.

Such changes in elements of identity are a legitimate subject for "negotiation" between groups whose identities clash, because the identity that one group chooses for itself has significant implications for the rights, interests, and identity of the other. Whenever one group translates the self-definition of its nationhood into action—"by making territorial claims, by demanding an independent state, by seeking to redraw borders, by declaring who is included in the national identity and who is excluded from it, or even by selecting a name for itself" (Kelman, 1997b, p. 337)—the other is inevitably affected. Each group, therefore, has a legitimate concern about the way the other defines itself, the way it formulates its national identity. It is not surprising, then, that identity issues play an important role in the formal and informal processes of pre-negotiation and negotiation—that is, in the efforts to open a way to the negotiating table and to reach agreement around the table.

To some extent, identity issues are part of the subject matter of the official negotiations. I have already referred to the territorial dimension of identity: insofar as Israelis and Palestinians are negotiating on the basis of a "land for peace" formula, they are accepting territorial limits to their national identities, which have, after all, been historically linked to the whole of the land. Similarly, the mutual recognition between Israel and the PLO, as expressed in the exchange of letters between Arafat and Rabin—which I have described above as the most important breakthrough of the Oslo agreement —can be viewed as a product of the negotiation of identity: an act of acceptance and legitimization of the other who in the past had been defined as the antithesis to the self.

Although redefined identities are thus promulgated around the official negotiating table, the "negotiation" of identity is primarily an informal, unofficial process in which members of the conflicting parties explore and invent ways of accommodating their group identities to one another. The purpose of negotiation in this looser sense of the term is not to produce political agreements, but to develop joint understandings and formulations that can help pave the road to political agreements at the official level. Implicitly and explicitly, this kind of "negotiation" has been a central focus for problem-solving workshops between Israelis and Palestinians that my colleagues and I have conducted over the past quarter-century.

Problem-Solving Workshops

Problem-solving workshops are the central instrument of *interactive problem solving*, an unofficial, third-party approach to the resolution of international and intercommunal conflicts, derived from the pioneering work of John Burton (1969, 1979, 1984) and anchored in social-psychological principles (see Kelman, 1972, 1979, 1992, 1998a). A workshop is a specially constructed, private space in which politically involved and often politically influential (but generally unofficial) members of conflicting communities can interact in a nonbinding, confidential way. The microprocess of the workshop provides them the opportunity to penetrate each other's perspective; to explore both sides' needs, fears, priorities, and constraints; and to engage in joint thinking about solutions to the conflict that would be responsive to the fundamental concerns of both sides.

Let me describe a typical "one-time" workshop for Israeli and Palestinian participants. By "one-time" I mean that this particular group of Israelis and Palestinians convenes only for this one occasion. Some of the individuals may have participated in more than one such workshop, and the one-time workshops that we have held over the years have had a cumulative effect within the two societies. But, until 1990, we made no effort to reconvene the same *group* of participants for another occasion. The workshops take place under academic auspices and are facilitated by a panel of social scientists knowledgeable about international conflict, group process, and the Middle East. The workshops usually begin with two pre-workshop sessions, about four hours in length, during which the third party meets separately with each of the two parties. The workshop itself typically lasts about two and a half days, often scheduled over an extended weekend. The participants include three to six Israelis and an equal number of Palestinians, plus a third party of three or more members.

The Israeli and Palestinian participants have included parliamentarians, leaders and activists of political parties or political movements, journalists, editors, directors of think tanks, and politically involved academicians—that is, scholars who not only publish academic papers but who also write for newspapers and appear in the media, who serve as advisors to political leaders, and some of whom move back and forth between government and academia. Some of our participants have been former diplomats, officials, or military officers, and many were later to become negotiators, ambassadors, cabinet ministers, parliamentarians, and leading figures in the media and research organizations. We look for people who are within the mainstream of their societies and close to the center of the political spectrum. At the same time, they have to be people who are at least willing to explore the possibility of a negotiated solution and to sit down as equals with members of the other party.

The central ground rule of problem-solving workshops is the principle of privacy and confidentiality. In the early days of our work, confidentiality was particularly important for the protection of our participants, because the mere fact that they were meeting with the enemy was controversial and exposed them to political and even physical risks. Confidentiality is equally important, however, for the protection of the process that we are trying to promote in workshops. We are trying to encourage the participants to talk and listen to each other, rather than focus on their constituencies, on third parties, or on the record. We want them to think out loud, to experiment with ideas, to explore different options, without having to worry about how others would react if their words in the group were quoted outside. We want them to engage in a type of interaction that is generally not feasible among parties engaged in a bitter conflict—a type of interaction that, indeed, deviates from the conflict norms that usually govern their behavior: an interaction that is analytic rather than polemical, one in which the parties seek to explore each other's perspective and gain insight into the causes and dynamics of the conflict; an interaction that is problem-solving rather than adversarial, one in which the parties sidestep the usual attempt to allocate blame and, instead, take the conflict as a shared problem that requires joint effort to find a mutually satisfactory solution.

The agenda of a problem-solving workshop is designed to allow this kind of interaction to unfold. The core agenda of a one-time workshop has four components. First, each side is asked to discuss its central concerns in the conflict—the fundamental needs that would have to be addressed and the existential fears that would have to be allayed if a solution is to be satisfactory to it. The parties are asked not to debate the issues raised, although they may ask for clarification of what the other says. The purpose is for each side to gain an adequate understanding of the other's needs, fears, and concerns, from the perspective of the other. Once they have demonstrated that they understand the other's needs to a significant degree, we move to the second phase of the agenda: joint thinking about possible solutions. What participants are asked to do in this phase is to develop, through an interactive process, ideas about the overall shape of a solution for the conflict as a whole, or perhaps, a particular issue in the conflict, that would address the needs and fears of both sides. They are given the difficult assignment of thinking of solutions that would meet not only their own side's needs, but the needs of both sides.

Once the participants have developed some common ground in this process of joint thinking, we turn to the third phase of the workshop: discussion of the political and psychological constraints within the two societies that would create barriers to carrying out the ideas for solution that have been developed in the group. We deliberately leave the discussion of constraints to the third phase, so that it does not hamper the creative process of jointly generating new ideas. Finally, depending on how much progress has been made and how much time is left, we ask the parties to engage in another round of joint thinking—this time about ways of overcoming the constraints that have been presented. The participants are asked to come up with ideas about what their governments, their societies, and they themselves might do—separately or jointly—that would help to overcome the barriers to negotiating mutually satisfactory solutions to the conflict.

The third party in our model enacts a strictly facilitative role. It does not propose solutions, nor does it participate in the substantive discussions. Its task is to create the conditions that allow ideas for resolving the conflict to emerge out of the interaction between the parties themselves. The facilitation of the third party, however, is an important part of the process. The third party sets the ground rules and monitors adherence to them; it helps to keep the discussion moving in constructive directions, tries to stimulate movement, and intervenes as relevant with questions, observations, and even challenges. It also serves as a repository of trust for parties who, by definition, do not trust each other: They feel safe to come to the workshop because they trust the third party to maintain confidentiality and to protect their interests.

Workshops have a dual purpose: to produce *changes*, in the form of new insights and ideas, in the individual participants; and to *transfer* these changes into the political process at the levels of both public opinion and decision making. These two purposes may at times create contradictory requirements—most notably in the selection of participants (Kelman, 1992). To balance these contradictory requirements, we look for participants who are not officials, but politically influential. They are thus more free to engage in the process but, at the same time, because of their positions within their societies, any new ideas that they develop in the course of a workshop can have an impact on the thinking of decision makers and the society at large.

The Israeli-Palestinian workshops we carried out until 1990 were all one-time events designed to create a climate conducive to movement to the negotiating table. In 1990, we organized our first continuing workshop, in which a group of high-level Israelis and Palestinians met periodically over a three-year period (Rouhana & Kelman, 1994). In 1994, Nadim Rouhana and I convened a Joint Working Group on Israeli-Palestinian Relations, which is still in progress.[2] For the first time in our program, this group has been engaged in producing jointly authored concept papers on some of the final-status issues in the Israeli-Palestinian negotiations and on the future relationship between the two societies. One of three papers that the group has published so far—a paper on the problem of Palestinian refugees and the right of return (Alpher & Shikaki, et al., 1999)—provides the starting point for my detailed illustration of the negotiation of identity, to be presented in the next section.

Much of the discussion in our workshops, from the beginning and until this day, has focused, in effect, on a process of negotiating collective identities. In our experience, such a process can be productive only if it is based on mutual respect for the core of the other's identity and on the principle of reciprocity. Each side must know that the other does not seek to undermine its group identity, and each must take care not to undermine the other's identity. And each must know that the risks it takes in acknowledging the other's claims, rights, and authenticity will be reciprocated by the other's acknowledgment of its claims, rights, and authenticity.

Starting from the understanding that neither side is prepared to negotiate the core of its identity—its peoplehood, its relationship to the land, the basic justice of its cause—or the general lines of its national narrative, there remain various elements of each group's identity that can be "negotiated" in the interest of mutual accommodation. Let me illustrate some of the possible changes in identity that can be and have been discussed in problem-solving workshops and similar encounters and that have, over time, begun to penetrate the Israeli and Palestinian political cultures.

1. Many members of both communities have become able to remove the negation of the other's identity as an integral part of their own identity. Though the other may still be seen as an obstacle to achieving one's own national goals, the other is not as often seen as the antithesis of one's own identity whose demise is a condition for one's own survival. Thus, many Israelis have come to accept the reality of Palestinian peoplehood, particularly after observing Palestinians' readiness to make sacrifices for their national cause during the *intifada* and Palestinians' celebration of the signing of the Oslo agreement in September 1993. Interestingly, Israelis saw parallels between these events and their own struggle for statehood and celebration at attaining it—a significant degree of identification with the other whose existence had previously been denied. Many Palestinians, on their part, now recognize the right of Israelis to their state, on the grounds that the state has existed for over half a century and that its dismantlement would create a new injustice to the generations that were born into it. Very few Palestinians, on the other hand, are prepared to acknowledge the historical links of Jews to the land, which might be seen as justification for the establishment of the Jewish state in the first place.

2. We have seen signs of softening of the exclusiveness of group identity, which allows for the recognition that—despite the validity of one's own claims—the other too has valid claims. The recognition of elements of identity shared with the other, such as a common identification with the land, opens the way to political solutions based on sharing territory and resources. In a recent workshop, for example, mainstream Israelis and Palestinians were able to agree—much to everyone's surprise, including their own—on a formula for sharing Jerusalem: a united city containing the capitals of both states. Public opinion polls on both sides also suggest greater willingness to share Jerusalem than had been widely assumed (Segal, 1999).

3. Workshop participants have experimented with disaggregating the monolithic nature of their identities, recognizing that there are different boundaries of group identity (such as ethnic boundaries, political boundaries, boundaries of sentimental attachment) that do not necessarily coincide. This recognition opens the way to the development of transcendent

identities, which might allow the two peoples to maintain a common attachment to the country while "owning" only part of that country as their political state. The concept of a "united country with divided sovereignties" was discussed in one of our workshops in the early 1980s. In a more recent workshop, the idea of establishing different kinds of boundaries was explored in the attempt to find solutions to the problem of Israeli settlements in the areas in which Palestinians hope to establish their state.

4. Workshop discussions can help to identify outdated elements of group identity, which refer to maximalist goals and dreams of glory or self-aggrandizing images that have no current political relevance but poison the climate for conflict resolution. Examples here might be Palestinian references to the armed struggle as the way to eliminate the Zionist entity, or Israeli references to the Zionist project of making the desert bloom. Workshops have often sensitized participants to words and images that humiliate and frighten the other and could be discarded with minimal cost to group identity.

5. In the course of workshop discussions, participants may decide to reorder the priorities within their national identities, such that certain elements (e.g., territorial ambitions), which may not have been given up but have become too costly to pursue, are relegated to low priority and thus become available for negotiated compromise. Thus, over time, Palestinians (in our workshops and in the larger society) decided to give priority to ending occupation and establishing a Palestinian state over recovering the lost land in its entirety. Israelis gave priority to maintaining the Jewish character of Israel over controlling the whole of the land.

6. Finally, workshop participants may "negotiate" changes in national narratives that accommodate the other's view of history as much as possible, such as accepting a share of the responsibility for the course of the conflict. The above-mentioned concept paper of our current Joint Working Group on Israeli-Palestinian Relations on "The Palestinian refugee problem and the right of return" (Alpher & Shikaki, et al., 1999) provides a good illustration of such an effort to negotiate identity. I shall conclude this chapter with a more detailed discussion of this concept paper, trying to show what made it possible to achieve common ground in this effort, what still remains to be done, and possible directions for achieving further progress.

The Problem of Palestinian Refugees

From the point of view of the struggle over national identity, the problem of Palestinian refugees is probably the most important and the most difficult issue to resolve in the Israeli-Palestinian conflict. It may ultimately be more important and more difficult than the issue of Jerusalem, because it bears directly on the contrasting views of the justice or injustice of the establishment of Israel presented by the two national narratives.

The problem of Palestinian refugees goes back to the 1948 war that followed the declaration of an independent State of Israel. In the course of that war, somewhere between 600,000 and 760,000 Palestinian Arabs—about half of the Arab population of mandatory Palestine—were displaced from their homes in what became the State of Israel (Morris, 1987, pp. 297–298). They were turned into refugees and most of them and/or their descendants remain refugees to this day. The precise number of Palestinian refugees today is in dispute. The figure given by UNRWA—the United Nations Relief and Works Agency, which is charged with the welfare of Palestinian refugees—is almost three and a half million (as of January 1998). This number includes Palestinians who registered as refugees with UNRWA after losing their homes in 1948, as well as their descendants. The majority of this population lives in refugee camps in Gaza, the West Bank, Jordan, Lebanon, and Syria. Palestinian refugees in Lebanon (some 350,000) and Syria (some 300,000) by and large remain stateless, as do many Palestinians living elsewhere in the Arab world.

Palestinians and Israelis have differed sharply in their account of the Palestinian exodus in 1948. According to the Palestinian narrative, "the Arab refugees were forcibly expelled by Jewish forces or left in a panic flight to escape massacre and . . . they were helped on their way by occasional massacres, committed by Jewish forces to keep them running" (Alpher & Shikaki, et al., 1999, p. 173). According to some Israeli accounts, the Arab population was urged by its own leaders to leave their homes in anticipation of an early return after the defeat of the Jewish forces by the Arab armies. The more recent writings of Israeli "revisionist historians" (e.g., Morris, 1987) support the claim that there were indeed some systematic efforts by Jewish forces to expel the Arab population at various times and places. No doubt, a combination of circumstances created refugees in a war that was fought in the midst of the country's towns and villages.

How the refugee problem is ultimately resolved raises major practical and symbolic issues for both sides that reach to the core of their respective identities. By *practical* issues, I refer to those relating to the *implementation* of any agreement on the refugees—that is, to the concrete steps that will be taken to deal with the plight of the current refugee population. By *symbolic* issues, I refer to those relating to the *principle* of the right of return of the refugees to their original homes.

At the practical level, Palestinians are concerned with normalizing the status of the refugees to the satisfaction of the individual Palestinians involved and of the entire Palestinian community. Normalization of the status of individual refugees could take any one or combination of the following forms: return to Israel (perhaps their original homes, where that is still feasible), return to the Palestinian state, financial compensation, resettlement in a country outside of Palestine, integration with citizenship in the state in which they are now living, or Palestinian citizenship and permanent status in the state in which they are now living. The options offered to the refugees must be such as to satisfy the entire Palestinian community that the final peace agreement was not achieved at the expense of any part of that community.

At the symbolic level, Palestinians are asking for an Israeli acknowledgment of the right of return as a matter of principle, even if they are prepared to compromise on the implementation of that right. From the Palestinian perspective, Israeli acknowledgment of the right of return presupposes admission of direct moral responsibility for the plight of the refugees. Such an acknowledgment and admission would confirm the Palestinian narrative about the consequences for the Palestinian people of the Zionist enterprise, of Jewish settlement in Palestine, and of the establishment of Israel. In confirming the Palestinian narrative, such an acknowledgment would also recognize the Palestinian national rights that are anchored in this narrative. There seem to be two interrelated, but separable, reasons for Palestinians' emphasis on this symbolic issue. Psychologically, they need an Israeli acknowledgment that Palestinians have a right to return to the homes from which they were wrongfully displaced, in order to satisfy their sense of justice and be able to let go of the conflict. Politically, they need this acknowledgment to support the validity of their claims (such as claims for compensation) in the bargaining that lies ahead.

For Israelis, too, major practical and symbolic issues are at stake in the resolution of the refugee problem. At the practical level, Israelis are primarily concerned with the impact of a return of Palestinians in large numbers to Israel proper (i.e., to Israel within its pre-1967 borders). A large-scale return of refugees (beyond a symbolic number of up to 100,000) would be disruptive to the society because it would raise many divisive questions about the ownership of homes, villages, and other properties that have changed hands or been destroyed after the 1948 events. To what precise destination would refugees return whose former houses are now inhabited by Jewish families or whose homes or villages no longer exist? Furthermore, and most centrally, Israelis are concerned about the impact of a large-scale return of Palestinians to Israel on the demographic balance and the Jewish character of the state. In short, they see a large-scale return of refugees to Israel proper as creating an existential threat to Israel by undermining the Jewish majority and the viability and stability of the state. There is also concern among Israelis about a mass return of refugees to the future Palestinian state because of the impact on the stability and economy of that state, but this concern is shared by the Palestinians themselves, who are at least as mindful as Israelis about the absorptive capacity of the Palestinian state.

At the symbolic level, Israelis have serious concerns about acknowledging the principle of a Palestinian right of return, even if Palestinians agree that this right will not be implemented through a large-scale return of refugees to Israel proper. Acknowledgment of that principle is particularly troubling, from the Israeli perspective, if it entails admission of moral re-

sponsibility for the plight of the refugees. Such an acknowledgment and admission would undermine the Israeli narrative about the rightful return of
the Jewish people to its ancestral homeland, the establishment of the State
of Israel, the Arab rejection of partition and attack on the new state, and the
resulting refugee problem. Again, there seem to be two reasons for Israelis'
stance on this symbolic issue and, in particular, for their reluctance to accept direct moral responsibility for the plight of the refugees. Psychologically, they are not willing to accept a national self-image that negates the
righteousness of their cause and implies that Israel was "born in sin." Politically, they are concerned that accepting the principle of the right of
return and moral responsibility for the refugee problem would keep the
issue open, even after a peace agreement has been signed, and make Israel
vulnerable to future claims.

Our Joint Working Group on Israeli-Palestinian Relations discussed, in
considerable detail, the divergent narratives of the two communities; the
fundamental needs, fears, and concerns of each community that would have
to be addressed if a solution of the problem of Palestinian refugees is to be
acceptable to each; and the general principles that must underlie such a solution. The joint concept paper that finally emerged from the group's discussion (Alpher & Shikaki, et al., 1999) starts with a review of the two narratives, of the basic needs of each side, and of the principles that must
govern a solution. It then proceeds to present four possible solutions to the
refugee/right of return issue. Solutions 1 and 2 reflect the traditional positions—conceivably, the opening negotiating positions—of the Palestinian
and Israeli sides, respectively. Solutions 3 and 4 are compromise solutions,
from a Palestinian and an Israeli standpoint, respectively. These two solutions represent serious efforts, on the part of each side—based on intensive
discussions within the group—to come up with a compromise that would
accommodate the concerns of the other side without jeopardizing its own
vital interests. The paper discusses the advantages and disadvantages of
each solution, highlights the areas of agreement between solutions 3 and 4
as well as the remaining gaps between the two sides, and points to possible
ways in which these gaps might be bridged.

Solutions 3 and 4 represent a considerable narrowing of the gap between
the two sides when compared to the opening positions of solutions 1 and 2.
Still, there remains a significant gap between the two positions, particularly
with respect to the symbolic issues that divide the two sides. Solution 3 calls
for an Israeli acknowledgment of the moral right of Palestinians to return
to their homes based on Israel's acceptance of responsibility for creating the
refugee problem (although it recognizes that the actual exercise of the right
of return would be limited). Solution 4, the Israeli compromise proposal,
acknowledges that Israel shares practical (but not moral) responsibility for
the plight of the refugees, and accepts the right of return to the Palestinian
state, but not to Israel proper (although it agrees to the return of a limited
number of refugees to Israel).

The third party tried very hard to encourage the participants to bridge the remaining gaps between solutions 3 and 4 and try to come up with a joint solution 5—a compromise of the compromises, as it were. We did not succeed in this effort, however. In part, further movement toward a joint position on the symbolic issues was blocked by the great difficulty of the assignment. We were dealing here with issues that reached to the core of each group's identity and associated narrative. For Israelis to acknowledge anything more than shared practical responsibility for the refugee problem and for Palestinians to accept anything less than an Israeli acknowledgment of moral responsibility would undermine their respective narratives, and most members of the group were not prepared to go that far. Furthermore, at least some of the participants may have preferred to leave the final bridging of the gap between the two sides to the official negotiators. Since that final bridging would inevitably entail large concessions on one or both sides, they may have felt that it could best be done in the context of an overall agreement, where concessions on the refugee issue could be made with appropriate trade-offs on other issues.

Even though the Joint Working Group did not come up with a joint solution to the refugee problem, the concept paper that it produced represents a significant contribution to the final negotiation of this issue. The publication of the paper is in itself significant, in that it is the joint product of a group of politically mainstream and influential Israelis and Palestinians, who worked on it over the course of two years and agreed to make it public. It is also significant that the Israeli and Palestinian authors of the paper explicitly premise their discussion on the assumption of a two-state solution, advocating the establishment of a viable, independent Palestinian state. In the paper, each group recognizes the other's narrative, without abandoning its own. The different options for resolving the refugee problem are evaluated in terms of their success in addressing the fundamental needs and fears of each side. What emerged from this effort is a considerable narrowing of the gap between the two sides, even though the paper does not entirely bridge that gap. Solutions 3 and 4 represent substantial movement from the initial positions reflected in solutions 1 and 2—movement based on each side's sincere attempt to accommodate the basic concerns of the other.

With respect to the practical issues—that is, the actual implementation of the right of return—the gap between the two sides was substantially narrowed in the Working Group's paper. "Solutions 3 and 4 concur that, at the practical level, the core of the solution involves four components: a 'return,' however defined, of a limited number of refugees to Israel proper; return of a larger number to the Palestinian state; permanent absorption in host countries (notably Jordan); and compensation. Both sides agree that a successfully negotiated solution should close the file on the refugee issue" (Alpher & Shikaki, et al., 1999, p. 184). The two solutions disagree about some important details. For example, the Israelis frame the limited return of refugees to Israel proper as part of a program of family reunification, whereas the Palestinians frame it as part of the exercise of the right of return. With regard to compensation, solution 3 calls for both collective and individual compensation for the refugees' losses, whereas solution 4 calls for collective compensation only. Furthermore, solution 4 stipulates a similar mechanism of collective compensation for Jewish refugees from Arab countries (albeit without an operational link to the compensation of Palestinian refugees), whereas solution 3 eschews any such linkage. These differences clearly require further negotiation. But what is important is that the two solutions agree on the crucial practical issues of implementing the right of return: Palestinians concede that there will be no large-scale return of refugees to Israel proper; and Israelis accept the refugees' right of return to the Palestinian state, agreeing to leave it up to Palestinian authorities to control the inflow of refugees in accord with the state's absorptive capacity.

With respect to the symbolic issues—those relating to the principle of the right of return—the concept paper represents significant movement toward a mutually acceptable formulation, although there is still a wide gap between the two positions. Solution 4, the Israeli compromise statement, acknowledges that Israel "shares practical (but not moral) responsibility, together with the other parties to the process that culminated in the 1948 war, for the plight and suffering of the refugees, and that rectification of that plight by all parties is a central goal of the Arab-Israeli peace process" (Alpher & Shikaki, et al., 1999, p. 181). This statement comes closer than past statements by mainstream Israelis to acknowledging the suffering of the Palestinian refugees and accepting a share of the responsibility for it, and thus beginning to address the Palestinians' sense of justice. The movement reflected in this statement was generated by an intensive process of negotiating identity within the Working Group. Though it represents significant movement, this acknowledgment is not sufficient to meet the Palestinians' call for full Israeli acknowledgment of the *principle* of the right of return, based on acceptance of direct *moral* responsibility for the plight of the refugees. Solutions 3 and 4, thus, still remain far apart at the symbolic level. This remaining gap is understandable in that the two solutions, though they represent serious efforts at compromise, have their point of departure in two sharply clashing national narratives. The question is whether it might be possible to bridge that remaining gap through a further process of negotiating identity.

Closing the gap at the symbolic level is clearly difficult because of the sharp clash in national narratives that gives rise to it. Neither party can be expected to give up the core of its narrative in the course of the current negotiations; it is likely to take several generations before such changes can occur. But it *is* possible, as part of the process of negotiation and reconciliation, for the parties to make changes in how they formulate their narratives, where they place their emphasis, how they present the other within their own narratives, and what they require by way of acknowledgment or validation of their narratives. Such changes at the edges of the narratives can potentially be "negotiated," in the sense of being explored and jointly formulated by the parties in a spirit of mutual accommodation.

Thus, in the case of the right of return, we can assume that Palestinians will not abandon their conviction that they have a moral right to return to the homes from which they feel they were wrongfully displaced by the Israelis, and that Israelis will not admit guilt for the plight of the refugees. The question is whether it is possible to jointly formulate an Israeli acknowledgment that would be substantially responsive to what Palestinians need to hear about the right of return without requiring either side to abandon these core elements of their narratives. In the terms of my summary, toward the beginning of this section, of the symbolic issues that the refugee problem raises for the two sides, the question would be: Can the parties formulate an Israeli acknowledgment that would provide significant (though probably not total) satisfaction of Palestinians' sense of justice and validation of their claims for restitution, without requiring Israelis to negate the righteousness of their cause and making them vulnerable to future claims?

Let me offer three possible approaches to answering this question, which can be seen as three steps in the negotiation of identity that might further narrow the gap between the two sides manifested in solutions 3 and 4.

First, it may be possible to *redefine the conception of responsibility* in a way that would not imply guilt and thus be acceptable to the Israeli public, and yet be viewed by Palestinians as confirming their narrative, validating their claims, and satisfying their sense of justice. One possibility here is for Israel to accept a degree of causal responsibility without necessarily accepting guilt. An Israeli acknowledgment might, for example, describe the refugee problem as a tragic and unjust outcome of a historical process that arose with the establishment of the State of Israel. It might go on to say that, while there are disagreements about the precise historical events and the distribution of blame, Israel acknowledges that it was an active participant in this historical process and, indeed, a beneficiary of it, and thus bears part of the responsibility for these events. The statement might conclude with an offer of compensation as an expression of that responsibility. A statement of this kind clearly implies causal responsibility without explicitly acknowledging guilt. It thus has the potential, if properly fine tuned, of an acknowledgment consistent with both the Palestinian and the Israeli narratives.

Second, it may be possible to *find a mutually acceptable moral basis for the right of return*, which satisfies Palestinians' need for an Israeli acknowledgment of the right of return as a moral principle without linking that moral right to the refugees' original homes in Israel. One approach here would be to anchor the moral basis for the right of return in return to Palestine: Israelis might acknowledge the Palestinians' *moral* right to return to *Palestine*, based on the proposition that both peoples have legitimate claims to the land and that sharing the land (by establishing two states within it) is, therefore, a just solution to the conflict. Although the two sides differ in their views of the justice and injustice of the events of 1948, the two-state solution allows them to develop a shared view of justice for the future. Israeli acknowledgment of the refugees' moral right to return to Palestine, while not fully addressing Palestinians' sense of justice, would do so to a significant degree. It would also strengthen the validity of Palestinian claims by confirming (in a context of reciprocity) Palestinian national identity and rootedness in the land. For Israelis, anchoring the moral basis for the refugees' right of return in return to Palestine, rather than to their original homes, would greatly reduce their concerns about future claims, even though it may not entirely eliminate them.

Third, in conjunction with the two approaches just discussed and possible other approaches to narrowing the gap between the two sides at the symbolic level, it may be possible for each side to find ways to *affirm the identity of the other.* Such affirmations, perhaps in the form of acknowledgments that the other has integral links to the land and national rights, could compensate each side for the concessions they make to resolve the refugee issue: the Israelis for the risks they take in accepting causal responsibility for the plight of the refugees, and the Palestinians for accepting something less than the right of the refugees to return to their original homes. Affirmation of the other's identity can take place only in the context of a process of negotiating identity, based on the principle of reciprocity, in which each side learns to uncouple negation of the other from affirmation of the self. Each can affirm the other's identity to the extent that it feels assured that it is not thereby jeopardizing its own identity and its own claims.

The three approaches to narrowing the remaining gap between the Israeli and Palestinian positions in our Working Group's paper on the problem of refugees all represent efforts to negotiate identity. As such, they search for ways whereby each group can accommodate the narrative of the other without undermining its own narrative. In such a process, each group is encouraged to affirm or protect the identity of the other if, in turn, its own identity is protected or affirmed. Each may be willing to grant something more to the other than it was originally prepared to offer, or receive something less from the other than it originally demanded, in return for a substantial concession by the other at the symbolic level.

Conclusion

In the Israeli-Palestinian conflict, as in other protracted ethnic conflicts, the ever-present disputes over territory, resources, and political control are exacerbated by perceived threats to national identity and national existence that underlie the actions and reactions of the opposing communities. Threats to identity and existence create obstacles to the settlement of conflicts, even when both parties have concluded that a compromise agreement is in their best interest. Moreover, even when specific issues in conflict are settled and political agreements signed—often with the mediation of powerful third parties—these agreements may not lead to stable peace, fruitful cooperation, and ultimate reconciliation between the two parties, unless they have formed a new relationship based on mutual respect for their national identities.

The experience of my colleagues and myself in problem-solving workshops on the conflicts in Israel/Palestine, Cyprus, Sri Lanka, and Northern Ireland, and experiences with similar efforts in other parts of the world, support the central argument of this chapter about the role of national identity in intercommunal conflict and conflict resolution. A central feature of such deep-rooted, protracted conflicts is the struggle over national identity between the two parties, which leads them to perceive their conflict in zero-sum terms, not only with respect to territory and resources, but also with respect to national identity and national existence. Long-term resolution of such conflicts and reconciliation between the former enemies requires changes in the groups' national identities; in particular, they require a redefinition of each group's identity so that affirmation of its own identity is no longer predicated on negation of the identity of the other. Such identity changes are possible, provided they leave the core of each group's identity and national narrative—its sense of peoplehood, its attachment to the land, its commitment to the national language, culture, and way of life—intact. Furthermore, such changes must and can be "negotiated" between the two groups. It is possible for the groups to accommodate their national identities and the surrounding narratives to one another, as long as each respects and acknowledges the other's peoplehood and thus reassures the other that the core of its identity will not be jeopardized by changes in the periphery. Although some negotiation of identity takes place around the negotiating table, it is primarily a process that must engage the entire body politic on each side, at all levels and through different media. Problem-solving workshops provide a specially constructed arena for engaging in this process and jointly developing new insights and formulations that can be injected into the public debate and can penetrate the political culture on both sides.

A central lesson from our experience is that national identity, though very much part of the problem in ethnic conflicts, can also become part of the solution. The way we talk about our identity affects the way we think about it and ultimately the way we act on it. In groups that are caught up in protracted conflict, identity depends on the conflict and is shaped by the conflict: Many elements of identity are constructed as vehicles for pursuing the conflict. It should be possible, within limits, to reconstruct these elements as vehicles for peace and reconciliation. What is needed is an investment of identity in conflict resolution and in a new relationship with the former enemy. Development of such a new, transcendent identity confronts many obstacles. It cannot bypass the political process of negotiating a mutually acceptable agreement, nor can it be allowed to threaten or undermine the particularistic identity of each group. But within these constraints, the potential for reconstructing the national identities of former enemies in the service of peace and reconciliation exists and needs to be nurtured.

Notes

1. The work reported here is carried out under the auspices of the Program on International Conflict Analysis and Resolution (PICAR), which I direct at the Weatherhead Center for International Affairs, Harvard University. I am grateful to the Center for providing a home for PICAR, to the William and Flora Hewlett Foundation for providing financial support for PICAR over a number of years; and to Donna Hicks, Nadim Rouhana, and my other PICAR colleagues.

2. I am grateful to the organizations that have provided financial support for the Joint Working Group over the years: the Nathan Cummings Foundation, the Carnegie Corporation, the Ford Foundation, the Charles R. Bronfman Foundation, the U.S. Information Agency, and the William and Flora Hewlett Foundation, as well as the Renner Institut in Vienna and the Weatherhead Center for International Affairs.

References

Alpher, J., & Shikaki, K., with the participation of the additional members of the Joint Working Group on Israeli-Palestinian Relations (1999). Concept paper: The Palestinian refugee problem and the right of return. *Middle East Policy, 6* (3), 167-189. (Originally published as *Weatherhead Center for International Affairs Working Paper No. 98-7.* Cambridge, MA: Harvard University, 1998.)

Anderson, B. (1983). *Imagined communities: Reflections on the origins and spread of nationalism.* London: Verso.

Burton, J. W. (1969). *Conflict and communication: The use of controlled communication in international relations.* London: Macmillan.

Burton, J. W. (1979). *Deviance, terrorism and war: The process of solving unsolved social and political problems.* New York: St. Martin's Press.

Burton, J. W. (1984). *Global conflict: The domestic sources of international crisis.* Brighton, England: Wheatsheaf.

Gerner, D. J. (1991). *One land, two peoples: The conflict over Palestine.* Boulder, CO: Westview Press.

Halpern, B. (1969). *The idea of a Jewish state* (2nd ed.). Cambridge, MA: Harvard University Press.

Harkabi, Y. (1986). *Israel's fateful hour.* New York: Harper & Row.

Hertzberg, A. (1973). *The Zionist idea.* New York: Atheneum.

Kelman, H. C. (1972). The problem-solving workshop in conflict resolution. In R.L. Merritt (Ed.), *Communication in international politics* (pp. 168–204). Urbana: University of Illinois Press.

Kelman, H. C. (1978). Israelis and Palestinians: Psychological prerequisites for mutual acceptance. *International Security, 3,* 162–186.

Kelman, H.C. (1979). An interactional approach to conflict resolution and its application to Israeli-Palestinian relations. *International Interactions, 6,* 99–122.

Kelman, H. C. (1982). Creating the conditions for Israeli-Palestinian negotiations. *Journal of Conflict Resolution, 26,* 39–75.

Kelman, H. C. (1987). The political psychology of the Israeli-Palestinian conflict: How can we overcome the barriers to a negotiated solution? *Political Psychology, 8,* 347–363.

Kelman, H. C. (1988, Spring). The Palestinianization of the Arab-Israeli conflict. *The Jerusalem Quarterly, 46,* 3–15.

Kelman, H.C. (1992). Informal mediation by the scholar/practitioner. In J. Bercovitch & J. Rubin (Eds.), *Mediation in international relations: Multiple approaches to conflict management* (pp. 64–96). New York: St. Martin's Press.

Kelman, H. C. (1995). Contributions of an unofficial conflict resolution effort to the Israeli-Palestinian breakthrough. *Negotiation Journal, 11,* 19–27.

Kelman, H. C. (1997a). Nationalism, patriotism, and national identity: Social-psychological dimensions. In D. Bar-Tal & E. Staub (Eds.), *Patriotism in the lives of individuals and nations* (pp. 165–189). Chicago: Nelson-Hall.

Kelman, H. C. (1997b). Negotiating national identity and self-determination in ethnic conflicts: The choice between pluralism and ethnic cleansing. *Negotiation Journal, 13,* 327–340.

Kelman, H. C. (1997c). Some determinants of the Oslo breakthrough. *International Negotiation, 2,* 183–194.

Kelman, H. C. (1997d). Group processes in the resolution of international conflicts: Experiences from the Israeli-Palestinian case. *American Psychologist, 52,* 212–220.

Kelman, H. C. (1998a). Social-psychological contributions to peacemaking and peacebuilding in the Middle East. *Applied Psychology: An International Review, 47*(1), 5–28.

Kelman, H. C. (1998b). The place of ethnic identity in the development of personal identity: A challenge for the Jewish family. In P. Y. Medding (Ed.), *Coping with life and death: Jewish families in the twentieth century (Studies in Contemporary Jewry XIV) (pp. 3–26).* Oxford: Oxford University Press.

Kelman, H. C. (1999). The interdependence of Israeli and Palestinian identities: The role of the other in existential conflicts. *Journal of Social Issues, 55*(3), 581–600.

Khalidi, R. (1997). *Palestinian identity: The construction of a modern national consciousness.* New York: Columbia University Press.

Mendelsohn, E. (1989). *A compassionate peace: A future for Palestine, Israel, and the Middle East* (rev. ed.). New York: Farrar, Straus & Giroux.

Morris, B. (1987). *The birth of the Palestinian refugee problem, 1947-1949.* Cambridge: Cambridge University Press.

Muslih, M. (1988). *The origins of Palestinian nationalism.* New York: Columbia University Press.

Muslih, M. (1990). Towards coexistence: An analysis of the resolutions of the Palestine National Council. *Journal of Palestine Studies, 19* (4), 3–29.

Rouhana, N. N., & Kelman, H. C. (1994). Promoting joint thinking in international conflicts: An Israeli-Palestinian continuing workshop. *Journal of Social Issues, 50* (1), 157–178.

Segal, J. M. (1999). Defining Jerusalem. *Middle East Insight, 14* (1), 27–28, 51–54.

Tessler, M. (1994). *A history of the Israeli-Palestinian conflict.* Bloomington and Indianapolis: Indiana University Press.

Richard D. Ashmore
Lee Jussim
David Wilder
Jessica Heppen

9

Conclusion

Toward a Social Identity Framework for Intergroup Conflict

We began this volume with two goals: (1) to review and organize social scientific knowledge, across several disciplines, about social identity and intergroup conflict; (2) to set the stage for future work by highlighting the theories, concepts, and methods with the most promise. These goals provide the basic structure for this concluding chapter. First, we take a look back: we summarize the chapters, distill the major points, and identify areas of agreement and disagreement. Second, we take a look forward: again drawing from the preceding chapters, we present a framework that highlights the ideas that we feel should be the highest priority as we and other social and behavioral scientists attempt to construct a more comprehensive and coherent social identity perspective on intergroup conflict.

A Look Back

As noted in the introductory chapter, the authors were given considerable freedom in how they carried out their task, and this shows in the types of contributions they have produced. Both chapters in Part I are conceptual analyses; however, Brewer presents a general theory, whereas Eriksen uses conflicts in three societies to illustrate his key points. In Part II, the chapters by Citrin, Wong, and Duff and Sidanius and Petrocik report empirical investigations, both based on survey data. In Part III, White presents a detailed analysis of the group-based violence in Northern Ireland, while Staub describes the place of self and identity within a general framework for understanding genocide. In the single chapter in Part IV, Kelman delineates the ways in which national identity is involved in problem-solving work-shops designed to help ameliorate the Israeli-Palestinian conflict. We turn now to a more in depth review of these chapters.

Although both Brewer and Eriksen present conceptual analyses, there are clear differences between these contributions. Brewer details a very tight theory addressing a very specific question, When does ingroup love become outgroup hate? This theory is stated in the most general and abstract form and is similar to the grand hypothetico-deductive theories of learning in the 1940s (e.g., Hull, 1943) and to social psychological models of the 1950s (e.g., Festinger's theories of communication [1950], social comparison [1954], and cognitive dissonance [1957]). And, as is true of this latter group of conceptual frameworks, it is individualistic in orientation, focusing on the thoughts and feelings of individuals, though admittedly in a complex social environment. Further, the model seeks support and testing primarily in laboratory experiments.

Brewer begins with Sumner's notion of ethnocentrism: social groups exist in a state of war with one another, and, as a consequence, ingroup love and outgroup hate are functionally interconnected sentiments necessary for group survival. Brewer, however, suggests that Sumner's theory can be decomposed into four separate propositions: (1) social categorization—individuals and groups partition the social world into categories, and this categorization involves ingroup assimilation and outgroup contrast, which make social categories more distinct in individual and collective representations than in reality; (2) ingroup positivity—given that self is a member of some groups and that self is positively valued, there is a tendency to view one's group (the ingroup) as good; (3) intergroup comparison—individuals compare their group to other groups, which can lead to judgments, not just that we are good but also that we are better than other groups; (4) outgroup hostility—the preceding steps, *together with certain additional conditions*, lead people to hate an outgroup and actively work to harm it. Brewer suggests that these four propositions are not highly correlated, as Sumner argued, but instead constitute a progression of possible relations between ingroup orientations and feelings about, and behavior toward, the outgroup.

Brewer further proposes that social categorization and ingroup positivity are likely universal. She also draws an important implication from the latter principle. Much discrimination is driven by ingroup positivity and is, thus, *favoritism for* one's own group, rather than *discrimination against* an outgroup. She presents laboratory experimental evidence in favor of this proposal. She also notes that an important task for future research will be to develop ways of disentangling pro-ingroup from anti-outgroup discrimination in real-world settings.

This raises the question that Brewer began with, When does ingroup love (and "discrimination for us") turn to outgroup hate (and "discrimination against them")? Brewer argues that it is not "realistic, objective conflict" that provides the significant impetus. Rather, she suggests that the answer lies within her optimal distinctiveness theory of social identity, which she links to evolutionary theory. Her argument is that humans evolved, not as isolated individuals or even in families, but instead as members of larger social groups. To allow the individual to learn from and cooperate with others, humans had to trust other people. However, to trust all others would be dangerous. Thus, human beings developed the propensity to trust all others *within their group* ("depersonalized trust"). When groups encounter one another, each operating according to this same orientation gives rise to universal ingroup-outgroup stereotypes: "we" are close knit and cooperative; "they" are clannish and treacherous.

The final ingredient in the progression to outgroup hate is provided by emotions. When members of different groups interact, they feel uncomfortable with one another and misattribute this negative emotional state to "*They* are_____." Under conditions of limited contact and little social mixing, the dominant emotions are likely to be contempt ("They are inferior and repugnant"), and this should motivate distancing (Karen Horney's "moving away from" [Ashmore, 1970]). However, under conditions of close contact and possible integration, people will likely feel invaded, and this will give rise to anger and fear ("They are violent and dangerous"). According to Brewer, it is these social conditions and associated feelings and attributions that turn ingroup love into outgroup hate and produce group-based harm-doing (Horney's "moving against").

In contrast to Brewer's development of a general theory of group identification and intergroup conflict with most evidence provided by laboratory research, Eriksen is concerned with identity politics, especially how social, especially ethnic, identities are manipulated by political elites, and experienced and enacted by everyday citizens, in real-world ethnic conflicts. Accordingly, his data are not from controlled experiments, but rather are case studies of three actual "ethnic conflicts," though it is clear from his analysis that he would not accept this label. Eriksen builds his case, not by a step-by-step elaboration of a small set of ordered propositions as Brewer does, but instead by first describing the current position in cultural anthropology concerning ethnicity and its implications for intergroup conflict. This position essentially argues that ethnicity is *not* primordial (a social category defined by shared biological descent or ancestry and thus a grouping that is fundamental and enduring for both the group itself and individual group members) and *not* centrally about what a group of people share. Instead, ethnicity is best seen as a set of *socially constructed* group and interpersonal performances that communicate to self and others the *boundaries* between groups, which are not fixed entities but rather collectives in flux. To capture this view, many anthropologists have turned from studying ethnicity per se to seeking to understand social identities. One implication of this position is that group identity is conceptualized as both conscious and strategic—individuals are aware of their multiple social identities and deploy them situationally in order to achieve personal and group goals.

Although Eriksen generally accepts this basic position, he notes that it leaves the person and his or her everyday experiences out of the ethnicity-identity-intergroup conflict equation. He proposes that, in addition to conceiving ethnicity as about social construction, boundaries, and strategic enactment, it is necessary to consider the personal identities of individuals and how these can become fused with social identities. More specifically with regard to intergroup conflict, he suggests that, when the lived experience of individual group members is consonant with the key elements of a social identity currently proffered by authorities, it sets the stage for destructive intergroup conflict fought in the name of that group identity. Thus, for example, although Bosnians and Serbs in Bosnia shared many cultural elements and in multiple ways were quite similar to one another, they had lived separate lives in the private sphere, with little intermarriage and few cross-group close friendships. This situation of separate private spheres allowed group myths and pejorative outgroup beliefs to be part of the everyday experience of members of each group. Thus, when leaders espoused the separate and conflicting religiously based social identities of Bosnian and Serb, the citizenry had personal selves and everyday experiences that made these appeals resonate.

Although they take two very different approaches and seem to offer incommensurate, if not incompatible, frameworks for understanding intergroup conflict, the Part I contributions are actually much closer than might appear at first glance. Brewer starts with the individual and does a nice job of identifying and ordering the cognitive and affective factors that set the stage for ingroup attraction and, in turn, outgroup hostility. She concludes by describing factors that moderate the model she has constructed. These moderators are all societal variables (e.g., social structural complexity), and it is precisely such factors that Eriksen elaborates in his contribution. Eriksen draws the circle complete by his insistence that only when socially propagated group identities fit with the lived experience of individuals and their personal sense of self will the stage be set for ethnically based violence. In complementary ways, then, both Brewer and Eriksen note the importance of individual *and* social factors in the ways in which social identity is implicated in intergroup hostility.

The foregoing should not be construed as meaning that Brewer and Eriksen are in total agreement about the personal and societal underpinnings of group-based harm doing. The clearest point of friction concerns the role of objective conflict between groups as a precipitator of hostile relations. Although he never uses the term, Eriksen at several points presents ideas consistent with the realistic group conflict (*RGC*) view of intergroup conflict (Ashmore & Del Boca, 1976; Boulding, 1962). According to this perspective, groups come into conflict over limited material resources—land, energy sources such as oil, and the like. Whereas Eriksen identifies objective competition as crucial to conflict development and proliferation, Brewer sees such "realistic" competition as much less important. In fact, she might be read as suggesting that tangible conflicts come only after the stage is set by the elements offered in her model.

The second major disagreement between Brewer and Eriksen is equally instructive. Brewer's presentation is all about the here and now, about individuals' thoughts and feelings about me, us, them, in the present moment. Eriksen, on the other hand, grounds his analysis in history. For each of his three examples, he describes what happened in the past, not just as stage setting but also as crucial to understanding why the groups are fighting now. This difference reflects, in part, two contrasting disciplinary paradigms. Brewer is a psychological social psychologist, and present-day practitioners of this social science continue to be much influenced by Kurt Lewin's proscription against "historical" or "genetic" accounts: do not explain a person's current behavior by recourse to what happened to that person in her childhood; instead account for action on the basis of the contemporaneous field of forces acting on the person. Although Lewin's ahistorical approach referred to the life history of the individual, many of his students who, in turn, shaped today's social psychologists, took Lewin's approach more generally to mean that the important determinants of action are *current* social factors. As a consequence, not only has the life history of the individual been left to developmental psychologists, but the past of social groups has been left for historians. In contrast, social and cultural anthropologists, viewing culture as, in part, something that one generation passes to the next, have been much more inclined to see a group's history as important to understanding its present organization and functioning—Thus, Eriksen's descriptions of current conflicts feature historical information.

One important next step will be to bring these perspectives together. One way, which will be elaborated below, is to extend the notion of life story and personal narrative into the analysis of social identity and group-based conflict. The basic notion is that, as individuals and groups, we make sense of who we are now, in part, by looking back and creating stories—about self, about our ethnic group, about our nation. And it is these stories, as part of personal and group identities, that may be crucial in setting the stage for violence and oppression done in the name of us vs. them.[1]

Part II: The Contribution of Ethnic and National Identities to Political Conflict in the United States

The two chapters in the second part follow very well from Eriksen's contribution. Methodologically, he suggests that it is useful to look closely at specific intergroup conflicts; substantively, ethnic conflict within nation-states is a major issue around the globe and is not limited to Third World or developing countries. In Part II, the focus is on patterns of ethnic divergence and convergence in just one nation, the United States, arguably the most economically advanced country in the world. Further, only one type of conflict is considered: political contentions among ethnic groups.

Citrin, Wong, and Duff's central concern is American national identity: What is it? Are there ethnic group differences in beliefs about American identity? How do individuals prioritize ethnic and national identity? How do ethnic and national identity relate to policy preferences? Citrin and his co-workers set the stage for their empirical research by carefully laying out their notion of social identity, in this case national identity. Following Tajfel (1978) they conceive of national identity as involving both "identification as," or self-categorization (e.g., "I am an American") and "identification with," or affective attachment to the nation. Regarding the latter, they further distinguish patriotism, or love for one's country ("Being American is very important to me") from chauvinism, or feelings of national superiority and degrading of other countries ("If only other countries were like America the world would be a much better place").

Citrin et al. suggest that they go beyond Tajfel (a point we return to below in considering the multiple dimensions of social identity) by adding a third component to national identity—normative content. The use of the word "normative" is deliberate and does not mean average. Instead, normative conceptions are assertions about how society should be organized, how people should behave to make society work well, and how society should treat groups and individuals in the nation. As political scientists, Citrin et al. bring an important theme to the volume—normative as pre- and pro-scriptive, not just descriptive. This reflects the subfield of political theory and the issue of how political systems should be constructed. Given the emphasis on ethnicity and national identity, Citrin and his colleagues stress three different normative views of how ethnic and national commitments should be related in multiethnic states: *liberal*, in which national membership depends on sharing a set of ideals (e.g., respect for the individual, freedom) and not shared ethnicity (hence, it is often termed civic, not ethnic, nationalism); *nativism*, in which American identity is equated with one ethnic group, white Anglo Saxons, and thus, to be an American means accepting the values and other characteristics of this dominant ethnic group; *multiculturalism*, in which ethnicity is prized above national identity.

Citrin et al. also preface their data reporting by introducing symbolic politics theory (Sears, 1993), which stresses that political orientations are socialized in childhood and maintained by adult engagements (e.g., work). According to the authors, national identity is widely socialized in the United States, and, thus, there should be more ethnic consensus than conflict concerning national identity.

Citrin et al. address their questions about national identity and predictions from symbolic politics theory using survey data collected from both a national sample and Los Angeles County respondents. Concerning their first question, What is American identity?, they found considerable agreement that, in regard to political issues, most Americans define self as "just an American" (self-categorization) and feel considerable pride in and patriotism for America, but not high levels of chauvinism. Also, there was considerable support for nativistic beliefs (though the pattern was uneven) and even more support for assimilation notions.

In answer to their second question, Are there ethnic group differences in views on American identity?, Citrin et al. concluded that there are few differences in defining American identity except on issues pertaining to ethnic groups per se (e.g., how the nation treats minority groups). A most intriguing finding was that, on average, African Americans were more nativist than whites. This was especially true for endorsing being a Christian as a criterion for being "a true American." As the authors note, this suggests yet another important social identity, religion.

Turning to the third question, How do individuals prioritize ethnic and national identity?, Citrin and colleagues found that, when given the option, about 50 percent of African Americans chose "both _____ [my ethnicity] and American," about one-third chose ethnicity as their primary identity, and about one-sixth chose "just American." Hispanics and Asians responded similarly, but were somewhat less likely to select "just American" and somewhat more likely to choose "both _____ [my ethnicity] and American" and ethnic identity. For whites, on the other hand, "just American" was far and away the predominate response.

The final question was, How do ethnic and national identity relate to policy preferences? As predicted by symbolic politics theory, race (given small sample sizes, only whites and blacks were compared) did not predict views on multicultural policies or international affairs (military spending or protectionism), whereas national identity did. On race-related policies, race did predict policy preferences. However, when ethnic identification was added to the predictive equation, felt closeness to one's ethnic group did not enhance support for race-based policies for blacks, but for whites felt closeness increased disapproval of programs that benefited minority groups. That it was among whites that identification with one's group related to political issues regarding race may seem paradoxical to some given that the practice of identity politics is most often associated with minority groups.

The Citrin et al. contribution highlights three points. First, social identity is multidimensional. Their chapter considers self-categorization, affective attachment, and normative content. Below we identify additional possible facets of social identification. Second, a particularly important aspect of experiencing ethnicity, though often neglected, is the "shoulds" attached to one's group. These are related to the notion of normative content, but they focus, not on broad issues of what it means, for example, to be a true American, but on the very specific group norms for how "one of us" should act—the food we should eat, the way we should talk, and the like—and the pressures an individual feels from members of her or his own group to abide by these "rules." To address this issue, Contrada et al. (in press) have recently developed a self-report instrument to assess individual differences in own-group pressure to behave in specific ways. Third, as Citrin and his colleagues note, social identities are not necessarily political identities. This raises the crucial question, How do people get from social definition to action?

In the second chapter of Part II, Sidanius and Petrocik take up much the same general topic as Citrin and his collaborators; the relationships between ethnicity and national attachment in the United States. And like Citrin et al., Sidanius and Petrocik identify three perspectives on this issue: melting pot (each ethnic group contributes something to an emergent national American identity, and, in the process, members of these ethnic groups lose their own sense of ethnicity and become identified with, and attached to, the nation); pluralism (individuals and groups retain their uniqueness, but all agree to be tolerant and to also identify with the nation); group dominance model (in all societies, groups are arranged in a hierarchy of prestige and power, and this means that groups not only maintain their distinctive identity, but also that, for those at the top, ethnocentrism and patriotism are positively linked, but for those at the bottom this correlation is negative). Again in parallel with the preceding chapter, Sidanius and Petrocik assess with survey data the predictions they derive from each perspective. These data come from five different samples, from university students, to Los Angeles residents, to a national sample.

Sidanius and Petrocik address three specific issues: the salience of ethnic identity; the relation between ethnicity and patriotism; the relationship between patriotism (attachment to the nation) and ethnocentrism (by which they mean a negative attitude toward American ethnic groups relative to one's own group). In regard to the first issue, Sidanius and Petrocik conclude that ethnic identity is salient for Americans and that this is especially true of minority-group Americans. With respect to the second issue, Sidanius and Petrocik find that white Americans are highest in patriotism and African Americans lowest. Concerning the third issue, Sidanius and Petrocik report that, for white Americans, patriotism and ethnocentrism are often positively correlated, but the correlation for minority Americans is generally negative.

Of the many excellent points in the Sidanius and Petrocik contribution, we underline just one, their group dominance model. Individuals develop their intergroup attitudes and ethnic groups come into conflict within society, and all known societies contain group dominance structures: Some social categories are privileged and others are disadvantaged. Thus, the societal context for intergroup relations is never neutral or even-handed, and this is true even in economically advanced nations with strong democratic traditions. This is a particularly important reminder at this time in the United States, where we surmise that a large portion of the dominant white populace believes that the civil rights and women's movements have somehow leveled the playing field for all Americans and now it is time to treat everyone as individuals and not as group members. Without denying the social changes that have occurred over the past four decades, it is simply not true that American society and culture treat all people and groups as equal.

The chapters by Citrin et al. and Sidanius and Petrocik present a paradox: both address the same basic issue (the interplay between ethnic and national identity in the United States), they deal with two similar folk models (though they use somewhat different labels—liberal [Citrin et al.] and pluralism [Sidanius & Petrocik]; nativist [Citrin et al.] and Americanization and melting pot [Sidanius & Petrocik]; see also Fredrickson [1999] for a historical review of models of American ethnic group relations), they both draw on similar previous studies (especially that by de la Garza, Falcon, & Garcia, 1996), and they take the same basic methodological approach (survey data; drawing in one case from the same survey). But they reach quite different conclusions: Citrin and co-workers see a small ethnic divide in the United States and little tension between ethnic and national identity, whereas Sidanius and Petrocik perceive a large ethnic divide and considerable conflict between ethnic and national attachment.

There are three factors that make this paradox more apparent than real. First, they use different items to assess ethnic/national self-categorization. Second, the two chapters are not really directed at precisely the same set of phenomena. Citrin et al. predict policy preferences from ethnicity and ethnic identity, whereas the primary outcome variable of interest to Sidanius and Petrocik is the correlation between national attraction (especially patriotism) and prejudice against U.S. ethnic groups other than one's own group. Third, and we believe most important, in reporting results, Citrin and colleagues concentrate on absolute levels of attachment to the United States (which are generally high) and play down group differences (which, for some measures, are substantial), whereas Sidanius and Petrocik stress group differences and deemphasize absolute levels of national attachment by ethnic group members.

The Citrin et al. and Sidanius and Petrocik chapters underline four important points. First, how one asks people to report their group self-categorization is crucial. Some items implicitly pull for "just American," whereas others pull for ethnicity and nationality self-codings either instead of, or in addition to, labeling self as "American." Our recommendation is that surveys concerned with ethnicity and national identity should use the 1995 LACSS item (described by Citrin et al.) that offers the respondent the following choices: "just an American," "_____ [whichever national or ethnic group the person sees self as a member of]," "both American and _____ [self-categorized ethnic group]." This seems to us to provide the most neutral way of getting at how respondents define and categorize self in terms of a superordinate national identity ("American") and more particular ethnic self-codings. Although the results reported by Citrin et al. are from a small and local sample, they suggest that the modal white American sees self as "just American," while minority Americans define self in three very distinctive ways: about half select a dual identity, about one in three categorizes self in terms of ethnicity only, and about one in six regards self as just American.

Second, the Citrin et al. and Sidanius and Petrocik chapters remind us that it is easy to slip from ethnic identity, or identification, to ethnicity, or simple ethnic group differences. Although both chapters report analyses dealing with individual differences in group identification (especially self-labeling), they also report analyses in terms of ethnic group differences. However, simple ethnic group differences do not necessarily mean differences as a function of ethnic or national identity. In addition, such an approach obscures the wide variation within any social category in the content and degree of identification with the group. For example, what other social identity, intergroup attitude, and public policy preference differences are there among minority group Americans who self-label as "just American," "American and ____," and minority group label only?

Third, ethnic groups are not monolithic. Obviously there is variation by age, socioeconomic status, and a variety of other variables that Citrin et al. and Sidanius and Petrocik partial out in some analyses. At the same time, some of these partialed-out variables constitute important social identifications. For example, there is considerable variation in the African-American (and white) community in terms of religious commitment, especially defining self as a "fundamentalist Christian."

Fourth, just as ethnic and national identity are multifaceted, so too is national attachment. Both chapters note that there is a positive form of national attachment (patriotism) and a more virulent brand (chauvinism/nationalism—basically "We are the best in the world . . . and others should emulate us"), as well as issues of willingness to leave the country and beliefs about what makes someone a true American.

The foregoing summary suggests that the Citrin et al. and Sidanius and Petrocik chapters have not resolved the question of how ethnicity and ethnic identity relate to national identity and attachment. They have, however, provided some important clues. In general, there is fairly high attachment to the United States in all groups, but there are also substantial differences between groups, especially on issues pertinent to ethnicity. More important, the two chapters begin to point us toward the necessary next generation of research. This will need to use multiple measures of ethnic or national self-categorization, especially items that do not tilt toward or away from ethnic (or national) identification, and multiple measures of national attachment. Thus, future work will be directed at two important questions: How do the various facets of ethnic and national identity (self-categorization, felt closeness, and the like) relate to the various components of national identity? How, in turn, do these sometimes competing and sometimes complementary forms of self-identification relate to variables pertinent to intergroup conflict (e.g., attitudes toward other groups, political policies and programs)?

Part III: The Contribution of Social Identity to Violent Intergroup Conflict

White continues the focus of Part II to look intensively at one conflict, but the site of his analysis is Northern Ireland, not the United States, and the type of conflict is deadly violence, not political strife. White begins his chapter in a very dramatic fashion by presenting a table indicating who has killed whom in the conflict. This table not only helps him make some very important points about the conflict but also reminds the reader that the ultimate outcome of identity-based disputes is that people may kill one another. Of the many excellent points made by White, we highlight three: (1) the past importantly shapes the contemporary conflict; (2) the violence in Northern Ireland is three- not two-sided; (3) identity is involved in the conflict in multiple ways.

First, the current fighting is rooted in a long history, and that past not only shapes the present conflict but also sets parameters for how the hostility might be reduced. White describes how the violence in Northern Ireland began with the Norman/English invasion of Ireland over 700 years ago, how religion was introduced into the conflict in the 16th century with the Reformation, how a Protestant ascendancy was created during the 17th century, how Northern Ireland was created in the early part of this century, and how the current protracted violent confrontation began in the 1960s.

This history is important to the current conflict in three major ways.

1. It underlines the importance of losing for group definition. On multiple occasions over seven centuries, the Irish have lost battles and wars to the English. These repeated defeats have been incorporated into the group narrative of the Republicans of Northern Ireland. This parallels the history and national narrative of Serbs as described by Eriksen (this volume; see also Staub this volume). This 700-year record also suggests why the Irish Republican Army may be so reluctant to "decommission," which, as this chapter is being written (spring 2000), may derail the recently agreed to peace accord. The Irish have lost many times to the English; they can not accept another "defeat," which is how many perceive decommissioning, even if the current agreement is widely supported by Protestants and Catholics.

2. The Protestants in Ireland were imported by the British and took over land and status from defeated Irish. They have always been in a minority in Ireland as a whole (though a majority in Northern Ireland), and in White's words, have a "siege mentality." It is likely that being a numerical minority with political and economic majority status (as whites in Southern Africa and the Tutsi in Rwanda until recently) also has important implications for social identity. Groups that have superior power but are numerically in the minority (power majority, numerical minority) likely stereotype the other group (power minority, numerical majority) as, at the same time, both immature and childlike (to justify their inferior position) and potentially violent in a primitive way (to make sense of past uprisings and fears of

what might happen if "they" won). This is much the same set of images that characterized U.S. whites' views of blacks during the slavery period (Boskin, 1970). In complementary fashion, the self-image of power majority yet numerical minority groups features traits such as grown up and mature (responsible, productive, and the like) and civilized.

3. As White notes, a long history of fighting an external oppressor also sets the stage for role identities in this struggle, a point to which we return below. Here we simply note that often roles are hard to give up, thereby making intergroup conflict difficult to reduce.

Second, what looks to an outsider as a simple two-sided religious conflict—Northern Ireland Catholics versus Protestants—is, upon more careful analysis, really a multisided political conflict with a religious gloss. White shows that there are three key contestants—Protestant paramilitaries (who are just a portion of the Protestant community); Irish Republicans (most IRA members are Catholic, but not all Catholics are affiliated with the IRA, and some IRA members are Protestant); and the state, especially British authorities. At the end of his analysis, White notes that there is actually a fourth important party, the people and government of the Republic of Ireland, and, with the current efforts at peace, the role of that party will likely be increasing. The United States has also been involved in the recent efforts to resolve the conflict, and thus there is a fifth "side." The crucial point for the present volume is that apparently "us against them" conflicts are seldom just two-sided; and the various parties are likely to have different "identity shares" in the conflict, which leads to the next major point we wish to underscore about White's chapter.

Third, identity is implicated in multiple and diverse ways in the conflict. To uncover how identity enters into the political violence, White focuses on accounts given by the various participants—quite simply how do various participants describe the conflict and their role in it? White begins his analysis by using Thoits and Virshup's (1997) distinction of "we" from "me" social identities. The former are collective social identifications (member of some social category [e.g., nation, ethnic group]), whereas the latter are role identifications (occupant of a particular role [e.g., parental, occupational]). White argues that for Republicans their involvement reflects both a collective social identity ("we") and role identity ("me"). Importantly, the collective self-definition is not me as Irish Catholic versus Irish Protestants, but me as Irish Nationalist versus the British. The role identity is a set of enactments that the person has learned from either growing up in a Republican home or as part of joining a Republican organization. White illustrates a Republican role identity by describing the hunger strikes of the early 1980s. He notes that hunger strikes have a long history in Republican efforts to get the British out of Ireland, and this means not only that these are part of the "Republican prisoner" role but also that there are specific men who have gone on hunger strikes (and often died) and who now serve as role models (see also Aretxaga, 1993).

White's suggestion that role identities can be important parts of involvement in intergroup conflict is a significant addition to role identity models (McCall & Simmons, 1966; Stryker,1987). Just as the normal everyday activities of society require roles, so, too, do protracted conflicts. What might these conflict roles be? Obviously, there are the roles of active fighter (soldier) and prisoner. But in addition, "armies" require that other functions be fulfilled. One important function is intelligence, or the collecting of information to assist in waging the fight. White describes a British soldier who slept outside a bakery; it is possible that the owner of the bakery could have provided intelligence reports to either the Republican or Protestant paramilitaries and, if so, would have taken on a conflict-related role identity. In addition, when an army is an insurgent one, other roles are necessary, among them, fund-raiser, politician, and civilian support. In one of the Republican narratives reported by White, the respondent describes his grandmother, of whom he said, "She never wavered." She may also have supplied a safe house to paramilitaries and fulfilled additional functions in support of others with active fighting roles and, in so doing, her role of "supporter" would have been active and not passive.

According to White, the Protestant Loyalists and British actors in Northern Ireland construe their involvement solely in "we" social identity terms. For the Protestant paramilitaries, the conflict is "us against them," where "We are British Protestants" and "They are Irish Catholics." For the English, White argues that the conflict is "them versus them," a religious conflict among the Irish.

White acknowledges possible role identities for Protestants and British, but we believe that he underplays them. Although in the earliest years of the current "troubles," the Loyalists may have been relatively unorganized with little sense of history, certainly as the conflict evolved it is probable that Protestant paramilitary groups became relatively well organized and developed systems of roles. Role identities are even more probable for the British or English first-line participants in Northern Ireland, the military personnel. It is likely that many English soldiers construed their involvement there as "me as a soldier doing a soldier's job," and not as "we British."

White's primary data are verbal accounts, and gathering such narratives in the midst of an armed conflict is very difficult. This difficulty raises some questions about White's conclusions. As he notes, the verbalizations he reports are not factual histories or descriptions, but instead they are stories that a person has told to someone else. As with any story, the content of the account depends, in part, on who is talking to whom for what purpose. This raises the most general question: Are the narratives given by the three groups of protagonists (Republicans, Protestant paramilitaries, English soldiers and elites) comparable? This can be partitioned into two more specific queries: Who gave the accounts? To whom were the accounts given and how did the respondent think the accounts would be used? Regarding the first or "who?" question, White acknowledges that the three groups were not equated: many of the Republicans were Sinn Fein members; Protestant paramilitary accounts were from former paramilitaries; the English voices were from soldiers at the start of the current conflict (late 1960s) and political leaders. Regarding the "to whom and how used?" question, the Republicans were all interviewed by White himself, and it is likely that they were assured confidentiality and told that the conversations were for research purposes. The Protestant paramilitary stories and statements by English actors were taken from secondary sources, most from memoirs and remembrances or from official statements. The question of how the respondents thought the accounts would be used is less certain, but at least some had clear public relations and political implications. As a consequence, these statements may have been tilted toward a "we" social identity perspective and away from explaining the individual's roles in the conflict.

While White presents a detailed analysis of just one violent conflict, Staub describes a general framework for understanding genocide that is based on, and applied to, several different murderous group conflicts. Basically, this model indicates that mass killing and genocide are the end result of a set of personal and social processes that are set in motion by one of two general types of instigators: difficult life circumstances (e.g., hyperinflation) and intergroup conflict. These instigators threaten basic needs, including those related to identity. This sets the stage for a spiral toward large-scale systematic violence as follows: the psychological elevation of the ingroup (and generally a derogation of the outgroup), which facilitates initial harmdoing; this, in turn, produces altered societal institutions and individual identities. These lead to the final step in the model, mass killing and genocide. To this causal sequence, Staub adds two moderators. The first, culture, involves a variety of societal-level factors (e.g., history of devaluation of an outgroup); the second, bystanders, indicates individuals both within and outside the group who are not (at least initially) involved in the harmdoing.

Among the many insights provided by Staub's model, we highlight five. First, both group and individual identity play important roles in intergroup violence. Regarding the former, Staub suggests that ethnic groups and nations vary in their "group self-concept," and this shared notion of "us" can lead some groups toward mass killing and genocide while directing others away from such harm-doing. In particular, Staub highlights as a cultural factor predisposing toward systematic intergroup violence, "unhealed victimization," the belief that "we" have been hurt coupled with no opportunity to personally and socially come to terms with this wound.

Second, and closely related to the first point, a personal and societal sense of vulnerability ("They have killed our people before, and they could attack us at any time") can not only predispose a group toward violence but also make preemptive violence more likely. As Eriksen noted regarding Serbs in the former Yugoslavia and White with regard to the Irish Republicans, these groups had histories of losing, which justified, in the participants' minds, acts of "getting them before they get us." This type of mind-set helps sustain these conflicts

Third, regarding the through-time set of factors leading to intergroup violence, most important for the present volume is that these involve changes in individual and group identities. Those in a society who engage in initial violence are more receptive to self-definitions that make their harm-doing not only acceptable but, in some cases, also morally right; those who at the outset are bystanders can come to see killing or support for killing as part of how "I ought to behave" and alter their self-conception accordingly.

Fourth, in terms of culture moderators, it is possible to identify societal-level identity types that are more likely to participate in mass killing, and these are not neatly divided along Eastern versus Western modal self-concept configurations. In fact, as Staub notes, both the autonomous individual self more common in Western industrialized societies and the more social and connected self-configuration that is more common in Eastern and less industrialized nations have their own vulnerabilities to genocide. The challenge for the next generation of researchers is to assess these types and test Staub's suggestions. (See Norenzayan et al. [1999] and Lyengar et al. [1999] for additional ideas about different types of cultures and the implications for intergroup strife.)

Fifth, third parties play significant roles both in creating conditions ripe for large scale group violence and as a major resource in limiting or stopping genocide. Staub describes how Belgians built on existing Hutu-Tutsi dominance systems and added the notion of "blood" to help make the society more manageable for them. Years later this made the violence more likely.

Part IV: The Role of Social Identity in Reducing Intergroup Conflict

Staub's emphasis on the importance of bystanders, especially external by-standers, as crucial to preventing the escalation to mass killing and genocide leads very nicely into the final part, which focuses on reducing conflict. The chapter in this section, by Kelman, describes problem-solving workshops as a conflict-reduction method that features third parties. Kelman begins his chapter by describing the history of the Israeli-Palestinian conflict. Just as Eriksen and White suggest that the past is important to understanding why and how intergroup harm-doing develops, Kelman proposes that efforts to reduce conflicts must take into consideration the historical foundations of current strife. Next, Kelman lays out his notion of national identity. He argues that, "Although national identity is carried by the individual members of a national group and can thus be studied as a property of individuals, the present chapter refers to it as a collective phenomenon—as a property of the group." In the simplest terms, national identity is the shared and consensual definition of us as a group and nation; this includes our claims to land and continuity over time, our beliefs about who we are, and what makes us distinctive. Kelman suggests that national identity is accompanied by a "national narrative—an account of the group's origins, its history, and the relationship to the land." Thus, for Kelman, social identity as a nation involves both a self-definition (national identity) and group story (national narrative).

In seeking to understand how national identity might underlie conflict, Kelman argues that in protracted intergroup fights, especially in which both sides have claim to the same land, the groups' national identities can become exclusive (e.g., "This land belongs to us and can belong to no one else") and monolithic (all the multiple dimensions of nationhood [religion, ethnicity, history, and the like] become seen as highly intercorrelated). Both of these properties make conflict resolution more difficult, identity exclusivity by making sharing impossible by definition, and identity unidimensionality by making us all the same and reducing any possibility that in some ways they are like us. One final aspect of protracted conflicts such as that between the Israelis and Palestinians is that the process of fighting can become part of the national identities—"We are the people who fight them." This echoes Staub's observation that engaging in intergroup violence changes individuals. Kelman proposes that intergroup conflict can change whole nations and become part of the shared collective self-definition and the consensual national narrative.

Kelman then describes how identity change, though difficult, is still possible. Here he makes two very significant points. First, although people and nations see their identities as fixed, they are, in fact, not. Identities, like all belief systems, are not immutable essences, but rather are socially constructed and, as such, are modifiable. Second, unlike land and other physical objects, identities are not zero-sum; the definition of "us" need not include the defeat or devaluation of "them".

How might these possible changes in national identity be achieved? Kelman describes the problem-solving workshops that he and his colleagues have been conducting for many years in the Middle East. These feature third parties who serve both to moderate the discussions and to provide an unbiased resource for both sides. Another key aspect of the workshops is that the participants are influential people in the Israeli and Palestinian communities (e.g., business leaders) but not formal political leaders. Thus, they have "clout" but do not need to represent a political position.

The workshops attempt to find ways to bridge the gaps between the two sides. Kelman highlights how this involves altering national identities. For example, workshop participants have considered what aspects of their national identity might be outdated and thus might be psychologically discarded. Kelman concludes his contribution with a detailed description of how one workshop grappled with a crucial issue in the Israeli-Palestinian conflict: what to do with, and for, the Palestinian refugees. A key feature of his analysis is that this question has both material (what Kelman terms "practical") and symbolic facets. On the material or objective side, how can Israel and Palestine accommodate the large number of refugees in other countries? On the symbolic side, how can each side resolve the refugee issue in such a way that it does not do violence to its national identity and group narrative?

A Look Forward: A Social Identity Framework for Intergroup Conflict

As the preceding "look back" indicates, our authors have done an excellent job of addressing the first goal of this volume: to survey what the social and behavioral sciences have learned about the ways in which social identity and intergroup harm-doing are interconnected. They have also succeeded in addressing our second goal in putting together this book: to identify the needed next steps in moving toward a more complete account of social identity and intergroup conflict. In this section we pull together and organize the next-generation conceptual and methodological tools identified by our contributors in the form of a social identity framework for intergroup conflict that is schematically depicted in figure 9.1. It is important to emphasize that this is not a tight deductive model such as proposed by Brewer; instead, we offer a heuristic scheme that identifies important constructs and suggests how they might be interconnected. We present this framework as follows. First, we provide a brief overview of the scheme. Second, the advantages of phrasing the framework in terms of a general threat or coping paradigm are described. Third, the details and implications of the framework are presented.

Overview of Framework

The figure depicts three general sets of constructs—threat and appraisal; destructive coping: intergroup harm-doing; and social identity—and identifies these as mutually influencing one another. The arrow from "threat and appraisal" to "destructive coping: intergroup harm-doing" marks this as a general threat/coping framework as used in psychological analyses of stress (Lazarus & Folkman, 1984). When members of a group perceive actual or possible harm to themselves and other ingroup members (threat), they seek to makes sense of this (appraisal), and if the other group is somehow judged as responsible for the threat, they may cope with the appraised threat destructively by harming that group and its members.

The return arrow from "destructive coping" to "threat" indicates that intergroup harm-doing can escalate threat and appraisal: when one group inflicts harm on another, it raises the possibility of retaliation (i.e., threat). The figure indicates that threat and appraisal and harm-doing are each connected to social identity, and also that social identity moderates the link of

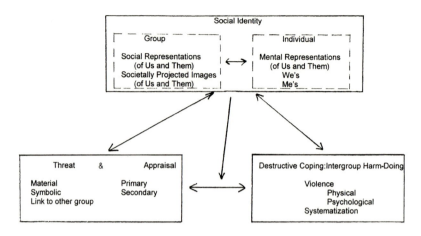

FIGURE 9.1 Social Identity Framework for Intergroup Conflict

threat and appraisal to intergroup violence. Social identity consists of both group (socially shared) and individual (personal) representations about own and other group. Group identities that feature own group as victim and other group as oppressor or aggressor heighten objective threat and appraisal of danger; the reverse path indicates that being threatened and seeing another group as responsible is likely to influence individual and group definition (e.g., living in a state of war, declared or not, with another group will help create social and personal identities congruent with this state).

Similarly, the "intergroup harm-doing" to "social identity" arrow indicates that groups that engage in outgroup violence will have their personal and group self-definitions altered, again to bring them into a psychologically consistent relation (e.g., "we are the people who are making the world safe/pure/ . . . by subjugating/killing . . . them"). Finally, "social identity" moderates the link between "threat and appraisal" and destructive coping." Groups that have a socially shared sense of "us" as victim and "them" as dangerous are more likely to cope with threat via intergroup violence than groups that do not have such a view of "us" and "them."

The figure is obviously simplified in several respects. First, the framework is from the perspective of only one group in relation to just one other group. As White's chapter in particular informs us, this is seldom the case in real-world conflicts, and the framework, if it is to prove useful, will need to be expanded to include additional groups beyond "us" and "them." Second, there are many other instigators to intergroup violence than threat. Often one group aggresses against another for material gain because the group's leaders believe that they can get away with it. For example, the people of West Africa in the 17th through 19th centuries posed no threat to Americans; slaves were introduced into the United States simply because Europeans and other slave traders had more power than Africans, and American plantation owners wanted cheap labor. Third, threat, even if it is linked clearly to some outgroup, does not always lead to violence. Fourth, there are many inputs into intergroup conflict in addition to threat and appraisal and social identity. At the societal level, type of economic system and political structures are important, and, at the individual level, personality and social attitudes are likely significant contributors to group-based harm-doing. Fifth, the figure suggests a static view of the links among the variables depicted. This is not the case. As Staub's chapter makes very clear, there is a through time path to mass killing and genocide. Thus, our figure stands for many causal paths that unfold through time. For example, a group might experience a large influx of immigrants to their country as an economic threat ("They will take our jobs"); this may, in turn, lead to discriminatory laws and outbreaks of violence against that group; if continued over time, these actions will likely come to be prominent parts of views of us and them; whether this would escalate to widespread and systematic harm-doing such as genocide would depend on threat and appraisal and social identity according to figure 9.1.

Advantages of Threat/Coping Framework

There are four major advantages to using a general threat/coping paradigm. First, as has been demonstrated at the individual level, unpredictable and uncontrollable threats are experienced as particularly stressful, and such threats often lead people to seek the comfort and security of the ingroup (Worchel, 1999). For most people, the world today is characterized by unpredictable and uncontrollable forces and events—modernization in many developing countries and globalization of the economy for all nations (Eriksen, this volume), rapid technological change, and often unplanned social change. Thus, the model suggests that intergroup strife will be more, not less, likely as we enter the 21st century, even though much of the globe is experiencing considerable material progress.

Second, as stress and health workers have demonstrated, it is fruitful to distinguish problem- from emotion-focused coping. In the former, the person, upon encountering a situation that signals current or future harm, attempts to deal directly with the source of threat (e.g., upon learning that she has high blood pressure, which it is explained to her increases the risk of health problems, the person changes her diet to reduce salt and fat). Emotion-focused coping, on the other hand, involves attempts to reduce the fear and anxiety that accompany threats. Thus, using the same example, the newly diagnosed hypertensive individual could drink alcohol to avoid thinking about the mysterious and scary condition about which she has just learned. As applied to intergroup conflict, the 1929 Stock Market Crash ushered in a worldwide depression. In the United States, one response was the set of political measures termed the New Deal, which among other things sought to provide assistance for the economically afflicted. This problem-focused coping can be contrasted with the rise of Nazism in Germany at about the same time. Hitler's programs sought more to alleviate feelings of despair and national impotence following the loss of World War I and the economic and political turmoil of the Weimar years, and these led to the "Final Solution" and the Holocaust.

Third, there are clear individual differences in styles of coping, and the preceding chapters suggest that there are likely reliable societal and group differences in styles of coping as well. Thus, for example, Staub notes that societies differ in degree of authority orientation. It is likely that those high in authority orientation will more likely accept violence-against-outgroup "solutions" for threats offered by leaders even if they contradict societal norms about harm-doing.

Fourth, and very important for the present analysis, there is evidence that self and identity are implicated in the threat-coping process (Contrada & Ashmore, 1999). Thus, there is reason to believe that an identity-intergroup conflict model based on a threat-coping framework may be fruitful.

Framework Details and Implications

Destructive Coping: Intergroup Harm-Doing.   As depicted in figure 9.1, our model seeks to account for intergroup harm-doing, by which we mean harm by members of one group to those of another group based on group membership. As suggested in the figure, we see intergroup harm-doing as multidimensional. Intergroup violence can involve physical and/or psychological hurting. For example, during the slavery and Jim Crow eras in the United States, African Americans were subjected to both physical violence (e.g., beatings, lynchings, poor housing) and psychological violence (e.g., societal stereotypes of innate inferiority and racial etiquette that made interracial contacts demeaning for blacks). Today the balance is much shifted toward psychological harm-doing (persisting cultural stereotypes), though physical violence against blacks has not been eliminated.

Another important dimension is the degree to which harm-doing is systematized. At one extreme, members of one group engage in local and spontaneous acts of violence against outgroup individuals. At the other extreme, there are elaborate societal systems for hurting the other group. In Nazi Germany, there was an organized set of institutions for carrying out the "Final Solution." It is not just open violence that can be highly systematized. The slavery system in the United States, the caste system in India, and apartheid in South Africa all were undergirded by complex sets of social institutions (legal, educational, and the like) that oppressed certain groups.

There are two other important dimensions of intergroup harm-doing not depicted in the figure: (1) extent—how widely across the other group is the violence extended? and (2) duration—how long has the harm-doing been going on? As both increase so too does the strength of the links of intergroup harm-doing to social identity and threat.

Threat and Appraisal.   According to our model, a significant contributor to intergroup harm-doing is threat and appraisal. Threat and appraisal are highly related but separable concepts. Just as work on social problems has profited from a distinction between actual conditions in the social environment and the public "seeing" and labeling of these as problematic (Thompson & Fine, 1999), we too feel it is useful to distinguish the objective threat and the individual and collective recognition and interpretation (or appraisal) of this condition (see also Northrup, 1989). Thus, for example, during the 1860s many Chinese immigrated to the United States to work on the transcontinental railroad. The societally projected image of Chinese during this period was relatively benign. However, when the railroad was completed and many Chinese became competitors for jobs, unions and other groups promoted public representations (in newspapers and the like) of the Chinese as dangerous, and these came to be shared widely enough that local discrimination occurred and national immigration restrictions were implemented. Thus, it was not the sheer numbers of Chinese that mattered or even the economic competition with whites, but the shared social representation of Chinese as dangerous.

Threat, like harm-doing, is viewed as multidimensional. Figure 9.1 identifies three important dimensions: material, symbolic, link to other group. Material and symbolic threat are often treated as opposite ends of a single continuum. We believe, however, that it is best to consider these as potentially independent dimensions. As noted above, material threat is the core of realistic group conflict (*RGC*) approaches to intergroup conflict (Ashmore & Del Boca, 1976). These are often contrasted with "symbolic politics" approaches (see Citrin et al., this volume; Sears et al., 1999). In symbolic politics (*SP*) models, groups come into "unrealistic" non-self-interested conflict over symbolic issues. For example, Whose language should be spoken in this country? Whose history should be taught in our schools? Our view is that the conflict between the RGC and SP positions is more apparent than real. Material things, especially land, often acquire symbolic meaning. And symbols may have significant material implications. Continuing the same examples, deciding "whose language" will, in turn, partially shape which group's members can make the better living economically. Whose history is taught will legitimate and buttress the economic and political status of some groups and undermine that of others. Thus, even symbolic conflicts have important material implications.

In his contribution to this volume, Kelman stresses that the Israeli-Palestinian conflict has both material, or "practical," and symbolic facets, and both of these need to be addressed in attempts to reduce the conflict. The other chapters in this book tend to emphasize either material or symbolic threat. As noted above, Brewer's primary argument is in terms of symbolic threat, whereas Eriksen stresses material conflicts. Citrin and his colleagues were guided by symbolic politics theory; Sidanius and Petrocik's group dominance model is, at its core, a materialist framework—group dominance in the service of material outcomes.

The third dimension of threat depicted in the figure is link to the other group. Some threats directly and clearly involve "them." Some examples: Chinese competing with whites in the United States after the completion of the transcontinental railroad, Hutus and Tutsi attacking one another in Rwanda (Staub, this volume), and laws in India designed to set aside jobs for the lower castes (Eriksen, this volume). At the same time, intergroup harm-doing can be triggered by threats that do not objectively arise from the other group. In Germany in the 1920s, the hyperinflation and other economic problems did not arise because of the actions of Jews. Hitler identified this group as a cause, however, and this appraisal was widely accepted given the longstanding societal representations of Jews as sneaky and dangerous (Goldhagen, 1996). Examples of types of threats that do not directly involve the outgroup that yet can start a cycle of intergroup harm-doing are economic instability and hardship (poverty, globalization that fractures traditional economic practices and procedures, inflation), political instability and corruption (changing governments, lack of societal agreement on political processes, widespread graft by public officials), and rapid social change (large-scale movements from rural to urban areas, changes in family roles, and other social changes associated with "modernization").

In sum, our conceptualization of threat underlines two major points. First, threats can be about tangible things (material threat) and about intangibles as represented in valued symbols (symbolic threat). Further, a given threat can have both a material and symbolic component. Second, conflict between groups can begin with factors that are not objectively related to the groups at all. Quite simply, some nongroup-related threats can initiate the set of processes that lead to intergroup violence. In these cases, leaders direct appraisal to "them" as the cause and away from the economic, political, and social factors, leading individuals to see themselves and their groups as in danger. In such cases, groups cope with the emotions aroused by the threat rather than with the threat itself.

There are two other important dimensions of threat that are not depicted in the figure, and these parallel those for intergroup harm-doing: (1) extent—how widely across the ingroup is the threat experienced? and (2) duration—how long has the threat been in existence? As both increase, so too do the links of threat to intergroup harm-doing.

Appraisal is necessary for threat to lead to collective group-based violence. Although the figure suggests that this is a static phenomenon, it is not. Instead, appraisal unfolds over time. To capture this idea we have identified both primary and secondary appraisal. Primary appraisal is an initial making sense of the threat: What is the problem? What or who is responsible? Thus, for example, when a society with many foreign workers (as is true of many nations) encounters an economic downturn, it might be explained relatively spontaneously as "them taking jobs from us," and this could lead, without much thought or organization, to isolated attacks on the foreign workers.

However, for violence to be systematic and widespread requires mobilizing a larger segment of society and providing more organized paths to action. This involves secondary appraisal guided by both group and individual social identities as indicated in the figure. Regarding the former, group identities must first be invoked to make sense of the threat. As Brewer, Eriksen, and Staub note, leaders are crucial in this process (see also Worchel, 1999). At least initially, these leaders are not likely to be national political leaders but instead proponents of "fringe" groups, labor leaders, or local religious figures. And, in an early coping stage, the efforts they direct, though more organized than a spontaneous attack or a "race riot," are still relatively reflexive.

But what makes individual citizens ready to accept a group-based ("them against us") explanation for their troubles? Eriksen's chapter points us in the right direction when he notes that the shared group social identities proffered by leaders must be consonant with the social and personal identities of individuals and also fit with their daily experience and enactment of these selves. This melding of a group identity with the identities of individuals can result in mobilization of substantial numbers of individuals for action, in this case a second stage of harm-doing.

As actions against the outgroup develop and widen, the ingroup engages in secondary appraisal where the "guilt" of the outgroup is solidified in societally projected images, and harm-doing is explained as a necessary or perhaps even a noble activity.

If mobilization is to be enduring, individuals will have to accept some personal costs. This raises the crucial question: Under what circumstances will individuals and groups be willing to endure personal hardship to either inflict harm or to experience harm? Stated somewhat differently, what are the factors that determine whether threat leads to mobilizing individuals and the group to undertake action? As figure 9.1 suggests, we believe that part of the answer lies in the content and structure of both group and individual social identity. With regard to the group narrative, a national or ethnic story that features being a victim will increase the likelihood of mobilization, and this will be true if there is also the sense of group vulnerability (Eriksen, White, Staub, this volume). At the individual level, we suggest that the relative lack of valued personal selves makes a society susceptible to group-based mobilization. Thus, for example, in a nation in which men and women are not able to successfully enact work and family roles because of poverty, discrimination, and the like, they will be more likely to be susceptible to social identities that involve outgroup violence or support others doing harm.

An important implication of this line of reasoning is that protracted conflicts create social identities, at both the group and individual level, that make the progression to widespread and systematic violence more likely. Harming others based on group membership or standing by while others do this changes people. Cognitive consistency models suggest that people and groups would develop personal and shared reasons that justify this behavior. These have included belief systems specifying that they are not human (and, thus, norms about hurting others do not apply), are inferior humans (and, thus, need to be taken care of as slaves), or are powerful and dangerous (and, thus, must be killed before they destroy us). These rationalizations become part of transformed group and individual identities as depicted by the arrow from intergroup harm-doing to social identity in figure 9.1. Given the focus of this volume on social identity, we turn now to a more detailed analysis of the group and individual identity portion of the scheme.

Social Identity. As indicated at the top of figure 9.1, and suggested at several places above, social identity is here viewed as a significant input to the threat-intergroup harm-doing relationship. In the proposed framework, we distinguish group from individual social identity.

• *Group Social Identity.* Group social identities are group-level phenomena. This means that both the referent and locus of the identity is the group. By referent we mean what the identity is about, the group—America/Americans; Serbia/Serbians, and so on. The content of the identity is the set of things that are thought to "define,"—for example, America and Americans, including geography (e.g., 50 states, mostly between Canada and Mexico), politics (e.g., democracy, two-party system), economics (e. g., capitalism), morals and values (e.g., caring, freedom), history (e.g., revolution, civil war), and the like. By locus of the identity, we mean that the group is also the level of representation of the identity. Such representation takes both psychological and socio-structural form. Regarding the former, labeled "Social Representations" in the figure, the group identity is a set of beliefs that are widely accepted in the society, even though many individuals do not know or endorse all of the beliefs (Thompson & Fine, 1999). The socio-structural form of group identity, "Societally Projected Images" in figure 9.1, is manifested in two primary and intertwined ways: (1) it is woven into the political, economic, and social structure of the society, often in implicit ways (e.g., institutional racism in the United States [Jones, 1997]); (2) it is conveyed by the societal mechanisms of socialization such as schools and the media (e.g., cultural racism in the United States [Jones, 1997, Worchel, 1999]).

In addition to the rather static group social identity notion ("We are _____"), we propose that there is a group-level analog to life story and personal narrative at the individual level (McAdams, 1997; Gergen & Gergen, 1988). That is, just as individuals develop stories that specify not only what "I am like now" but also "how I got here" and "where I will likely go in the future," we propose that groups develop narratives that tell the story of their group. This proposed construct is explicit in only one of the foregoing chapters; Kelman makes national narrative a central part of his analysis, but he draws no link to life story or self-narrative at the individual level. The notion of group narrative, however, is implicit in several other contributions. For each of the three case studies of intergroup conflict described by Eriksen, a group narrative was propagated by political leaders who identified "us" as noble and deserving and "them" as dangerous (e.g., in Bosnia the Serbian national narrative featured past defeats at the hands of powerful outsiders, especially the Turks, and the local Muslim community was defined as representing external invaders even though this definition was inaccurate). In describing the role identities of Republicans, White emphasized the importance of a family history of involvement in the cause and the fact that this history was often passed down from one generation to the next. We suggest that, as one generation of Republicans socialized the next, they not only told the story of "our family's" involvement but also told the story of "We Republicans," the narrative of this group.

There are four additional important points about group narrative:

1. Group stories can lie relatively dormant for periods of time. For example, in Yugoslavia during the Tito period, the divergent group narratives of the Serb, Croat, and Muslim communities were not in the foreground of societally projected images or social representations of the citizenry.
2. At certain times and under certain conditions, there are forces pushing for demonstrating and featuring a national narrative. Threat, in the form of societal crises or outgroup actions, can bring group stories to prominence and political leaders can use such narratives (Brewer, Eriksen, this volume).
3. Group narratives can change. As Kelman noted, history is not fixed, and, thus, groups can alter their story (Rothman, 1997).
4. Group narratives often contain folk theories of ethnicity, and these generally do not match scientific understanding of this concept. As Eriksen notes, most current-day anthropologists reject the notion that ethnicity is primordial, and yet it is precisely this version of ethnicity that activists and politicians use in mobilizing people to action on the basis of ethnicity.

• *Individual Social Identity.* At the individual level, identity components are generally partitioned into social identities and personal identities (Ashmore & Jussim, 1997b), and we follow that convention here even though drawing the line between personal and social is not always easy (Deaux, 1992). Social identities are those self definitions that identify self in terms of, or in relation to, other people and groups (e.g., "I am a teacher" which specifies a role that I and other teachers enact in relation to other people who fill the role of student; "I am an American," which specifies that I am a member of a social category along with others). Personal identities are self-definitions that identify me as a unique individual (e.g., "I am obedient"). Personal identity also includes self-narrative (an organized story about me, again as an individual).

Given the thrust of this volume, we feature social identity here, though we briefly describe below how individual-level personal identity might be important to intergroup conflict. We follow Thoits and Virshup (1997) in partitioning individual-level social identities into "we's" (i.e., self as a member of a collective group [e.g., "I am an African American"]) and "me's" (i.e., self as fulfilling a role [e.g., "I am a mother"]).

1. *Individual social identity: "we selves."* In the application of social identity to intergroup conflict, "we selves" are obviously important and have been the most often studied. Thus, in this volume, all authors have been concerned with how individuals define self in relation to an ethnic or national group. And, they have done this in a variety of ways: self categorization in terms of an ethnic label such as black or white, felt closeness to one's group, beliefs about one's group and another group, and the like. This diversity of approaches raises an important question for the next generation of work on social identity and conflict: what are the components of "we" social identities?

Most researchers regard self-definition in terms of collective social groups as multidimensional, but there is far from consensus on what these dimensions are. To illustrate, table 9.1 lists the distinctions and components that three research groups have proposed for ethnic identity, racial identity, and cultural identity, perhaps the most often studied types of "we" social identities. On the same line are listed dimensions that are the same or highly similar. It can be seen that there are five areas of partial agreement on what are the major dimensions of "we" social identity. Two of the three articles included: (1) salience/centrality; (2) evaluation and feelings/private regard; (3) values and attitudes/ideology; (4) interest and knowledge/familiarity; (5) behaviors and practices/behavior and language.

At the same time, no dimension is mentioned by all three authors. And, there are three components listed by just one author: (1) self-identification, (2) commitment, (3) public regard. De la Garza et al. and Sellers and his associates may have omitted self-identification because they were proposing scales to measure discrete dimensions of a specific social identification, and, in so doing, they may have taken for granted that the first step in social identification is placing self in a social category. At the same time, it is likely that a comprehensive assessment of "we" social identity will require attention to self-identification, including such issues as preferred ethnic label and the possibility of self-subtyping. Just as perceivers discern subtypes within age (Brewer, Dull, & Lui, 1981), gender (Clifton, McGrath, & Wick, 1976), and racial categories (Devine & Baker, 1991), it is likely that people may define self in terms of such subtypes (e.g., Eriksen noted that Yugoslavians living in Belgrade and other urban areas had very different views of being a

TABLE 9.1 Dimensions of "We" Social Identity Proposed by Three Research Groups

AUTHOR(S)	Phinney (1995)	de la Garza et al. (1995)	Sellers et al. (1998)
CONSTRUCT	Ethnic identity	Latino(a) cultural identity	African-American racial identity
DIMENSIONS	Self-identification	—	—
	Salience	—	Centrality
	Evaluation of and feelings about group	—	Private regard
	—	—	Public regard
	—	Values and attitudes	Ideology
	Interest in and knowledge of group	Familiarity with Latino(a) culture American culture	—
	Ethnic behaviors and practices	Behavior and language Spanish proficiency English proficiency	—
	Commitment	—	—

Serb, Muslim, or Croat than those in rural areas, and this may involve subtyping). Regarding commitment, most would agree that something akin to the Eriksen/Marcia notion of the developmental path that the person took to her or his current sense of group identification is a potentially important component of racial/ethnic/cultural identity. Cross's (1995) work is a related but different approach to social identity as a developmental construct. Finally, even though only Sellers et al. explicitly include a public regard dimension as part of social identity, it is likely that others would regard this as a potentially important dimension.

Table 9.1 illustrates one other complication in conceiving "we" social identities: to what extent must the "other" group be included within the concept of collective social self-definition? De la Garza and associates are very clear that Latino cultural identity includes familiarity with and language skills relevant to both the ingroup and the "other" group. Should aspects of identification in terms of "them" routinely be included in assessments of social identities?

As is apparent, table 9.1 suggests a large number of possible components of "we" social identities. As researchers grapple with which are necessary to include, it is important to consider construct validity. In the simplest terms, where does collective social identity end and related variables (causes, correlates, and consequences) begin? For example, is "interest in and knowledge about" one's ethnic group part of one's social identity, or is it best seen as an outcome predictable from identification? This question becomes even more difficult regarding behavior: are ethnic behaviors part of social identity or an outcome that can be used to assess the construct validity of social identity measures?

One of the most important messages of the present volume is that even conflicts that appear to be simple "us against them" on the basis of one social identity distinction (e.g., religion in Northern Ireland) also involve multiple other social identities. These other social identifications are not just regarding ethnic group and nation, which have been the focus of the foregoing chapters. For example, in Part II of the volume addressing ethnic and national identity in the United States, there was evidence that gender, socioeconomic status, and religion were associated with ethnic and national identifications and with the intergroup attitudes and policy positions under investigation. Thus, as highly social creatures, people have multiple identifications with collectives, and these interrelate with one another in complex ways to shape orientations toward other groups and toward political issues.

2. *Individual social identity*: *"me selves."* As White's chapter reminds us, how people relate to their own and other groups depends not just on collective self-definitions ("we's"), but also on thinking of self in terms of social roles ("me's"). As noted above, role identities pertinent to group conflict are especially likely to arise and be important in protracted conflicts where many "supporting" roles are needed to carry on the fight. Also as noted above, there is a second major way in which role social identities are important to understanding intergroup conflict: to the extent that societal conditions allow individuals to have and successfully fulfill valued role identities (e.g., husband and father), it will be more difficult to recruit them for doing violence against others. On the other hand, when poverty, oppression, modernization, and other social forces make it difficult for large numbers of people to fulfill social roles, it makes it easier for them to be drawn to social identities that provide feelings of positive evaluation and potency even if they also explicitly or implicitly involve doing harm to others.

In addition, the relation between social role organization and group boundaries is likely to have important implications for group-based violence. Eriksen's observation that Bosnians and Serbs had separate private spheres means that they did not have role identities (husband-wife, in law, and the like) *across social category lines*. Social roles organized largely along in-group lines may make it easier to recruit people to intergroup harm-doing. Further, it is likely that friendships, too, were predominantly within group. We suggest that cross-group friendship is likely to reduce intergroup violence (Ashmore, 1970; Pettigrew, 1998). If I see myself as Richard (Bosnian) friend of Mel (Serb) and we have extensive first-hand experience with one another, it will be harder to mobilize either of us for "us against them" identity conflict.

Personal Identity.   Although social identities are most pertinent to inter-group conflict, we suggest that personal identifications (self-construals that identify me as a unique individual) are also likely important. We offer two illustrative examples. First, although Staub treated "authority orientation" as a societal-level construct, it is likely to have an individual-level representation also, with substantial individual differences even within a society high (or low) in this orientation. To the extent that I define myself as obedient to authority, I will be a more likely recruit for group-based violence fomented by political leaders. Second, as noted above, we believe that self narratives are important to identity at both the group and individual level. White's chapter suggests that self stories are most likely to be conflict-related in societies characterized by protracted conflict. White notes that many current-day Republicans come from families with a long commitment to the cause of freeing Ireland from England. Further, in these families, that tradition is a central part of the stories that parents and grandparents tell to children, and, in turn, this history of one's family's involvement becomes part of the individual's personal story. Thus, just as Kelman noted that the group narrative can feature "We are the people who fight them," so, too, at the individual level, a central part of an individual's narrative can be that "My family and I are people who fight them."

Whose Social and Personal Identities?   It is useful to distinguish three general types of actors in intergroup conflict situations:

1. Elites—individuals who have political, economic, or information power. As Brewer, Eriksen, Staub, and Kelman note, elites play a pivotal role in social strife, often in propagating "us versus them" social identities to mobilize citizens (Worchel, 1999).
2. Agents of violence—people who actively and directly carry out the harm-doing (e.g., in White's chapter, the Protestant and Republican paramilitaries and English soldiers).
3. "Ordinary _____s" (as per Goldhagen's [1996] "ordinary Germans")—general citizens or average group members. Whatever the merits of Goldhagen's arguments, he has highlighted a crucial point, How do ordinary citizens become participants in organized violence between groups? Staub suggests that bystanders who "do nothing" while organized violence is done will be touched, possibly even taking on the identity of the hurting party.

Caveats

We reiterate that the proposed framework is not a tight deductive theory, but instead a heuristic scheme intended to highlight the possible roles of identity in intergroup conflict. Thus, it is necessary to note two significant caveats.

One of the most important caveats about the model is what is left out. Many factors that contribute to intergroup violence are not depicted. As noted above, these omissions are made to underscore the importance of social identity. At the same time, as with any framework, our scheme hides as well as highlights. Even some factors that we feel are quite important (e.g., the role of political, economic, and religious leaders in promoting identity-based conflict) are only indirectly represented in the figure (e.g., as societally projected images under group social identity).

A second caveat concerns context. As depicted in figure 9.1, we have essentially frozen in time a conflict between two groups and also wrenched that conflict out of its regional and global context. As is clear in the chapters by Eriksen, Sidanius and Petrocik, White, and Kelman, however, many ethnic and national conflicts unfold over a relatively long time period, and, as noted above, early events profoundly influence the current situation (Fisher, 1990; Northrup, 1989; Rothman, 1997).

White's chapter highlights the "space/place" context caveat for our model: In the case of Northern Ireland, England/Britain is an "outside" (not "them" or "us" if one focuses just on the two groups in Northern Ireland) yet potent factor (and if White is correct, the "them" party for Republicans). Further, White notes but does not emphasize other important outsiders—the Republic of Ireland and the United States. The differing responses of the world community to the conflict in Yugoslavia and Rwanda suggest the importance of regional context, together with associated strategic interests and belief systems (e.g., racism). The fighting in Kosovo, on the edge of Europe, led to a military campaign by NATO, whereas the genocide in Rwanda resulted in action from the world community that was "too little too late" (*New York Times*, December 16, 1999).

Identity and Conflict Reduction

Given that we anticipate a future volume of the *Rutgers Series on Self and Social Identity* completely devoted to reducing intergroup conflict, here we discuss just two issues important to defusing intergroup conflict: social psychological mechanisms and types of interventions.

Regarding social psychological processes, several of the preceding chapters noted that getting people to accept higher order, superordinate identities might be useful in ameliorating intergroup strife (Eriksen, Staub, Kelman). Brewer, too, raised this possibility, but also noted that according to her optimal distinctiveness model and the present extension and elaboration of it, overarching identity units could create conflict under some conditions. The possible utility of higher order identities for conflict reduction is the direct focus of Gaertner and his colleagues. In multiple experiments, they have demonstrated that intergroup bias is significantly reduced when members of different groups adopt a superordinate or common group identity (e.g., Gaertner, Dovidio, Nier, Ward, & Banker, 1998)

Perhaps the furthest extension of the concept of superordinate categories is that of "global culture." The goal of global culture is to unite all people on the basis of characteristics shared as humans, thereby changing group boundaries so members of currently different groups see themselves as belonging to the same group (Worchel, 1999). However, it is important to note that global culture violates the basic need of identity uniqueness as specified by Brewer's optimal distinctiveness model (see Brewer, this volume). It also requires that individuals deny all previous group identities (e.g., national, ethnic) in favor of the global identity. Thus, although the notion of global culture builds on research on higher order identities, it conflicts with evidence that the benefits of superordinate identities occur even when subordinate identities are also strong. These findings suggest that intergroup conflict reduction does not require that people give up their ethnic identity or other relatively specific collective social identities (Gaertner et al., 1998; Citrin et al., this volume).

Although the notion of higher order identities is appealing and Gaertner and his co-workers have provided evidence for such an approach, we would note that the power of transcendent identifications is not just inside the head. Rather, we believe that it is action based on shared goals that is important. This was Sherif's (1958) basic insight when he introduced the idea of "superordinate goals"—goals that members of both groups desired but that could not be achieved by either group on its own; as a consequence the groups had to work together. Ashmore's (1970) shared coping model took Sherif's logic a step further by proposing that shared goals induced cooperative action and that such behavior promoted cross-group positive affective ties, especially friendships, and these emotional ties promoted stereotype destruction, dissonance reduction, and the like that, in turn, produced prejudice reduction (see also Pettigrew, 1998). The importance of cross-group friendships as a mediator of intergroup contact fits with Eriksen's emphasis on lived experience. Just as the separate private spheres of Bosnians and Serbs provided fertile ground for religiously based hostility, so, too, could changes that promote cross-group friendship help in reducing conflict and making citizens of Bosnia more resistant to identity politics appeals from leaders.

The second issue related to reducing intergroup strife to be addressed is implementation of conflict reduction strategies. Here we discuss two approaches: educational programs designed to promote learning about other groups, and third-party interventions. Many school-based programs have been designed to foster intergroup learning (Aboud & Levy, 1999; Gurin, 1999). Bilingual and multicultural educational programs and materials have been shown to have positive effects on intergroup relations among students (Bigler, 1999; Genesee & Gandara, 1999; Stephan & Finlay, 1999). The goal of these programs is to create an environment that allows groups to maintain their cultural identity and, at the same time, accept other groups (Fisher, 1990). Through these programs, individuals may see that they are less different from members of other groups than they thought (Stephan & Finlay, 1999). The danger, of course, is that individuals may find learning about their group highly involving and satisfying, while ignoring or denigrating lessons about other groups. If so, such curricula might unintentionally magnify group boundaries and increase intergroup friction.

Another approach to conflict reduction, designed for groups engaged in active, often violent conflict, is third-party intervention (e.g., Worchel, 1999; Rothman, 1997). Although the positive role of third-parties in reducing conflict is most obvious in Kelman's chapter in the present volume, it is also clear in the contribution by Staub. Fisher (1990) suggests that it is important to distinguish different types of third-party interventions, and presents a taxonomy of four types of third-party interventions that differ in terms of whether or not the third-party focuses on the subjective (including perceptions and evaluations of the conflict) and objective (including conflicts over both scarce resources [material] and over values [symbolic]) aspects of the conflict. Third-party consultation, the type performed by Kelman and his colleagues, is seen as the most desirable because it involves a clear emphasis on both the objective and subjective aspects of the conflict (Fisher, 1990). In contrast, there are numerous examples of conflict interventions carried out by other nations or aggregations of nations that focus only on objective facets of the conflict. Worchel (1999) suggests that such third-party interventions can sometimes save ethnic groups from persecution and destruction, but that they rarely lead to long-term peace. It is possible that these interventions are often unsuccessful, in part, because they fail to adequately address the identity issues of the conflict.

The chapters by Kelman and Staub raise an important question regarding third-party intervention: *When* should third parties intervene? At the roundtable discussion at the conference associated with this volume there was clear agreement that early intervention was desirable, though Citrin pointed out that there is little political incentive for leaders to intervene until major conflict has emerged with clear evidence of harm-doing. Further, Rothman (1997) notes that negotiating too early in a conflict may instead escalate identity conflicts.

Summary and Suggestions

In this concluding chapter we both summarized the preceding chapters and offered a conceptual framework that might guide future research.

Part I of the volume was, in part, concerned with the issue of the locus of social identity—does social identification reside in the individual or in society? Brewer and Eriksen did not resolve this starting question, and, in fact, these authors answered that social identity is both "in" society and "in" the individual. Thus, social identity, as with self and identity more generally, is both personal *and* social (Ashmore & Jussim, 1997b). Brewer and Eriksen identified the individual and societal building blocks of social identity, especially as they are linked to conflict between groups.

In Part II we asked the contributors to address one type of conflict (political strife) in one society (the United States). Not only did they share this charge, the authors also used a similar method, survey research. Yet given this shared topic and empirical approach, Citrin et al. and Sidanius and Petrocik reached contrasting conclusions, the former seeing generally low levels of ethnically based political conflict and the latter concluding that the ethnic divide is wide and deep. As noted above, the difference in conclusions is more apparent than real, reflecting, in part, methodological and interpretational differences. The Part II authors leave us with many important ideas, including the multifaceted nature of ethnic and national identification.

In Part III, White and Staub addressed violent conflict, the first in an analysis of Northern Ireland and the latter with a general model of the factors contributing to mass killing and genocide. These two chapters dovetail well in highlighting the importance of history and action for understanding the links between identity and conflict. White detailed the history of the violence in Northern Ireland and showed how the distant past was influential in shaping the most recent protracted fighting beginning in the late 1960s and is still much alive as the contestants seek to build on, and extend, the 1998 peace accord. Staub underlined that identities are not just in the head but, instead, both influence action and are shaped by action (and inaction).

Kelman, in the single Part IV chapter, described the problem-solving workshop approach that he and his colleagues have developed to ameliorate protracted conflicts. In so doing he underlined the central role that national identity plays in maintaining such conflict, and, at the same time, he offered the very optimistic message that national identity as a social construction can be altered.

The second part of this concluding chapter was devoted to a "look ahead." We presented a social identity framework for intergroup strife. This scheme, depicted in figure 9.1, identifies three major constructs: threat and appraisal, destructive coping: intergroup harm-doing, and social identity. It is proposed that these are mutually causally linked and further that social identity moderates the threat and appraisal to intergroup harm-doing link.

We offer three general suggestions for theorists and researchers undertaking the next generation of work on social identity and intergroup conflict. First, we believe it will yield dividends if intergroup relations researchers looked to the concepts and methods of the general field of "self and social identity." Except for White's use of role identity models, all the chapters in this book were guided by social identity perspectives specifically intended for understanding intergroup relations (e.g., Tajfel, 1981; Turner, Hogg, Oakes, Reicher, & Blackwell, 1987). There is, however, a broad interdisciplinary field concerned more generally with the issues of self and social identity (Ashmore & Jussim, 1997a). We urge scientists interested in intergroup conflict to look more systematically at this field. We illustrated what we have in mind above in linking "national narrative" as described by Kelman to the individual-level concept "life story" (McAdams, 1997) and personal narrative (Gergen & Gergen, 1988).

Second, we suggest that those interested in the interface between identity and group conflict consider a broader range of conflicts than here addressed. Because we anticipate a future volume directed at identity and gender, we did not include female-male relations in this volume. Yet gender and other forms of intergroup conflict are likely to share some features with ethnic and national conflict but also to have some unique facets.

Third and finally, we hope that the general framework we have proposed will generate both empirical work and conceptual debate. Our broader hope is that the heuristic scheme, and the volume as a whole, will spur others to develop a more comprehensive and coherent social identity paradigm for intergroup conflict

Note

1. History is also important for knowing the "objective" ways in which present day material realities and symbols are constructed. For example, the Rwandan genocide was made more likely by the distant and recent past of Rwanda: Several centuries ago, the indigenous Hutu were subdued by Tutsi invaders (Smith, 1998), who were physically different (e.g., taller); the Tutsis implemented a feudal system that subjugated the numerically superior Hutus and propagated a value system that exalted Tutsi physical attributes. Early in the twentieth century, colonial Belgians used these economic and value systems to help maintain order and their control over both Hutus and Tutsis. In addition, they added the notion of "blood" to explain group differences. These historical "facts" shape today's material and symbolic realities that guide action.

References

Aboud, F. E., & Levy, S. R. (1999). Are we ready to translate research into programs? *Journal of Social Issues*, *55*, 621–625.

Aretxaga, B. (1993). Striking with hunger: Cultural meanings of political violence in Northern Ireland. In K. B. Warren (Ed.), *The violence within: Cultural and political opposition in divided nations* (pp. 219–253). Boulder, CO: Westview Press.

Ashmore, R. D. (1970). Prejudice: Causes and cures. In B. E. Collins (Ed.), *Social psychology: Social influence, attitude change, group processes, and prejudice*. Reading, MA: Addison-Wesley.

Ashmore, R. D., & Del Boca, F. K. (1976). Psychological approaches to understanding intergroup conflict. In P. A. Katz (Ed.), *Towards the elimination of racism* (pp. 73–123). New York: Pergamon Press.

Ashmore, R. D., & Jussim, L. (Eds.) (1997a). *Self and identity: Fundamental issues* (Vol. 1). New York: Oxford University Press.

Ashmore, R. D., & Jussim, L. (1997b). Toward a second century of the scientific analysis of self and identity. In R. D. Ashmore & L. Jussim (Eds.), *Self and identity: Fundamental issues* (Vol. 1, pp. 3-19). New York: Oxford University Press.

Bigler, R. S. (1999). The use of multicultural curricula and materials to counter racism. *Journal of Social Issues, 55*, 687–705.

Boskin, J. S. (1970). Sambo. In G. Nash and R. Weiss (Eds.), *The great fear: Race in the mind of America*. New York: Holt, Rinehart and Winston.

Boulding, K. E. (1962). *Conflict and defense: A general theory*. New York: Harper.

Brewer, M., Dull, V. & Lui, L. (1981). Perceptions of the elderly: Stereotypes as prototypes. *Journal of Personality and Social Psychology, 41*, 656–670.

Clifton, A. K., McGrath, D., & Wick, B. (1976). Stereotypes of woman: A single category? *Sex Roles, 2*, 135–148.

Contrada, R. J., & Ashmore, R. D. (Eds.) (1999). *Self, social identity, and physical health* (Vol. 2, pp. 3–20). New York: Oxford University Press.

Contrada, R. J., Ashmore, R. D., Gary, M. L., Coups, E., Egeth, J. D., Sewell, A., Ewell, K., & Goyal, T. (in press). Measures of ethnicity-related stress: Psychometric properties, ethnic group differences, and associations with well-being. *Journal of Applied Social Psychology*.

Cross, W. E. (1995). The psychology of Nigrescence: Revising the Cross Model. In J. G. Ponterotto, J. M. Casas, L. A. Suzuki, and C. M. Alexander (Eds.), *Handbook of multicultural counseling* (pp. 93–122). Thousand Oaks, CA: Sage Publications.

Deaux, K. (1992). Personalizing identity and socializing self. In G. Breakwell (Ed.), *Social psychology of identity and the self-concept* (pp. 9–33). London: Academic Press.

de la Garza, M. F-O., Newcomb, M. D., & Myers, H. F. (1995). A multidimensional measure of cultural identity for Latino and Latina adolescents. In A. M. Padilla (Ed.), *Hispanic psychology: Critical issues in theory and research* (pp. 26–42). Thousand Oaks, CA: Sage Publications.

de la Garza, R. O., Falcon, A., & Garcia, C. (1996). Will the real Americans please stand up: Anglo and Mexican an-American support of core American political values. *American Journal of Political Science, 40*, 335–351.

Devine, P. G., & Baker, S. M. (1991). Measurement of racial stereotype subtyping. *Personality and Social Psychology Bulletin, 17*, 44–50

Festinger, L. (1950). Informal social communication. *Psychological Review, 57*, 271–282.

Festinger, L. (1954). A theory of social comparison process. *Human Relations, 7*, 117–140.

Festinger, L. (1957). *A theory of cognitive dissonance*. Stanford: Stanford University Press.

Fisher, R. J. (1990). *The social psychology of intergroup and international conflict resolution*. New York: Springer-Verlag.

Fredrickson, G. M. (1999). Models of American ethnic relations: A historical perspective. In D. A. Prentice & D. T. Miller (Eds.), *Cultural divides: Understanding and overcoming group conflict* (pp. 23–34). New York: Russell Sage.

Gaertner, S. L., Dovidio, J. F., Nier, J. A., Ward, C. M., & Banker, B. S. (1999). Across cultural divides: The value of superordinate identity. In D. A. Prentice & D. T. Miller (Eds.), *Cultural divides: Understanding and overcoming group conflict*. New York: Russell Sage.

Genesee, F., & Gandara, P. (1999). Bilingual education programs: A cross-national perspective. *Journal of Social Issues*, *55*, 665–685.

Gergen, K. J., & Gergen, M. M. (1988). Narrative and the self as relationship. In L. Berkowitz (Ed.), *Advances in experimental social psychology* (Vol. 21, pp. 17–56). New York: Academic Press.

Goldhagen, D. (1996*). Hitler's willing executioners: Ordinary Germans and the holocaust*. New York: Alfred A. Knopf.

Gurin, P., Peng, T., Lopez, G., & Nagda, B. A. (1999). Context, identity, and intergroup relations. In D. A. Prentice & D. T. Miller (Eds.), *Cultural divides: Understanding and overcoming group conflict* (pp. 133–170). New York: Russell Sage.

Hull, C. L. (1943). *Principles of behavior*. New York: Appleton-Century-Crofts.

Iyengar, S. S., Lepper, M. R., & Ross, L. (1999). Independence from whom? Interdependence with whom? Cultural perspectives on ingroups versus outgroups. In D. A. Prentice & D. T. Miller (Eds.), *Cultural divides: Understanding and overcoming group conflict* (pp. 273–301). New York: Russell Sage.

Jones, J. (1997). *Prejudice and racism* (second edition). New York: McGraw-Hill.

Lazarus, R. S., & Folkman, S. (1984). *Stress, appraisal, and coping*. New York: Springer.

McAdams, R. C. (1997). The case for unity in the (post)modern self: A modest proposal. In R. D. Ashmore & L. Jussim (Eds.), *Self and identity: Fundamental issues* (Vol. 1, pp. 46–78). New York: Oxford University Press.

McCall, G. J., & Simmons, J. L. (1966). *Identities and interactions*. New York: Free Press.

New York Times, 16 December 1999.

Norenzayan, A., Choi, I., & Nisbett, R. E. (1999). Eastern and Western perceptions of causality for social behavior: Lay theories about personalities and situations. In D. A. Prentice & D. T. Miller (Eds.), *Cultural divides: Understanding and overcoming group conflict* (pp. 239–272). New York: Russell Sage.

Northrup, T. A. (1989). The dynamic of identity in personal and social conflict. In L. Kriesberg, T. A. Northrup, & S. J. Thorson (Eds.), *Intractable conflicts and their transformation* (pp. 55–82). Syracuse, NY: Syracuse University Press.

Pettigrew, T. F. (1998). Intergroup contact theory. *Annual Review of Psychology*, *49*, 65–85.

Phinney, J. S. (1995). Ethnic identity and self-esteem: A review and integration. In A. M. Padilla (Ed.), *Hispanic psychology: Critical issues in theory and research* (pp. 57–70). Thousand Oaks, CA: Sage Publications.

Rothman, J. (1997). *Resolving identity-based conflict in nations, organizations, and communities*. San Francisco, CA: Jossey-Bass.

Rosenberg, S. (1997). Multiplicity of selves. In R. D. Ashmore & L. Jussim (Eds.), *Self and identity: Fundamental issues* (Vol. 1, pp. 23–45). New York: Oxford University Press.

Sears, D. O. (1993). Symbolic politics. In S. Iyengar and W. J. McGuire (Eds.), *Explorations in political psychology* (pp. 113–149). Durham: Duke University Press.

Sears, D. O., Citrin, J., Cheleden, S., & Van Laar, C. (1999). Cultural diversity and multicultural politics: Is ethnic Balkanization psychologically inevitable? In

D. A. Prentice & D. T. Miller (Eds.), *Cultural divides: Understanding and overcoming group conflict* (pp. 35–79). New York: Russell Sage.

Sellers, R. M., Smith, M. A., Shelton, J. N., Rowley, S. A. J., & Chavous, T. M. (1998). Multidimensional model of racial identity: A reconceptualization of African American racial identity. *Personality and Social Psychology Review, 2,* 18–39.

Sherif, M. (1958). Superordinate goals in the reduction of intergroup conflict. *American Journal of Sociology, 63,* 349-363

Smith, D. N. (1998). The psychocultural roots of genocide: Legitimacy and crisis in Rwanda. *American Psychologist, 53,* 743–753.

Stephan, W.G., & Finlay, K. (1999). The role of empathy in improving intergroup relations. *Journal of Social Issues, 55,* 729–743.

Stryker, S. (1987). Identity theory: Developments and extensions. In K. Yardley & T. Honess (Eds.), *Self and identity: Psychosocial perspectives* (pp. 89–103). New York: Wiley.

Tajfel, H. (1978). *Differentiation between groups: Studies in the social psychology of intergroup relations.* London: Academic Press.

Tajfel, H. (1981). *Human groups and social categories: Studies in social psychology.* Cambridge: Cambridge University Press

Thoits, P. A., & Virshup, L. K. (1997). Me's and we's: Forms and functions of social identities. In R. D. Ashmore & L. Jussim (Eds.), *Self and identity: Fundamental issues* (Vol. 1, pp. 106–136). New York: Oxford University Press.

Thompson, L., & Fine, G. A. (1999). Socially shared cognition, affect and behavior: A review and integration. *Personality and Social Psychology Review, 3,* 278–302.

Turner, J. C., Hogg, M. A., Oakes, P. J., Reicher, S. D., & Blackwell, M. S. (1987). *Rediscovering the social group: A self-categorization theory.* Oxford: Basil Blackwell.

Worchel, S. (1999). *Written in blood: Ethnic identity and the struggle for human harmony.* New York: Worth Publishers.

Index of Subjects

Index of Names

Lightning Source UK Ltd.
Milton Keynes UK
UKOW04f1811290116

267413UK00001B/83/P